"If you have a daughter with autism or Asperger's Syndrome, this book will be your primary source of information and inspiration as well as becoming your 'best friend' who understands and supports you."

—*Tony Attwood, Clinical Psychologist and author of* The Complete Guide to Asperger's Syndrome

"Eileen Riley-Hall writes as an old hand, reassuring new recruits that they, too, will survive the shock of getting a diagnosis, and showing them how to be their own child's advocate, while maintaining a healthy balance in their own lives and the on-going life of their family. This is a heartening, and at the same time no-nonsense, look at what it means to be the parent of not one, but two daughters on the autism spectrum. The author speaks with the insight, compassion and wisdom that only come from first-hand experience…enabling new parents to make better-informed choices on their own child's behalf."

—*James Coplan, MD, author of* Making Sense of Autistic Spectrum Disorders

"Eileen Riley-Hall has encouraged her daughters to grow into beautiful and delightful young women and has developed distinctive strategies to develop their potential."

—*Gayle Buckley, MD, pediatrician, New York State*

"Eileen Riley-Hall, a parent of two girls on the autism spectrum, has demonstrated with great clarity the differences between girls and boys on the spectrum. Her book addresses the complexities of girls being a 'minority in a minority group.' Without doubt her book is inspiring, positive and practical providing excellent tips on living with, understanding and supporting girls on the spectrum. A must read for all of us who care about this 'hidden' group."

—*Dr. Judith Gould, Clinical Psychologist and Director of the NAS Lorna Wing Centre for Autism*

Parenting Girls on the Autism Spectrum

of related interest

Girls Growing Up on the Autism Spectrum
What Parents and Professionals Should Know
About the Pre-Teen and Teenage Years
Shana Nichols
With Gina Marie Moravcik and Samara Pulver Tetenbaum
ISBN 978 1 84310 855 9
eISBN 978 1 84642 885 2

Aspergirls
Empowering Females with Asperger Syndrome
Rudy Simone
Foreword by Liane Holliday Willey
ISBN 978 1 84905 826 1
eISBN 978 0 85700 289 1

Stand Up for Autism
A Boy, A Dog, and a Prescription for Laughter
Georgina J. Derbyshire
ISBN 978 1 84905 099 9
eISBN 978 0 85700 285 3

Kids in the Syndrome Mix of ADHD, LD,
Asperger's, Tourette's, Bipolar, and More!
The one stop guide for parents, teachers, and other professionals
Martin L. Kutscher MD
With a contribution from Tony Attwood PhD
With a contribution from Robert R. Wolff MD
ISBN 978 1 84310 810 8 (hardback)
ISBN 978 1 84310 811 5 (paperback)
eISBN 978 1 84642 241 6

The Social and Life Skills MeNu
A Skill Building Workbook for Adolescents
with Autism Spectrum Disorders
Karra M. Barber
ISBN 978 1 84905 861 2
eISBN 978 0 85700 433 8

Autism All-Stars
How We Use Our Autism and Asperger Traits to Shine in Life
Edited by Josie Santomauro
Foreword by Tony Attwood
ISBN 978 1 84310 188 8
eISBN 978 0 85700 600 4

Parenting Girls on the Autism Spectrum

Overcoming the Challenges and Celebrating the Gifts

Eileen Riley-Hall

Foreword by Shana Nichols

Jessica Kingsley *Publishers*
London and Philadelphia

Copyright Acknowledgements
Every effort has been made to trace copyright holders and to obtain their permission for the use of copyright material. The authors and the publisher apologize for any omissions and would be grateful if notified of any acknowledgements that should be incorporated in future reprints or editions of this book.
Quotations on p.11 and p.228 from *The Four Loves* by C.S. Lewis. Copyright © C.S. Lewis Pte. Ltd. 1960. Reprinted by permission of The CS Lewis Company Ltd.
Quotation on p.19 from *The Story of My Life: The Restored Edition* by Helen Keller, p.16. Reprinted by permission of Random House, Inc.
Quotation on p.100 reprinted by permission of Temple Grandin.
Quotation on p.128 reprinted by permission of Eustacia Culter.
Quotation on p.143 from *Man's Search for Meaning* by Victor Frankl. Copyright © 1959, 1962, 1984, 1992 by Viktor E. Frankl. Reprinted by permission of Beacon Press, Boston.
Quotation on p.187 from *Mere Christianity* by C.S. Lewis. Copyright © C.S. Lewis Pte. Ltd. 1942, 1943, 1944, 1952. Reprinted by permission of The CS Lewis Company Ltd.
Quotations on pp.189, 200, 220 and 237 from *Charlie Brown* by Charles Schulz. Reprinted by permission of PEANUTS Worldwide.

First published in 2012
by Jessica Kingsley Publishers
116 Pentonville Road
London N1 9JB, UK
and
400 Market Street, Suite 400
Philadelphia, PA 19106, USA

www.jkp.com

Copyright © Eileen Riley-Hall 2012
Foreword copyright © Shana Nichols 2012

Library of Congress Cataloging in Publication Data
Riley-Hall, Eileen.
  Parenting girls on the autism spectrum : overcoming the challenges and celebrating the gifts / Eileen Riley-Hall ; foreword by Shana Nichols.
    p. cm.
  Includes bibliographical references.
  ISBN 978-1-84905-893-3 (alk. paper)
  1. Autistic children--Family relationships. 2. Parents of autistic children. 3. Mothers and daughters. 4. Parenting--Psychological aspects. I. Title.
  RJ506.A9R55 2012
  618.92'85882--dc23
                    2011046695

British Library Cataloguing in Publication Data
A CIP catalogue record for this book is available from the British Library

ISBN 978 1 84905 893 3
eISBN 978 0 85700 612 7

Printed and bound in the United States

This book is dedicated to my amazing daughters, Elizabeth Anne and Caroline Grace. Thank you for the many gifts you have given to me; you are my greatest blessings. I love you forever and always.

"All good gifts around us
are sent from heaven above,
then thank the Lord, O thank the Lord
for all his love."

—*Traditional hymn*

Contents

Foreword

In my work with families of females with autism spectrum disorders (ASDs), and with women themselves, I have been asked many questions related to my clinical experience and about what families can expect and hope for. A few of those questions have become "universals" over the years—questions that almost all families and women ask. They include questions such as "Are there other families like us?" "Where are the other girls/women with ASDs?" "Is it common for girls with ASDs to be missed?" and "Are there any books or resources written for parents of *girls* with ASDs?"

These questions come from a place of parents of daughters often feeling very alone in their journey and in the autism community. As we begin to understand more about female ASD, we realize that what we have learned and written about to date is based primarily on a male conceptualization and male experiences. In his August 2007 *New York Times* article "What autistic girls are made of," Ami Klin wrote that females with ASDs are "research orphans"—girls and women are typically not included as participants in the studies where the goals are to increase our knowledge of ASD. If we take that metaphor further, females are orphans *twice over*—first, they are not included in research because their numbers are too small, second, they are not included in research because they haven't been identified as having an ASD. Many girls and women are living their lives having been misdiagnosed, and they are subsequently misunderstood, often leading to feelings of self-doubt, sadness, anxiety, and isolation. Whether or not we believe that labels are important in and of themselves, the understanding that can come from an appropriate diagnostic evaluation can be the turning point in a female's life and that of their family—it can create an "Aha" moment, and it can lift the weight of feeling inadequate or feeling that you're not trying hard enough. An accurate diagnosis, and the label it arrives with, can provide an explanation for many of life's challenges—for a young girl who is trying to make friends but can't seem to get it right, or a woman whose relationships with co-workers fall apart at every job she has. As a field, we have begun to make strides during the past five years towards recognizing that the experience of females with ASD is different from that of their male peers. As a clinician who specializes in working with girls and women, I realize that we still have a long way to go. And we need to be able to answer "Yes" to the last of the universal questions I included above: we need more books and resources for families of females with ASD. Thankfully, this book will be part of the answer.

I met Eileen in October 2010 when I was presenting about the experiences of females with ASDs at a conference, sponsored by the State University of New York, at Albany Center for Autism and Related Disorders. We spoke afterwards and she shared that she was a mother of two girls on the autism spectrum and that she had written a manuscript about what she has learned from raising her daughters. She wondered if I would be interested in reading it, and whether she thought other parents might find such a book helpful. My answer to both questions was a resounding "Yes!" I encouraged Eileen to focus on her experiences raising girls as I knew this was something so many parents have been asking for. Today I am honored to be writing the Foreword to *Parenting Girls on the Autism Spectrum: Overcoming the Challenges and Celebrating the Gifts*.

As a teacher and a fellow lover of literature, Eileen brings to her story quotations from writers whose messages are both powerful and hopeful. Take, for example, the incredible Louisa May Alcott, who created for us a cast of unforgettable characters in her treasured classic *Little Women*; girls who are beautiful, spunky, soulful, and kind—in whom we can all find a part of ourselves—and a part of the amazing girls with ASDs. Alcott wrote, "I am not afraid of storms for I am learning to sail my ship." With quotations such as these, and her voice of optimism and hope, Eileen invites families to embark on their journey with their daughters with the reassurance that, though the road ahead will have its bumps, it will be a beautiful and empowering adventure full of unimaginable gifts.

The wonderful characters of Eileen's own narrative are her amazing and vibrant daughters Lizzie, 14 (Asperger's), and Caroline, 12 (autism). From their birth, to how her daughters were diagnosed, and over the course of their experiences in school, Eileen shares a wealth of personal stories that will resonate with parents of girls across the full range of the autism spectrum and abilities. Most importantly, she does so with a powerfully positive approach. Eileen poses a challenge to all parents and to everyone who works with their daughters: to see that labels are just words, that there is room for talking about differences rather than disabilities, and that optimism and hope are what fuel positive growth. Eileen herself states that others may see her positivity as a Pollyanna-ish attitude to the experience of raising daughters with ASDs, yet one of Eileen's gifts is her ability to eloquently balance acknowledgement and acceptance of the challenges while at the same time embracing and believing in the small steps and successes. Chapters are dedicated to helping parents with the emotional challenges of raising their daughters, encouraging the all-important self-care and development of a supportive network, and allowing yourself to have a not so great day. At the same time, parents are encouraged to help their daughter discover her gifts and to believe in their daughter's potential.

The story of Lizzie and Caroline is deeply embedded in what I think of as Eileen's *optimistic realism*. In a later chapter she chooses to bravely share with us, her readers, her "Outtakes, Mistakes, and C is for Crazy." Realism accepts that perfection is not an option—besides the fact that being perfect would be terribly boring! Eileen's stories of her worst moments and embarrassing mistakes are accompanied always by humor and hope, and the message of acceptance and moving on. Parents of girls with ASDs need a tribe, a family of other parents with whom they can open up and share their experiences without editing. In another quotation from the book, that sense of connection and community is highlighted. Author C.S. Lewis said, "Friendship is born at that moment when one person says to another: 'What! You, too? Thought I was the only one.'" How many times have you been the only parent of a girl in a support group? How many times have you been asked, "Can girls have autism?" How often have you felt that you are the only one?

Eileen shares with her readers the unique experiences of females with ASDs and the challenges that they and their families face; challenges such as minority status within a minority, social expectations for females to be good at social communication, the risks of depression and anxiety, handling mean girls who bully in ways that are different from the bullying of boys, hygiene and fashion, and making friends. Whether your daughter is a spunky spitfire or a quiet little lady, you will find her somewhere in Eileen's words, and I guarantee that you will not feel alone.

Passionate and strong-minded, Eileen is a champion for her daughters and their futures. Lizzie and Caroline are blessed, and I look forward to hearing more about their journey as they reach the next milestones in their lives. I also hope that all parents of girls with ASDs will be able to read about Lizzie and Caroline. Eileen has written an emotional and practical guidebook for parents of girls with ASDs that is bound to touch hearts and provide much-needed encouragement.

If parents who read this book are able to develop their own optimistic voice, a chorus will blossom and grow, shaping the future of the ASD sisterhood—*celebrating the gifts*.

What a wonderful future to look forward to.

Shana Nichols
August 2011

Acknowledgments

My sincere thanks to Shana Nichols for agreeing to read the manuscript of a mom, believing it could be a worthy contribution to the literature about girls and autism, and for writing such a beautiful foreword. Thank you also to my amazing editor, Sarena Wolfaard, for her patience, guidance, and support. Thank you to Lucy Buckroyd for answering every one of my endless questions and working so diligently on all the permissions. My great thanks to Jessica Kingsley Publishers for giving a mom of girls the chance to participate in the conversation about autism.

A heartfelt thanks to the teachers and school professionals who have been exceptionally devoted and kind to my girls over the years: Evelyn Baltis, Stephanie Bowen, Eileen Chera, Jane Cutler, Sandra Hess, Kristin Huntsman, Rosemary Kukuk, Jessica Mann, Catherine Powzyk, Debra Rainville, Barbara Scanlon, Nicole Viscusi, Linda Weiss, and Debra Wisner. Thank you to Dr. Buckley, our pediatrician, and Dr. Susan Britain, our psychologist. Thank you to all the wonderful people at Helping Hands Preschool, Chango Elementary School, and Gowana Middle School. A very special thank you to Joan Frolish, speech teacher extraordinaire, who taught Miss Caroline so much.

Many thanks to our extended families, especially the girls' grandparents, for their love and support of Lizzie and Caroline. I also wish to thank my close family and friends for their support and faith in me. A special thanks to my loving husband, Harlan Hall, for his patience while I asked him the same questions time and again, and made him listen to long passages read aloud, frequently interrupting myself to change something and start over. Thank you to my Lizzie for her encouragement and support, and bringing me cups of coffee and Pop-Tarts. And thanks to sweet Caroline for sharing the computer with me as I wrote, in her words, "a story about me." As always, my deepest thanks to the Lord who makes all good things possible.

Preface

When I was pregnant with my first daughter, Elizabeth, I visited several pediatricians to choose who I would like to be my baby's physician. After years of infertility treatments, I was finally pregnant with a baby girl, and I was determined to make sure she had the best pediatrician around. So on a chilly Thursday evening in October 1996, when I was around seven months pregnant, I met with Dr. Gayle Buckley, a seasoned pediatrician who is kind, forthright, and has the wisdom gained from many years of experience caring for children. Smiling at me with twinkling blue eyes, she listened as I explained my struggle to start a family and tremendous excitement at finally being pregnant. I also confessed that I was a bit nervous at that point in my pregnancy because I had declined the alpha-fetoprotein test (AFP) blood test, which is given to women at 16 weeks of pregnancy to detect birth defects in their babies. If the AFP is positive, obstetricians normally recommend an amniocentesis, which can potentially harm a pregnancy. And if amniocentesis shows birth defects, the parent is offered no options but a worry-filled pregnancy or the choice to abort. I knew I would never abort, and I didn't want to risk my pregnancy, so I declined the AFP test. But at seven months pregnant I was wishing I had taken it, to have the reassurance that my baby was perfectly "normal."

After I finished explaining my hopes and fears, I looked to Dr. Buckley for reassurance. I wanted her to tell me that, in all likelihood, my baby was normal, that I was worrying for nothing. Instead, she leaned forward in her chair, took off her glasses, looked directly at me, and said with total conviction, "All babies are perfect." Then she was silent for a moment, and so was I. I felt a little judged by her declaration and surprised at her directness. We concluded our visit with a tour of the cheery office, decorated with dinosaurs, dolls, and cowboy boots. That night I lay with my hand on my pregnant tummy and contemplated her words. My baby suddenly seemed very real to me as a person, and I understood what she meant: my baby was exactly who she was meant to be. It wasn't about what I wanted or needed; it was all about her. I think that may have been the moment I became a mom. Dr. Buckley is still my girls' pediatrician today.

Little did I know how powerful those words and the love they demand would become in my life. And in a moment of grace or serendipity, whichever you choose to believe, I heard that same sentiment again years later, when I was in the midst of doubt and fear. All children are perfect just as they are. Once you realize that, you are on your way.

Introduction

"Hope is itself a species of happiness, and perhaps the chief happiness which this world affords."

—*Samuel Johnson*

Since I was a child, I always loved books. Books were my favorite pastime and often my escape during a stormy childhood. As an adult, I chose literature to study in college, and books helped me understand history, the complexities of human nature, and even, at times, myself. Throughout my life, both in times of stress and promise, books have offered me solace and direction. So when I was 36 and my daughters, Lizzie and Caroline, were both diagnosed on the autism spectrum, I immediately drove to a bookstore and searched the shelves for a book to guide me through this new challenge. I wanted desperately to hear from someone who knew how I felt and could share with me what to expect. More than anything, I wanted someone who would tell me it would all be okay.

Instead, I found a dizzying array of clinical books describing autism in grim terminology. There were encyclopedia-thick volumes which overwhelmed me with recommendations of intensive behavioral interventions, diets and supplements, blood transfusions, and even oxygen chambers. The advice in the books was conflicting and confusing, and yet every author was adamant that their advice be followed exactly and immediately. Even the few books of personal stories were descriptions of lives consumed with the agonies of fighting autism. With every book I read, I became more panicked, as if I was in a desperate race against time to save my girls. What I wanted was a book to give me the hope and confidence to face the challenges ahead. I needed to hear an optimistic voice to relieve the fear, sadness, and loneliness I felt when I was told my daughters had autism. I promised myself that if I found a way to cope with this challenge, I would write that book for parents of girls like mine. Well, I made it through and discovered many wonderful surprises along the way. So here is the book.

Pay it forward

This book is for you, the parent of a very special little girl, to provide comfort and perspective in a world where parents of children with autism are being pulled in a million different directions and being made to feel guilty about whatever choices they make for their children. I hope this is one of the first books you read after your daughter is diagnosed because you need reassurance and hope, as much as you need information, for the road ahead. I hope you will turn to it when you have a question or just need a friend who understands how you feel. Although I am not an expert on autism, as a mom and teacher, I know the challenges special parents face, especially parents of girls, and I have benefited from the wisdom of other special moms and dads. I am nearly ten years along now in the journey of raising my extraordinary girls, and I have learned a great deal through research and experience, along with plenty of trial and error. I also talk with other parents all the time about our shared struggles and triumphs, and I have always found my greatest comfort in the camaraderie of other special families like mine. Even though we have different experiences, there are common threads that run through all our stories and a wealth of knowledge born of experience. As best I can, I want to pass that on to you.

Each of the following chapters addresses a topic of concern to parents of girls with autism. This is the landscape of autism as I have experienced it in my life: a road map through education, therapies, relationships, and the many hidden blessings of having a daughter with autism. It is true that you have many challenges before you, and at times it will be hard, but do not give up hope. Your life will be different, but it will also be beautifully enriched in more ways that you can possibly imagine. You already have all the basics you need to help your daughter. This is a journey that doesn't require anything extraordinary, just patience, hope, and a lot of love. So take a deep breath, hug your little girl, and believe you can do it.

Chapter 1

Defining Autism and Meeting My Girls

"Knowledge is love and light and vision."

—Helen Keller

What autism is and what it is not

Autism is defined as a group of developmental disorders, including Pervasive Developmental Disorder (PDD) and Asperger's Syndrome, that "affect a child's ability to communicate and interact with others" (Mayo Clinic 2011). Simply put, people with autism struggle with expressing their thoughts and feelings, and it is equally challenging for them to interpret what is happening in the world around them. However, this does not mean that a person with autism feels less or experiences less than the rest of us. In fact, some studies indicate they may feel more deeply at times. A person with autism is still a whole person, just one who can't as easily express all of who she is or, at times, understand what you are saying or feeling. While you and your daughter may struggle with autism, she is still perfectly complete and full of potential. Never hesitate to remind everyone in her life of that truth. People with autism have a neurological condition which makes communication difficult, but it does not diminish their worth or wholeness as human beings.

Possible causes

The cause of autism is unknown, although most experts now agree there is a genetic basis for autism, perhaps augmented by exposure to environmental factors, most likely during prenatal development. In this context, environmental factors can mean anything that contributes to the "environment" in the womb and affects development. Some of those factors may include "parental age, maternal genotype, maternal-fetal immunoreactivity, in vitro fertilization, maternal ingestion of drugs, toxic chemicals in the environment during pregnancy, and maternal illnesses during pregnancy such as maternal diabetes or infections" (Szatmari 2011, pp.1091–2). Just a couple of notes of explanation: "drugs" does not mean illegal substances, but any number of prescription medications taken during pregnancy; "maternal genotype" refers to a mother's genetics; and "maternal-fetal immunoreactivity" refers to a mother's possible immune system reaction to a pregnancy. And this is just the beginning of the list of potential "environmental" factors. Many scientists are now looking into the way a genetic vulnerability could leave a developing fetus more susceptible to environmental influences in the womb. It is hoped, as research continues to explore both genetic and environmental factors, and examines the possible interaction between the two, that we will have a better understanding of the causes of autism.

Signs and symptoms

Often the first sign of autism is a delay in a child's language development between the ages of one and three. Usually, both expressive language (your daughter talking to you) and receptive language (your daughter understanding what you say) are affected. However, a diagnosis of autism is only made once a more complete developmental evaluation has been done. Children are typically diagnosed with autism because they exhibit deficits in three areas: delays in language and non-verbal communication, limited or difficult social interaction, and engaging in repetitive behaviors. The delay in acquiring language can isolate a child from family and the world. Unable to communicate with the ease of a typical child, a child with autism may appear detached and self-absorbed, unaware of social situations. This is often reflected in the manner in which a child with autism plays. You may notice that your daughter often tends to play games that are orderly and routine (building with blocks) and solitary, rather than playing house or dolls. Playing dolls or house is imaginative play which requires that a child understand and be aware of social situations in order to recreate them in play. This is difficult for children with autism because they often do not have the level of social awareness necessary for imaginative play. Recent studies, however, indicate this lack of social awareness may not be as true for girls on the spectrum, some of whom do play imaginatively.

Although autism is a communication disorder by definition, people with autism may also have other neurological conditions that impact both fine and gross motor skills, and potentially affect other parts of the brain as well. Studies show that children with autism are at greater risk for developing seizures and epilepsy (Autism Speaks 2011a). Therefore, it is important that your daughter is under the care of a pediatrician who is familiar not only with autism but also with the possible complications it can bring. In addition, children with autism may also be sensitive to sights, sounds, smells, and textures because their nervous systems may not be processing stimuli in a typical fashion. Some children with autism are not as comfortable being hugged or held; however, that does not indicate a lack of feeling or attachment. It can simply indicate a sensory overload to their nervous systems. These sensory overloads can result in repetitive or ritualistic activities, also called self-stimulatory behaviors, which are often attempts to calm an overwhelmed nervous system.

The truth is that most everything your daughter is doing she is doing for a reason. Our children's behaviors are really marvelously ingenious coping mechanisms. Self-stimulatory activities allow an overstimulated brain to focus and thereby calm down; deep pressure—for example, squishing into the sofa—often has the same calming effect. Repeating phrases from films or books, known as echolalia, may be an attempt at communication, no matter how clumsy. Or echolalia could be her way of sharing an interest and may provide a glimpse of what is running through her mind. Rituals and routines, while sometimes maddening, are markers on the road of a life filled with neurologically overwhelming experiences. Imagine if your brain was being routinely inundated with stimulation it could not properly process or filter—a kaleidoscope of sights, sounds, and smells; you too would want some familiar signposts along the way to keep your balance, whether it was the same breakfast every day or the same pajamas every night. A wonderful way to understand the experience of autism from the child's perspective is to read *Emergence*, an autobiography by Temple Grandin (Grandin and Scariano 1996). Dr. Grandin is an adult of tremendous accomplishment who has autism, and she documented her childhood experiences and the reasons for her sometimes confounding behaviors in *Emergence*. Reading *Emergence* allowed me to understand how a mind with autism might work and the possible meaning behind certain behaviors. It also revealed beautifully all of the feelings behind the silence and struggles with communication.

Autism is not a lack of feeling or attachment

Many people misunderstand autism. Because people with autism have more difficulty communicating, people often assume they do not think or feel as typical people do. That is not true. Autism is not a lack of feeling or attachment to the world. My daughters have taught me that people with autism feel deeply, love fully, and think complexly. Many adults with autism, such as Temple Grandin, give testimony to all they were feeling and thinking as children, things they simply could not express when they were younger. Some people with autism have revealed an amazing complexity of thoughts and feelings once they were given the means to communicate. Even when people with autism seem to be in their own worlds, they are often still aware of the world and the people around them. I am amazed at how much my daughter Caroline remembers about her early childhood, from periods when her communication was very limited. The mystery and hope in autism is that there is so much in our children; our goal should not be to change who they are, but to help them express what is already inside. There is an enormous depth of love, hope, and intellect in people with autism. So never give up on your daughter's potential. I promise she will surprise you!

My sweet girls: Some background

I would like to tell you a bit about my daughters because in many ways they typify life at both ends of the autism spectrum, and, by sharing stories about their struggles and triumphs, I think you will be encouraged that together you and your special girl can accomplish many things. My older daughter, Elizabeth Anne (Lizzie, as she prefers), is now 14; she was diagnosed at five years old with pervasive developmental disorder (PDD), but has now been reclassified as Asperger's. My younger daughter, Caroline Grace, is now 12, and was diagnosed with autism at two years old. They are the loves of my life, and being their mom is my greatest privilege. Both of my girls were challenging infants for different reasons, but never did I think there was anything about my girls that indicated autism. However, the stories of their infancies may sound familiar to you, as I now realize there were tell-tale signs all along.

Lizzie

Lizzie was an absolutely beautiful baby—big brown eyes, fair skin, a full head of soft brown hair, and a look of skeptical curiosity on her face. She weighed in at a healthy, if petite, six pounds and one ounce. Lizzie was smart and observant from the minute she was born, wide awake and hyperaware of her surroundings. Almost immediately I noticed she was tremendously sensitive to sounds and lights and temperatures. Nursing was a disaster with Lizzie. She just refused to do it. After 14 days of trying to nurse her 24 hours a day, I surrendered and gave her a bottle. She didn't really take the bottle much better, and feeding her became a daily struggle.

Lizzie's infancy was not easy, to say the least. She always wanted to be awake, vigilantly examining everything; she was a very serious little person. I also learned early on that the temperature of her bath water needed to be warm but not hot, the tags had to be removed from all her clothes or she would squirm in discomfort, and the house had to be completely silent if she was to sleep at all. It was as if she was missing an outer layer of skin, just exposed to the elements and the mercy of every breeze that blew by. Pretty much the whole first year of Lizzie's life, all I did was try to feed her and rock her to sleep. However, as tough as that year was, Lizzie grew to be a happy baby—sweet and affectionate and bright. With a lot of hard work on my part, she gained weight well and made her milestones pretty much on time. And she was one of the prettiest babies I have ever seen.

Caroline

Two years later, Caroline came bouncing along. Her expression at birth was just the opposite of her sister's serious stare. Caroline was born ready for a party: chubby and smiling, hungry and happy. Nothing seemed to bother her. She was on a mission to do her own thing, and what the rest of us wanted or said never altered her path. I loved her independence and zeal for life. Caroline loved to cuddle; she had several favorite stuffed animals and wouldn't go anywhere without her blankie. She was as adventurous as Lizzie was cautious. They seemed a perfect balance for each other and loved each other from the start.

Unlike Lizzie, Caroline was a great sleeper as a baby. She went full-throttle while she was awake, passing out like a drunken sailor after. In fact, Caroline slept so soundly that it used to kind of worry me. I was always checking to make sure she was breathing. As soon as she learned to crawl, she was everywhere! Once she began walking, she would walk outside if a door was unlocked and just keep going. I had to watch her like a hawk because she was such a daredevil, and I nearly went crazy making sure I knew where she was at every moment. Once, when she was about two and a half, she escaped through the back door, stripped off her clothes as she crossed the yard, and was heading for the neighbor's plastic kiddie pool. Luckily, Lizzie saw her as she went streaking by, and alerted their dad who caught her just in time. Scary! There was never a dull moment when Caroline was little.

Early signs

For the first several years, nothing really struck me as unusual about my girls. I knew that Lizzie was extremely sensitive and thoughtful, and Caroline had boundless energy and a tendency to climb like an acrobat. But to me they just seemed to be individuals with all the quirks and spirit of ordinary children. And as far as their early developments went, both of my girls seemed somewhat typical. They did things late, but they seemed to be getting there. They both started to babble around eight months, spoke their first words around a year, and walked around 14 months. Lizzie's language developed more quickly than Caroline's, but neither of them showed a troubling lag. Because I knew so many people with kids whose children varied so greatly in reaching their developmental milestones, I never really worried too much if my girls did things later.

In retrospect, I can see the signs of autism. Lizzie's was a tendency to repeat lines of dialogue from movies when upset, and Caroline's was always lining everything up in rows around the house. But, like so many of us, my love for my girls made me blind to many of their quirks and lags in development; I just thought that was my Lizzie and Caroline. I was so happy to be a mom that, even when it was hard, I was still amazed at my good fortune. It never occurred to me to ask their pediatrician about their leisurely development because I just assumed they would catch up in time. To me they were two perfect and extraordinary little people. Sometimes our love and optimism can cloud our vision for a time; however, in the long run, seeing all that is amazing in our daughters may just be what they need from us the most.

Words we use to describe our daughters

When I look at both of my daughters now, I see miracles. I refuse to use the words "disorder" or "disability" in reference to my daughters because I just see them as different, not deficient. Therefore, in this book, I will use the words "special needs" or "developmentally challenged" to describe our children. I am not denying that autism brings struggles and at times puts our daughters at a disadvantage, but I think it is a form of brainwashing when people with special needs are repeatedly called "disabled." I believe we all have gifts and challenges; we are all capable in some areas and limited in others. So I encourage you right now to erase the words "disabled" and "disability" from your vocabulary as it relates to your daughter. And don't let other people define your daughter that way either. I wish we could erase those words from the human dictionary because they are discriminatory. Words are powerful, and the language we use to describe our children can, in many ways, be a choice about their destiny.

The heart of the matter about autism

1. Autism is a neurological condition that makes communication difficult.

2. Autism in no way diminishes a person's value or wholeness as a human being.

3. Children with autism usually have difficulties with language and social interactions, and engage in repetitive behaviors.

4. Sometimes, as parents, we miss things because we see only the best in our kids. Don't sweat it; ultimately, being your daughter's biggest fan will help her more than anything.

5. Remember, the words you use to describe your daughter will help to shape her future, so always speak with optimism and faith.

Chapter 2

The Diagnosis

"When it is dark enough, you can see the stars."

—*Ralph Waldo Emerson*

If you are reading this book, your daughter has probably already received a diagnosis of autism spectrum disorder. And, honestly, whether or not you have been told it is pervasive developmental disorder or autism or Asperger's doesn't matter because they are just words to describe a hill you now know your daughter has to climb. The day your daughter is diagnosed is a tough day, no doubt about it. I used to think of it as a sad day in my life, but I don't see it that way anymore. It was just the day I finally had the words to explain why I saw my daughters struggling with so many things that other children did with ease. If you have yet to get your daughter a full evaluation, I would like to share with you how that appointment will likely proceed and how to try to keep it all in perspective. If your daughter has already been evaluated, I want to reassure you that it is not the final word on her potential. I would also like to share my experience to show that you will get beyond that bleak moment. The gloominess of that day does not need to be the air you breathe for the rest of your life. It will get better. Life will be different, but it can still be wonderful.

The appointment
When we start off as parents, we don't know very much, no matter how many days we spent babysitting or how many baby books we read. That is because babies are unique, as all people are unique. They are quirky little beings when they first arrive—crying and spitting and turning their little faces bright red. It is very hard to know what is

typical and what is not, especially with your first child. And the baby books tell us that children meet milestones on all sorts of different timelines, so we wait. And sometimes we wait some more. And we convince ourselves that is it the ear infections that delay words, and that our kids are just sensitive or quiet, or perhaps too energetic and busy to start talking in sentences. Whatever the case, when it is your baby, you see only the best and most wonderful, and that is normal and loving. So, it may have been your mother, or your mother-in-law, or a friend who first told you they were concerned about your daughter's unusual pattern of development. And, of course, as moms, we become immediately defensive. We think they just don't understand our children and their sweet peculiarities that we have mastered so well. Don't beat yourself up if you dragged your feet a bit about getting an evaluation. That is human and normal; nobody wants to face a tough reality, especially when it involves your child.

At some point, however, the pediatrician, a daycare provider, or even your spouse convinced you to get a complete evaluation for your daughter. You may have seen any one of a number of professionals who are qualified to diagnose autism spectrum disorders: a child psychiatrist, a child psychologist, a developmental behavioral specialist, a pediatric neurologist, or a developmental pediatrician. The appointment is a tough day for parents of children with developmental challenges. You find yourself in the waiting room of a specialist, not wanting to be part of this new club—the parent of a child with a developmental challenge. There are some things we would rather not know. You want to believe in your heart that your daughter will grow out of it, even as your head is starting to accept the inevitable truth. This is again completely normal. It takes a while for our brains to accommodate a new reality that is so life-changing.

The meeting with the doctor is usually congenial and reassuring. Doctors who work in this field tend to understand that this diagnosis is tough for parents, so they usually ease you into it. The doctor will usually chat with you while simultaneously watching how your daughter plays with the toys in the room. Sometimes there will be a nurse or social worker who will interact with your daughter, while you provide information to the doctor. There is a list of questions, and as the doctor reads methodically through them, all your daughter's quirks may start to line up neatly, like the blocks she is arranging on the floor. Usually, the doctor will make an attempt to interact with your daughter, engage her in play or conversation, and you will see the list of symptoms you just heard come into focus before your eyes. Then the doctor will make his initial diagnosis. And, in that moment, you know your life has changed. But take heart; this is by no means any kind of certain prediction of your daughter's future.

When your daughter is first diagnosed, you may pray to hear a less dire diagnosis—maybe Asperger's, which focuses more on social challenges. You do not want to hear the word "autism," but maybe you will. Do not worry too much about what the specific diagnosis is; the spectrum is just that—a spectrum. At that initial diagnosis, there is no way to tell for sure just where on the spectrum your daughter will ultimately end up. In truth, if your daughter is diagnosed with autism, although it sounds more ominous, it can be a helpful thing; with a more severe initial diagnosis, your daughter may qualify for more intervention services, which can lead to greater progress. After working with children of all ages for over 20 years, it is my opinion that the specific diagnosis, made at a young age, is not the important part. What matters is the realization that your daughter is struggling with communication and social skills for a reason. Lots of children have their specific classification change over the years—for example, from PDD to Asperger's. Think of the diagnosis as one more piece of information you now have about your daughter. And resist the natural impulse to start worrying about every day from now to eternity. One day at a time is the only way to do it.

Follow-up

Even if you already have the diagnosis, I would suggest that you go to a developmental pediatrician, if you have not done so already. The developmental pediatrician will look at your child as a whole, addressing both the neurological and medical implications of the diagnosis. Although most kids with autism are healthy, there can be related physical issues, so it is best to have your daughter under the care of someone who can test for and address everything. These tests may include an electroencephalogram (EEG), hearing and visions tests, and genetic testing. It is important to note that at this time there is no genetic test for autism, just for other disorders that may have autism as a symptom. For most children with diagnoses of autism, there are no underlying medical or genetic conditions. The Centers for Disease Control and Prevention (CDC) estimates that only 10 percent of children diagnosed with autism spectrum disorders have an "identifiable genetic disorder, such as Fragile X syndrome, tuberous sclerosis, Down syndrome and other chromosomal disorders" (CDC 2011a). The easiest way to find a developmental pediatrician is to investigate the pediatric services at your top local hospital; teaching hospitals, in particular, often have the best and most up-to-date services. Or, obviously, your daughter's pediatrician can guide you to the appropriate person. It is a good idea to make the appointment as soon as you suspect there may be an issue, because there are usually long waiting lists for these physicians, and it is important that your daughter begins to receive the most complete services she needs to help her as soon as possible.

There are also follow-up evaluations with psychologists, teachers, and therapists to see what is to be done next. There will be an array of specialists enlisted to identify your daughter's strengths and weakness and to provide direction and help. These may include speech therapists, psychologists, and occupational and physical therapists. It is a tough adjustment, because all of a sudden your job as parent includes a host of strangers upon whom you must rely. You may feel kind of invaded as you explain the daily routine of your daughter over and over again to different people. Just remember, these professionals are trying to help you. I know as I described the craziness of our household, I felt embarrassed by what I thought was my ineptitude as a parent. I was actually reassured by most of the people I met that I had been doing a valiant job alone thus far under difficult circumstances. It is hard to give up some of the control in the job of raising your child, but think of it as extra help; not replacing you, but augmenting the awesome job you are already doing. It is only by creating a complete profile of your daughter that a truly helpful and comprehensive program can be put in place. So go for all the evaluations you need to in order to justify the most services you can obtain for your daughter. Think of all of these sessions as gathering information to help your daughter. And remember that your daughter is an individual, full of potential, so no one can tell you with any certainty at this point what her limits will be. It can be a rough entry into the world of autism, but, I swear to you, it will get better.

How my girls were diagnosed

When Lizzie was four, it became apparent to me that she needed more interaction with other children than the occasional play-date could provide. She was content at home with Caroline and me, but she was painfully shy outside of the house. I had tried placing her in nursery school at three, almost four, but she had severe separation issues and would not interact with the other children. Since I was a stay-at-home mom after the girls were born, I attributed her reluctance to her attachment to me. And because she had such a sensitive nature, I thought it was inevitable that the transition to school would be difficult for her. However, by the time the next year rolled around, and I knew kindergarten was in sight, I was determined to find her a nursery school.

After a long search, I found a sweet, relaxed nursery school, taught by a gentle woman who had decades of experience with preschool children. It was the perfect fit for Lizzie's timid temperament. However, on the very first day the teacher recognized that Lizzie's persistent crying after I left her was something more than separation anxiety. For the entire first week, after I dropped her off, Lizzie would go into a crying state where she didn't hear the teacher talking and seemed unreachable by any comfort or reason. I would be called to come and pick her up. The teacher was alarmed and concerned, so she suggested that I have Lizzie evaluated by a developmental pediatrician. Reluctantly, I agreed, although I really felt Lizzie just needed time to adjust. I assumed the teacher just didn't understand my daughter.

Clinical verdict

I made an appointment for Lizzie with a very well-respected local developmental pediatrician. This physician specialized in diagnosing children on the autism spectrum, although I didn't know that at the time. The day of the appointment I brought Caroline along simply because I had no one with whom to leave her. My daughters' dad met me at the physician's office and stayed with Caroline in the waiting room while I brought Lizzie in to meet the physician.

During the evaluation, the physician noted Lizzie's shyness and initial lack of eye contact; however, in this small, one-on-one setting, he found her to be bright and verbal. He seemed to be debating a diagnosis, mentioning her anxiety and shyness. To gather more information, he asked me to bring Caroline in, so he could see how Lizzie interacted with her sister. By this time, "Hurricane" Caroline had pretty much decimated the waiting room toys and was sitting in the middle of the room, smiling at her destructive triumph.

As soon as Caroline entered the exam room, oblivious to the physician, she headed right to the toys. At this point, Caroline was just shy of three, and she had a functional, if limited, vocabulary. I glanced up and a look of sudden awareness appeared on the physician's face. I could almost see the cartoon light bulb above his head. Lizzie continued to make a doll-house dad and mom run laps up and down the stairs, while Caroline lined up a group of blocks by shapes and size. She always spent time carefully sorting things into categories, which had never struck me as quite so peculiar until that moment. The physician watched them for about ten minutes while I helplessly tried to direct their play into something more conventional. I tried to make them acknowledge each other and play with the toys in the "right" way. I felt myself sinking, and all I wanted to do was cover up whatever he saw that was not "normal." I wanted to hide it from the physician and myself.

After many questions and answers, and some less than successful attempts to interact with my girls, the physician took a breath and said, "Well, your younger daughter is autistic, and your older daughter has a slighter degree of autism as well." He tried to comfort me by saying that this was just the initial diagnosis, and kids make enormous progress through intervention. But I was numb, trying to absorb what he said. I had worked with children severely affected by autism at a summer camp during my college years. It had always seemed like something so remote from my life. Many of those children didn't speak and avoided hugs. My girls were happy, they spoke, and they loved hugs and kisses. I asked the physician about the ways in which they didn't fit my stereotypical view of autism. The physician then pointed out that my girls' play was repetitive and not creative. Caroline's language was largely rote phrases. And both of my girls' eye contact was minimal and fleeting. At that moment, I had a flash of a sweet little boy with blond curly hair at that summer camp; he always looked at me out of the corner of his eye, just like Caroline did. I knew it was true. I felt a sudden surge of panic; I had no idea what to do next. With a few pleasant words of encouragement, the physician walked us back out to the front desk and handed Lizzie's chart to the receptionist. He advised me to make another appointment to have Caroline formally evaluated, so she could receive services. Shortly after filling out some paperwork and collecting the names of educational psychologists and special needs nursery schools, we left.

Still my girls

In the parking lot, my girls' dad told me he was certain the physician was wrong. He was anxious to just get in his car and drive away from the whole revelation. Seconds later I was alone and bewildered, standing in the parking lot, holding my girls' hands. I put the girls in their car seats and just sat there for while. I was filled with images of special education classrooms sealed off from the rest of the school kids, weddings that might never happen, adult group homes, lifetimes of opportunities never to be realized. I was too numb to cry. I was in shock. Both of my girls had been diagnosed with forms of autism, and I had no idea how to help them.

After a few minutes, Lizzie spoke. "McDonald's?" she asked hopefully, with a big smile on her face. Caroline was smiling too at her sister's suggestion. I looked back at my girls in the car; they didn't look any different to me than they had before that appointment. They were still Lizzie and Caroline, still sweet, smiling, happy girls. Nothing had changed, certainly not how much I loved them or how much joy they brought to my life. What I didn't know then is that the diagnosis of autism is just one way of describing certain traits of theirs, and that it in no way defines who they are. They were and are so much more than a clinical diagnosis of a few words. What I didn't realize then is that my girls and I were and are powerful. The physician let me know their challenges, but what he couldn't see was all the potential that was still there, untapped, unknown, and unstoppable.

A diagnosis is just a word, not a prophecy

I wish someone had told me then what I am telling you now: autism is just a word. Your daughter is exactly the same person as she was before the diagnosis; you just have some new information about her now. Autism is not a child, it is not a person, and it is not prediction of a certain future. The truth about autism is that we don't know how much potential there is in our daughters. There is intelligence, sensitivity, even brilliance in people with autism. The job of the parent is just to love, defend, and advocate for their child, to help her discover all of the gifts inside of her. The gifts are there; sometimes it is just more difficult to let them out. The following chapters will help you understand the many therapies, services, and people available to help your daughter. I will also share the victories and challenges of my girls to illustrate all the ways in which your daughter will grow, struggle, and blossom. When my children were initially diagnosed, I felt lost. However, though I didn't realize it at the time, that day began a wonderful journey. As I found out, it was not a journey to discover what my children could not do. Rather it was a journey to help them uncover what their many talents are, to help them become the miraculous girls they are today. Once you get your balance and bearings, you will find a world of people who see your daughter's potential and beauty and are anxious to be a part of her success story. Like I said, it is a rough entry, but you will be just fine, and your special girl will be amazing.

The heart of the matter about a diagnosis

1. The day your daughter is diagnosed on the autism spectrum is a tough day, but it will get much better with time.

2. Think of the diagnosis as important information to describe certain areas in which your daughter is struggling. It is not the definition of who she is.

3. Try to think of all the subsequent evaluations as gathering further information in order to get your daughter the most help possible.

4. A diagnosis is not a prophecy. Your daughter's early diagnosis is just an estimate; no one can predict her potential.

5. Your daughter is exactly the same sweet, amazing little girl as she was before you heard the word "autism."

Chapter 3

Girls on the Spectrum

"I am not afraid of storms for I am learning how to sail my ship."

—Louisa May Alcott

What's different about girls on the spectrum?

Before we begin to explore the various aspects of life with our girls, I wanted to take a moment to address our unique situation as parents of daughters on the autism spectrum. Current estimates indicate there are four or five boys for every one girl diagnosed on the spectrum (CDC 2011b). That certainly makes us the minority. It is difficult enough to have a child diagnosed with a lifelong developmental challenge, but then to discover you are a curiosity in that group makes life even harder. When my girls were first diagnosed and I shared that news with people, the usual comment was, "Really? Your *daughters* have autism?" It made me feel even more inadequate, if that was possible. Not only had I produced two children who had to face such challenges, but somehow I had even managed to bungle that. Even specialists in the field found the fact that I had two girls on the spectrum a novelty. I remember one appointment with a specialist whose eyes opened wide as he stared at us, mesmerized, repeating, "Both girls, fascinating, just fascinating." I felt like Mrs. E.T. with my two junior aliens. This feeling of "alienation" only added more loneliness to my already full plate of troubles. And when Caroline started nursery school at a preschool for kids with special needs and I joined the parent support group, it was the same: it was nearly all boys who had autism and the parents of those boys. I found no one with whom to talk about the special hopes, concerns, and fears of having a girl on the autism spectrum.

This minority status in the autism community has created other problems for girls and their families as well. First of all, the overwhelming majority of research done on autism has focused on boys; girls are what one researcher called "research orphans" (Bazelon 2007). The few studies available highlight the need for more investigation. One of the most startling revelations was published in June 2011, in the medical journal *Neuron*; researchers found autism in girls may be caused by different genes than autism in boys (Gilman *et al.* 2011). This discovery may well change the way autism is viewed in girls. It only stands to reason that if autism originates differently in girls, it may affect them differently as well. We obviously need research focused specifically on the ways in which girls on the autism spectrum develop, learn, and behave.

Since it has always been assumed that girls were no different from boys on the spectrum, most of the treatment paradigms and educational interventions have been designed based on the symptoms and needs of boys on the spectrum. This does not mean those programs are not relevant or useful to girls. However, it could mean that the interventions and treatments presently used may have to be modified or changed to be more helpful to girls. Furthermore, it does appear that some of the key issues and challenges specific to girls on the spectrum are not addressed in the current body of knowledge. Another hurdle for girls has been in diagnosis: because girls with autism may behave more passively than their male counterparts, some have gone undiagnosed until elementary school or later, with parents struggling to help their daughters on their own, long after the early intervention years have passed (Giarelli *et al.* 2010). Even for the girls whose autism is obvious, their struggles and strengths may still be different from those of boys, and those distinctions need to be investigated so we can offer our girls the best interventions to create the possible outcomes.

Most of what I know about the specific issues of girls on the spectrum has been gained not from reading articles or journals but from my personal experiences with my daughters and my students. From what I have seen, the special challenges for girls on the spectrum seem to arise out of the fact that they are *still girls*, and having a social communication challenge can be even more difficult when you represent the half of humanity that is supposed to be really good at making friends, carrying on conversations, exhibiting good manners, and generally being more civilized. This paradox can make life a rocky path for our girls to walk. However, with knowledge and a little extra care, you can help your daughter navigate that path successfully.

The following are the most striking differences the research has uncovered thus far, many of which you may see in your own daughter. In each of these areas, two facts are clear: girls on the autism spectrum are different from boys in some crucial ways, and they are also regarded differently by the world in some difficult ways.

Girls tend to be less aggressive than boys
Quiet little ladies

Generally speaking, research has found that girls on the spectrum are often less aggressive than their male peers (Giarelli *et al.* 2010). Some, in fact, are very timid and compliant. This more passive presentation may account for the fact that many more girls are diagnosed at later ages. As Judith Gould of the National Autistic Society explains, "Characteristics such as shyness and over-sensitivity, common to people affected by autism, are sometimes deemed to be typically female traits" (BBC News 2008). Many girls on the spectrum simply do not fit the more aggressive profile doctors and teachers expect of a child with autism. Children with autism are presumed to act out and resist when faced with frustration and confusion. Therefore, it is easy to pass over a shy, reticent little girl. And while a gentle nature may help these girls fit in better, it can make it harder for them to have their needs met socially and academically in school.

My older daughter, Lizzie, was one of those girls. When she was young, she was content to play with her dolls and watch her videos for hours without complaint. At nursery school, she just watched the other children play, and amid the hustle and bustle rarely interacted with anyone. Once she became accustomed to nursery school, she never caused a problem or said a word, and it would have been easy just to ignore her. Needless to say, if not for the special efforts of her teacher, the whole experience might have been a waste for her. So while it is easier for parents and teachers to have a sweet, docile little girl on the spectrum, you must be sure that your daughter's needs are still being met by her school program. Since the majority of students with special needs in general are boys, and within the autism group the overwhelming majority are boys, it is easy for a quiet, compliant girl to be ignored. Before I returned to teaching full-time, I worked at the special needs preschool Caroline had attended. I remember one non-verbal girl with autism at the preschool who was so silent and meek that it was easy for her to get lost amid her classmates' meltdowns and rollicking play. It was essential that she spend some time working with the teacher and just one other girl in order for her to get the instruction and attention she needed. In fact, if you know your daughter is very timid, include as much one-on-one instruction time in her school programming as you can.

But not all girls
Spunky spitfires

Although some girls on the spectrum may be quiet and meek, there are still many who are just as loud and aggressive as the boys. As many parents know, girls on the spectrum can have meltdowns that rival those of any boy on the planet. And while those girls who do fulfill the profile of a more aggressive child may be more easily diagnosed, those disruptive behaviors may be less tolerated by adults and peers who find the behavior even more unacceptable in a girl. People are often not prepared to see aggression and loss of control in girls because it flies in the face of gender stereotypes about boys' and girls' behavior. As early as nursery school, girls are expected to be more polite, more sensitive to others' feelings, and more composed. Boys are expected, even encouraged, to be aggressive, boisterous, and physically active. These stereotypes continue all through school. Even in the high school in which I teach, there is much less tolerance for aggression and poor behavior in typical girls than their male peers. Is this fair? Absolutely not. You have to remember yourself not to project that same unfair bias on to your daughter and not to let any family member, friend, or teacher do so either. Our girls are susceptible to the same kind of sensory overload as any boy on the spectrum, and there should not be more stringent expectations of them. Make sure the school knows how to handle your daughter's behavior, so they can respond appropriately. And be sure to remind them that while you want to help your daughter learn to control her impulses, she shouldn't be held to a higher standard than the boys.

Imaginative play
Girls on the spectrum often like to play imaginatively

How children play is usually one of the first indicators of autism, especially in very young toddlers and babies. Parents are asked if their child plays rigidly with toys such as blocks and Lego. Does a child repeatedly line up objects or organize them by colors and shapes? This is the standard image of a child with autism. Or does a child play more imaginatively, creating free-flowing scenarios with dolls, putting on plays, imagining pirates and princesses? Imaginative play is seen as a sign of typical play in a child. Recent studies have found that some girls on the spectrum also have the capacity for and interest in playing imaginatively (Nichols, Moravcik, and Tetenbaum 2009), although they may not do so as well as their typical peers. This is one of the many promising strengths of girls on the autism spectrum. It shows a potential flexibility in the way their minds work, as well as a social nature. Girls on the spectrum often excel at creative endeavors such as reading and writing, rather than mechanical ones such as math and science (Bazelon 2007), and this may indicate a very different kind of autism than the one we have envisioned for so long. All these differences can be signs of potential for our girls to connect with people.

Both of my girls loved dolls and stuffed animals from the time they were very small, always sleeping with one beloved toy. And while I can see now that Caroline also played in ways very typical of children on the spectrum, lining up crayons and blocks, Lizzie never played that way. Lizzie always played imaginatively with her dolls. She would play for hours, making her dolls go to school and put on plays. This is one of the reasons her diagnosis came as such a shock to me. As time went on, however, her imagination actually provided me with lots of opportunities to teach social skills to Lizzie, as we created social scenarios for her dolls. Eventually we were able to have Caroline join us as well. So, if your daughter does like to play imaginatively, you can use that interest to teach social skills and help foster her understanding of emotions and relationships. This is topic explored further in Chapter 5 ("Friends") and Chapter 10 ("Autism Truths and Myths").

Studies are now finding that older girls on the spectrum are also imaginative. Many of them enjoy artistic pursuits such as drawing and painting, reading and writing, activities in which they can also work out feelings about relationships and people. I know Lizzie loves to read and write, and she also loves musicals. She often works through feelings by journaling. Caroline also loves drawing pictures of her favorite television characters, the Little Einsteins and the Peanuts kids, and talking about their relationships with each other. Although Caroline's creative "play" is more limited, it still represents an interest in understanding open-ended human relationships. I can see how these imaginative pastimes in both of my girls reflect their interests in people, feelings, and relationships.

Social skills

Girls on the spectrum want to be social and have friends

The capacity for and interest in imaginative play relates to another important feature of many girls on the spectrum: a longing for social interactions and friends, which points to greater social awareness in many girls. In one study, even girls with significant cognitive impairments show "more prosocial behavior than boys" (Bacon *et al.* 1998, p.139). Both of my girls have always loved other children and wanted friends. However, knowing how to make friends and keep friends has not always been easy for them. Research shows that even though language and social skills are difficult for our girls, their need for friendships is often profound, and the lack of friends is a source of tremendous heartache at times (Bazelon 2007). This is one of the ways in which being a girl with autism may be distinctly different. I know many boys on the spectrum who are often quite content pursuing their particular interests in a solitary way and maintaining relationships with only family. However, the girls on the spectrum whom I know seem to really want girlfriends of their own age with whom to spend time, share experiences, and feel a sense of belonging. I imagine this is because, autism or not, they are still girls.

When I look at my friendships with women, I see so much love, support, and validation. They are emotionally intimate relationships, and I know I would be very lonely without my girlfriends. My husband has friends for different reasons—shared activities, interests, humor, and banter. I can say with a great deal of certainty that my husband and his friends do not regularly share secrets and talk about their feelings. I know this is a generalization, but it often seems to me that women need close friends in a much more essential way than men do. Perhaps it has some evolutionary purpose in maintaining our role as mothers and nurturers. Whatever the genesis of our need for close female friends, it only makes sense that the need for friendships in girls on the spectrum would be deeper and more profound than that of their male counterparts. Unfortunately, this is not an easy thing for our girls to accomplish.

The difficulties our daughters face when trying to make friends arise out the fact that they are socially awkward girls often trying to win friendships with typical girls. The girl factor is at work again. Boys are often oblivious to and more forgiving of quirks and social gaffes in their peers. However, typical girls are more tuned in to subtle social nuances; they have adept social skills and stronger intuition when someone is "different," which makes our daughters' deficits all the more apparent. In addition, girls hold their peers to more stringent standards of "acceptable" behavior and are often much less tolerant of quirky or unusual behavior. Our daughters' deep desire for friendships, combined with their lack of social sophistication, can too often lead to painful rejection. To compound that, the flip side of the wonderful friendships girls can maintain is the incredible unkindness they are at times capable of displaying. Our girls are more likely to be ostracized and bullied than typical girls. Their awkwardness, together with their inability to discern insincerity and mockery, make them easy targets.

I remember, when Lizzie was in kindergarten, there was a little girl who created the "cheerleader game" at recess; she would line the girls up and judge who was pretty enough and skinny enough to participate. At five years old, this little girl was choosing her friends based on these hurtful, superficial standards. Lizzie told me this one day and was sad that, halfway through the school year, she had still never been chosen. Girls can be very unkind at times. It is so important to be aware of the other girls at your daughter's school and try to have the school intervene to create opportunities for friendships for your daughter. Our daughters' social awareness underscores how important it is to help them find friends with whom they feel connected and accepted. I will discuss how to do this and how to help your daughter help and maintain friendships in Chapter 5 ("Friends"), but it is important to note that this deep need for friendships is one of the more challenging and important issues faced by girls on the autism spectrum.

Social stereotypes
A challenge for our girls

Another special consideration in having a daughter with autism is finding a way to help her fit in with her peers in the more traditional ways of clothing and appearance. Although no one is suggesting that you become a pageant mom, it is in your daughter's best interest not to stand out dramatically from her peers because of unusual clothing or a generally unkempt appearance. The difficulty arises out of the fact that studies show that girls on the spectrum often have no interest in or idea how to go about grooming themselves or generally fulfilling those superficial social norms (Nichols *et al.* 2009). While boys can often get by in sweats and T-shirts, girls have no such options when attempting to fit in with their peers. As many of us can attest, clothes, hair, and style are a huge part of our "girl" culture and require a lot of effort, time, and ability to master. Even the sportiest typical girls I teach in high school have a good grasp on grooming and wearing stylish athletic clothing. Even the girls who chose to be "Goth" or counterculture do so with style and finesse.

When our girls dress inappropriately or neglect their grooming, they stand out even more from their typical peers. Even more distressing for some girls on the spectrum, their lack of interest or understanding in appearance can leave them at a loss to know how to connect with their typical peers, when something that has no appeal to them is the focus of so much of their peers' time, conversations, and concerns. Additionally, since many girls on the spectrum struggle with fine motor skills such as handwriting, you can imagine how the finer points of fashion and make-up can be a struggle. Be understanding with your daughter as she tries to process it all. I draw a line between hygiene and fashion. Some things are non-negotiable in my house, such as cleanliness and grooming. I am militant about daily showers. Other things, such as fashion, take more patience and creativity to figure out.

Finally, there are girls on the spectrum for whom the whole issue of gender is confusing. They know they are girls, but what that means in social terms is confusing for them, especially if their interests are more in line with the things boys like. This issue takes sensitivity and care on your part. You never want to make your daughter feel ashamed of who she is, just as you want to help her feel at home in the world. Sometimes it just takes longer for girls on the spectrum to mature enough to understand gender as a concept. Your priority is to consider how to help your daughter fit in, while still respecting who she is as an individual. And remember, it is not just about superficial appearances; finding an appropriate sense of style and grooming underlies our daughters' greater need to be accepted by and included with their peers as much as possible.

Depression
Our girls are at greater risk of depression

One of the most sobering truths I have read about repeatedly is that our girls are at greater risk of depression than both typical children and their male counterparts on the spectrum (Kim *et al.* 2000). You can certainly see why this would be so. When you combine the emotional nature of girls with feelings of confusion and inadequacy in making human connections, it is easy to see how depression could follow. Trying to live up to standards you don't understand and adhere to rules that are invisible and absurd to you must be so frustrating. When what you most desire—friends and acceptance—are elusive and hard to maintain, it must feel hopeless at times. Even more discouraging, when talking is a struggle, let alone articulating feelings, it can seem impossible to seek help for depression. As parents, we must be watching carefully for the non-verbal clues of depression, such as appetite changes, sleep patterns, and overall mood and temperament. However, I do not believe depression has to be an inevitable by-product of autism. I firmly believe if we are proactive and optimistic as parents, we can help our daughters overcome their difficulties and develop healthy self-esteem based on the very real contributions they can make to this world. They will look to us to believe they are worthy, capable, and lovable just as they are.

Our girls' differences can also be their strengths

If you are feeling dismayed at this point, do not be. Identifying the challenges is just the first step in helping our daughters. I can attest to the fact that there are many ways to help our daughters become happy, well-adjusted, and successful girls. The most important way is just to believe in them. And while the things that make our daughters different from boys on the spectrum can sometimes make their lives more difficult, they can also provide pathways for progress. The behavior issues our girls face, whether too passive or surprisingly aggressive, can be dealt with and used as opportunities for growth and advocacy. We are the ones who will widen the understanding of what it is to be a girl with autism. The capacity for imaginative play, if present, can provide unique opportunities to teach and develop emotional understanding. And even when my girls have felt the sting of rejection by an unkind classmate, the desire for friends is still a positive and healthy emotional need that connects our daughters with the world.

Our daughters may also represent enormous potential for the entire community of people with autism and their families, as they seem to have a greater need and capacity for self-expression. Just as Temple Grandin has done, our girls may well be able to articulate to the world what it means to have autism. And while we may not be painting our nails with our daughters, the world of clothing and grooming is another opportunity to bond and find positive ways for your little girl to express her beautifully unique self. One of the coolest things about having a daughter on the spectrum is that she will never be a replica of any other image, brand name, or social stereotype. Whatever she does, she will do it her way, with her distinctive brand of quirkiness. I love my daughters and the girls on the spectrum whom I teach for always being unabashedly true to themselves. What a refreshing quality in the world today! Although our girls do face some tough challenges, helping your daughter discover the unique person she is can make having a girl on the spectrum a spectacular experience.

The heart of the matter about girls on the spectrum

1. Girls on the autism spectrum may be different from their male counterparts in significant ways that have not yet been thoroughly researched.

2. Girls on the spectrum may be quieter and more passive, possess stronger imaginative play skills, and have a deeper need for friendships than boys on the spectrum.

3. Girls on the spectrum may be at higher risk of depression due to struggles with social pressure and gender roles.

4. Our girls' greater social awareness and need for self-expression may just prove to be their best assets, and they may teach the world a great deal about autism.

5. Girls on the autism spectrum are simply amazing!

Chapter 4
Education

"Education is not filling a pail but the lighting of a fire."

—William Butler Yeats

Testing and evaluation

After your daughter is diagnosed on the autism spectrum by a physician, one of the first steps you should take is to have her undergo a complete educational and psychological evaluation to assess her educational needs. This lengthy test is meant to identify your daughter's strengths and weaknesses. In the US, you can usually have this done through your health insurance, or the school district in which you live will provide it. Sometimes it is even good to have two evaluations done (one through insurance and one through school) to see if the results are consistent and therefore likely to be more accurate. However, it can be a trial getting a child to cooperate, so don't torture your daughter or yourself if getting one evaluation is an ordeal. In the UK, your daughter's GP (general practitioner) should be able to refer you to the appropriate specialists for evaluations.

In the both the US and the UK, these evaluations typically look at your daughter's developmental and cognitive abilities using a variety of tests. The validity of these results is questionable with children on the spectrum. The test most often used in both countries is the Wechsler Intelligence Scale for Children (WISC-IV), which uses a "great deal of language" (Caldwell 2008). If your challenge is communication, how well can a test that relies on language accurately assess your intelligence? Therefore, I am not sure how reliable the WISC-IV can be in judging our daughters' cognitive abilities. Recent studies have found that testing children on the spectrum with the Raven's Standard Progressive Matrices (RSPM), which evaluates skills such as inference and creative thinking through visuals, yields significantly higher test scores than the WISC-IV (Thomas 2009). An important question to ask is: What kind of intelligence is the test being used to examine? One of the most important distinctions with children on the spectrum is how their crystallized intelligence compares with their fluid intelligence. Crystallized intelligence refers to "our store of memorized facts" (Coplan 2010, p.117). This is what you see when your daughter can memorize facts, dates, dialogue from movies, and so on. Fluid intelligence is "our ability to recognize patterns or relationships, either verbal or non-verbal" (p.117). Fluid intelligence is what helps us put things in context, and in a sense this is the more practical kind of intelligence; it is what helps people problem-solve, predict, and comprehend general concepts. Our children usually have trouble with fluid intelligence because it involves generalizing or translating groups of facts into concepts. It is important to understand that your daughter may have great strengths in some areas and weaknesses in others. However, don't let those weaknesses discourage you. Any kind of intelligence is potential and reason for hope.

Also, keep in mind that no matter what intelligence test the psychologist uses, if your daughter is not feeling particularly accommodating, the results will not be accurate. Lizzie was a proper little angel at her evaluation and scored well. Caroline spilled blocks all over, ignored everyone, and scored low in all areas. Lizzie's results showed deficits in some areas, but lots of average and above-average scores as well. Caroline's early test results indicated her IQ was well below average in nearly every area. However, now at the ages of 12 and 14, I can say that both of my girls are pretty smart. So I am not sure how accurate any of those test results were. Bottom line: learn what you can from the intelligence testing, but don't take it as any kind of absolute verdict on your daughter and her potential.

Your daughter will probably also be evaluated by speech, occupational, and physical therapists to assess her needs in these areas. I know that having all of your daughter's abilities evaluated can be overwhelming and scary, but remember this is a necessary precursor for your daughter to receive help and make the greatest strides possible. Sometimes, as parents, we have an inclination to downplay our daughters' struggles out of a sense of protection or pride. Try not to do that here because you want the various people evaluating your daughter to provide the most help possible for her, not the least. After all the testing is done, you, your daughter, and her complete evaluation are off to school.

Starting school: Crafting a program

School is a huge part of any child's life, and feeling happy and capable at school is essential to a child's success there. For a child with special challenges, it is even more important that school be a place of joy, acceptance, and opportunity for growth. Navigating the school system can at times be a frustrating endeavor for parents of special children. I know this only too well as both a parent and teacher. I have been a teacher for most of my adult life. Although I am a general education English teacher, I work with many special education students in an inclusive co-teaching program which integrates regular and special education students. It is one of many models now offered in schools, designed so that students of all ability levels can learn together. Obviously, I am also a parent dealing with the school district, overseeing my daughters' educational programs. Therefore, I have the opportunity to look at education from both a teacher's and parent's perspective. I hope to help you create the best educational experience possible for your daughter by providing all the information I can.

The meeting

The first step in your daughter's education will be a meeting with the school or agency providing her services to discuss her education plan, along with the teachers she already has or will have. Before I explain the particulars, allow me to offer some general advice. First, take a picture of your daughter with you to the meeting and show it everyone present before you begin. This reminds them that your daughter is a person, not just a program to be created in a cost-effective manner. Second, tell them some of the sweeter things about your daughter—things she loves, what makes her smile, and some of her talents. Remind them of your little girl's unique identity and worth, so they see a child and not just a disability. It is far too easy for schools simply to identify your daughter by her disability throughout school. How unfair and absurd that is! For example, I have no sense of direction; I can get lost in my own neighborhood if I veer off my regular route. I am also tremendously clumsy and I have problems with depth perception. I routinely bump into woodwork, chair legs, and counters. I know I should probably look into this, and some mythical day, when I have time, I will. However, when I meet people, I don't say, "My name is Eileen, and I am directionally and spatially disabled. That's the most important thing about me, so please think of me that way." But that's exactly what we do with children with special needs when we only view them one way. And school is especially guilty of having myopic vision when it comes to our kids, and of lowering expectations as a result. So always start every meeting about your daughter with reminders of the sweet, special human being for whom the meeting is being held.

Your daughter's program in the US: It's all about the IEP

In the US, depending on the age of your child, you will meet with a different agency to create a plan for your daughter. Early intervention, for children ages birth to three, will typically be handled through an agency in your state's or county's Department of Health. Your daughter's pediatrician can put in you touch with the appropriate agency. If your daughter is a preschool student (ages 3–5), you will meet with the Committee on Preschool Special Education (CPSE), and if your daughter is school age, you will meet with the Committee on Special Education (CSE). The CPSE will likely take place through your daughter's school district as they will participate in creating her preschool program. Obviously, the CSE meeting takes place at your daughter's school. One thing you *must* do before you have your daughter's CPSE or CSE meeting is visit the federal website: http://idea.ed.gov (Individuals with Disabilities Education Act 2004)

This website will explain in detail your daughter's rights in school. It covers preschool through post-secondary education. The United States' Individuals with Disabilities Education Act of 2004 guarantees children with disabilities (and all autism spectrum conditions qualify as such) the right to a "free and appropriate" education, in the least restrictive environment possible, funded by the government. "Least restrictive" means your daughter has the right to be educated side by side with her typical peers with access to all the opportunities school has to offer. It is also a very good idea to visit the Department of Education website of your home state, which will detail how the CPSE or CSE meeting will take place and will likely have user-friendly parent guides for you.

The CPSE or CSE meeting will typically include in attendance: the special education chairperson for the district, a school counselor, a special education teacher, a general education teacher, and you. There may also be a speech teacher and an occupational or physical therapist present. At the CPSE or the CSE meeting, an individualized education plan (IEP) will be developed by the school district with your input. In the US, every student with a disability is entitled to an IEP by law. The IEP is the document that will detail all the services your daughter will receive. The IEP is a legally binding document, meaning that by law the school must abide by what is agreed upon in the IEP. Therefore, it is essential that your daughter's IEP is comprehensive and addresses all her needs.

The IEP identifies your daughter's classification (for example, autism, PDD), outlines the setting of her education, the supports she will receive, and the goals and outcomes of her program. The IEP will include any other therapies your daughter needs, such as occupational, physical, and speech therapies. Do not be afraid to have your daughter classified accurately. Some parents prefer more general classifications, such as other health impairment (OHI) or learning disabled (LD), to autism because they fear stigma or discrimination. An accurate classification can only help your daughter and the teachers working with her. Among educated professionals, an autism classification is just another piece of information. It may also give your daughter access to more services than a more general classification. You want to advocate for your daughter to receive as many services as possible, as early as possible. You can always reduce services, but increasing them can be difficult, so err on the side of more services. Your input as a parent should be welcomed and valued at your daughter's IEP meeting. You know best how your daughter struggles and in what areas she needs the most help. Crafting a thorough IEP is one of the most important steps you can take to ensure your daughter is successful in school.

Your daughter's program in the UK:
It's all about the "statement"

The process is similar in the UK. If your daughter is too young for or not enrolled in nursery school, you may contact a Sure Start Children's Centre for information and direction about obtaining services for her. In the UK, services for children under three are delivered through a program called the Early Years Action or Early Years Action Plus. If your daughter is in preschool or primary school, the process will be conducted through her school and handled by the school's special education needs coordinator (SENCO). The program and level of support chosen for your daughter will depend on the degree of her special needs.

If your daughter is on the milder end of the autism spectrum, the school may first try to assist her through School Action or School Action Plus, programs designed to support students with a variety of special needs in the general school setting. However, if your daughter's challenges are more significant, the SENCO may proceed with a "Statutory Assessment" for your daughter, which is a detailed educational evaluation generated by the school. The "Statutory Assessment" will then be used to create a statement of Special Education Needs (SEN), which will outline your daughter's challenges and the support she is to be given in school. The statement of SEN is a very comprehensive document which will address all the areas of your daughter's educational plan. Sometimes the school may delay carrying out a Statutory Assessment in the hope that the School Action will be enough support. This can inhibit your daughter's progress. If you feel that your daughter's services are not adequately addressing her needs and supporting her progress, as a parent, you have the right to request that the LEA (local education authority) carry out a Statutory Assessment to fully evaluate your daughter's challenges and thus increase her support. Don't wait if you see your daughter floundering in school; she deserves the best chance to succeed.

Another issue that can prevent a child from receiving fully supportive services is that some parents fear their daughter being stigmatized by a statement of SEN, so they do not advocate for the Statutory Assessment. You do not have to feel that way. Think of the statement of SEN simply as more accurate and detailed information to support your daughter's success. The more information you can provide to the school, the better the school will be able to help your daughter. The more the school knows about your daughter's needs, the greater their obligation to provide services for her. By law, the school must provide the assistance, called the "special education provisions," outlined in the statement of SEN. Make sure you advocate for your daughter every step of the way.

As in the US, it is wise for you as a parent to familiarize yourself with the law and your daughter's rights under it, before your initial meeting with your daughter's school. The UK's Special Educational Needs and Disability Act 2001 guarantees children with special needs the right to be educated in mainstream schools with their typical peers. You can visit the UK website at: www.legislation.gov. uk/ukpga/2001/10/contents.

This document outlines in detail the many rights your daughter has to a complete education, with as much access to curricula and school resources as her typical peers. You should also visit the UK Department for Education website (www.education.gov.uk), where special education parent guides are available. Another incredibly informative website that helps parents of children with special needs to advocate for their children in school is IPSEA (Independent Parental Special Education Advice): www.ipsea.org.uk. This website provides parents with the information they need to advocate for their special children.

Both the US and the UK have progressive laws to protect and provide for our special children in school; however, it is your job as a parent to ensure that the school does all that it should and can to support your daughter's academic and social progress in school.

Preschool: Shapes and colors

Preschool services are usually fairly comprehensive for any child with a developmental issue in both the US and UK. You may have to advocate for your daughter to get the most services offered; however, government agencies and school districts (LEAs in the UK) are usually accommodating in the preschool years. By providing children with comprehensive preschool services, these agencies hope to avoid more expensive services later when children are older. In the US, services and resources may vary, depending upon availability in your area. In fact, if you live in a very sparsely populated area, you might even want to consider moving, so that your daughter can have access to all the therapeutic preschool services available. A good preschool program should include instruction at a school designed to address your daughter's specific needs, combined with at-home instruction from a special education itinerant teacher (one who travels to your home). This ensures that your daughter has one-on-one instruction, as well as the opportunity for socialization. If home instruction is not available in your area, be sure that ample one-on-one instruction is built into your daughter's preschool day. In the UK, the structure also varies, depending upon what is available in your area, but all children ages three and four are guaranteed preschool education by law.

The key is to begin these services as soon as possible after your daughter's diagnosis. The preschool program will typically include behavioral therapy and/or developmental-relational therapy, as well as the standard preschool curriculum. Since there are a variety of therapies recommended for children on the spectrum, you may find the preschools in your area offer a number of different programs. Chapter 7 ("Causes, Treatments, and Acceptance") explains the guiding philosophies of the various therapies as well their practices. In addition, special education preschool services usually include speech therapy, occupational therapy, and physical therapy, if necessary. Children on the spectrum may struggle to some extent in all these areas since autism is a neurological condition which can affect the entire nervous system. Some preschools are solely for children with developmental challenges, and others are a mixture of special needs kids and typical toddlers. As long as your daughter can have the full array of therapies necessary, I would opt for the integrated school, so your child can benefit from the role-modeling of typical peers. Visit the schools to learn about what they advocate and offer, and to find the best match for your daughter.

One thing to remember: it is incredibly important that any program you choose has speech therapy as a central component. You may find this surprising if you are envisioning the kind of speech services offered when many of us were in school, which focused on enunciation skills, remedying lisps and stutters. A good speech program is about communication, both verbal and non-verbal. Speech therapists can work on signing and other alternative modes of communication if your daughter is non-verbal. They also offer pragmatic language instruction (social language) and social skills practice. Since autism is at its heart a communication challenge, speech therapy is an absolute must. In addition, some schools may offer social skills training through speech services, and that is tremendously beneficial as well.

The most important resource any preschool must have is energetic, happy teachers who are devoted to working with your daughter. Visit programs and look for children who are enthusiastic, engaged, and constructively active. Make sure your daughter receives the most intervention she can in her preschool program because great strides are made in the early years. Most parents are happy with the preschool services their children receive.

Elementary or primary school: Advocating and negotiating

The school situation becomes more challenging and complicated once your child enters the public school system in kindergarten or primary school. As a teacher, I know there are professionals in schools who genuinely want what is best for your daughter. However, there are also administrators who want to provide your daughter with an education at the least possible cost. They are answerable to taxpayers and want to keep costs downs. Therefore, you must understand from the beginning that you and the school are at times coming at this process with very different goals. Your only goal is to get the best education for your daughter at any cost, so there will be times when you will be at odds with the school. It does not, however, have to be an unpleasant or adversarial situation. I have just always kept in mind that the school and I have different priorities at times. I try not to take it personally, but I never back down! I know the law is on my side.

Even if the process proves difficult, you will get much farther working with the school in a polite and professional manner than by coming across as a bitter, emotional special education parent. It is not fair, but you may be scrutinized more than the average parent by the schools, so you must always be on your game. Come prepared, know what you want for your daughter, and be firm. Err on the side of more services for your daughter rather than fewer, since it is much easier to pull back services than add them. Also be very wary of reducing services prematurely. Be sure your daughter doesn't need something before it is taken away, because chances are you will not be able to get it back. Don't be afraid; most teachers are truly dedicated to helping your daughter. Just remember, no one cares more about your daughter than you do, and no one has her best interests at heart more than you. So listen to the school's advice, but do what you believe in your heart is best. The bottom line is that no matter what the school says, generally speaking, the choice of programming for your daughter is yours.

What are the options?

Long ago, when I was a student, the children with special needs in my school were cloistered away somewhere in the basement of the school. We never saw them except for the occasional furtive glimpses in the hallways. They were mysterious to us, slightly scary, and they cowered when seen, as if shame was part of their DNA. It makes me so sad now to think of what that must have been like for them. Thank the Lord that times have changed, and our children have the right to be a part of school and are being acknowledged for their talents and contributions. Now children with special needs have the chance to be fully educated and to educate their typical peers in the process. This progress leaves parents with more choices, but often feeling bewildered at what to choose.

What is meant by the "least restrictive environment"?

The US's Individuals with Disabilities Education Act of 2004 requires that your daughter be educated in the "least restrictive environment," which means she has the right to be educated alongside her typical peers. Similarly, the UK's Special Educational Needs and Disability Act of 2001 guarantees that students with special needs have the right to be educated in mainstream schools with full access to the school curriculum and resources. In both countries, this means that the general education setting must be considered first, and there must be a compelling reason to remove a child from the general education classroom into a self-contained model or special school. Before that is done, the school must have exhausted every support possible in the general education setting to keep your daughter there—for example, aide services, assistive technology, modified curriculum. The legislation also guarantees that your daughter be educated in her home school, which means she should attend the same school she would have attended if she did not have special needs.

Even though your daughter has the right to be educated in the general education classroom, the choice of setting is dependent on your daughter's needs and your wishes. The spectrum of programming goes from full inclusion, which means a child is integrated into general education classes with ample support, to fully self-contained programs, which seek to teach your daughter in a smaller setting, with a more individually tailored program. Some parents may even wish for the school district (or LEA in the UK) to cover the cost of programming at a private school that specializes in autism and other developmental challenges. It is usually a fight to get a school district/ LEA to pay for private schools, but if you believe it is best for your daughter, fight for it. The key is deciding what is most productive and beneficial for your daughter.

Shortcomings of self-contained special education classes

Self-contained special education classrooms are meant to help students with significant special needs to learn at individual rates and make academic progress through remediation. If you choose this programming for your daughter, the special education classroom will be her "home" classroom. At first glance, it might seem to you that a self-contained program is best, as it promises to meet your daughter exactly where she is. And while that may be true in part, you need to investigate your options fully before you decide. Too often children with special needs are automatically put in self-contained classrooms, sequestered away from their peers. Although some self-contained programs do an excellent job of tailoring instruction to individual students, these programs are not without their downsides.

Full-day, self-contained special education classes in primary or elementary school can actually hinder a child's success in school for a number of reasons. First of all, too often children in self-contained models actually fall farther behind rather than make academic gains because they are not in an environment of high expectations. In addition, when students are isolated in a special education class, they are deprived of opportunities to interact with and learn from the role-modeling of their typical peers. Furthermore, since their home classroom is a special education class, they are often viewed as outsiders by the kids and the teacher in the general education class when they do have opportunities to join them. In essence, children in self-contained classes often seem to be orbiting around the outer edge of school, not really able to enjoy and learn from the full range of social and academic opportunities school can offer.

Another factor to consider with a daughter in special education classes is that the majority of children in special education are still boys, and that is even truer for children on the spectrum or those diagnosed with attention deficit hyperactivity disorder (ADHD). Therefore, if you do choose a self-contained model, it may be that much harder for your daughter to find girls with whom to be friends. Not only will she lack the company of girls, but she may well be in class with boys who are modeling less than stellar behavior. The worst Caroline's behavior ever became was the summer when she was six and she attended a program for children on the spectrum that was comprised of almost all boys except for her and one other girl. She copied many of the most disruptive behaviors she saw. If you do choose for your daughter to spend some time in a self-contained program, try at least to be sure there are other girls there with whom she can connect. And be sure the teachers give your daughter just as much time and attention as the boys in the classroom often command.

There are two goals to keep in mind when designing a program for your daughter: giving your daughter the best chance to build skills, academic and social, and making her a part of her school community and the wider world. So do not be too quick to allow the school to place your daughter in a self-contained program that makes it easiest for them. Make sure you choose the very best program to meet her needs.

Inclusion, not seclusion: What your daughter gains being a student in the general education classes

What is inclusion? Inclusion is the philosophy that children with special needs deserve to be educated with their typical peers, enjoying the opportunities offered by the general education curriculum. I believe strongly as a parent and educator that, in elementary or primary school, children with special needs should be included in the general education classroom as much as possible. While your daughter may need to spend a portion of the day in a self-contained, smaller setting to focus on improving academic skills, she also needs to be included in meaningful activities with her typical peers on a regular basis.

What inclusion offers: The three S's

I call the philosophy behind inclusion the three S's—socialization, stimulation, and structure. First, our daughters need to have the social opportunities provided by their more typical peers. Watching their peers teaches them norms of behavior and social interaction in a natural, organic, and consistent manner. They absorb through daily opportunities how people speak, interact, learn, and behave. There is no book on earth that can teach what being surrounded by more able children can teach. Second, they need and deserve the stimulation of a regular curriculum. Of course, the curriculum may have to be modified, but they will learn so much more by being stimulated and included than by being allowed to "work at their own pace." Caroline learned at least as much by watching her typical peers master a skill as she did from individual instruction. I truly believe the joy and bustle of the general education classroom wakes them up and keeps them eager to develop. The self-contained classrooms often do not provide the opportunity for children to stretch to their potential.

Also, children with special needs, especially kids with autism spectrum issues, thrive on structure. The general education classroom is nothing if not structured, full of reliable rituals, a comforting schedule, and smiling faces of familiar peers every day. Our children need a variety of activities and environments to stay engaged in school. The general education classroom moves energetically from one activity to another in affirming groups, and our daughters can benefit from being a part of this structure. Let your daughter at least try the general education setting first, before you confine her academic activities solely to the self-contained special education class. And no matter where your daughter learns her reading and math skills, she should belong to a general education "home" class, for special events such as field trips and parties and to attend classes such as physical education and art and music. It is the right of our daughters to be offered the most, not the least, the schools can deliver.

What an inclusive model looks like

An inclusive model means that your daughter's "home" classroom is the general education classroom, and her program builds out from there. She is a member of a general classroom, and, if necessary, goes from there into smaller group settings for other therapies such as speech therapy. This allows your daughter every opportunity to stay in with her peers for as much of the day as possible and identifies her as part of the general education classroom and student body. Your daughter may need a one-to-one aide (called an individual needs assistant (INA) in the UK) to participate in the general education classroom, and that is fine. Caroline still has a one-to-one aide going in seventh grade, and she is still in the general education setting. Insist the school provide a one-to-one aide if that is what's necessary. By law, the school needs to exhaust every possible support for keeping your daughter in the general education setting before moving her to a self-contained classroom. In other words, if you place your daughter in the general classroom, the school has to try very hard to make it work. That's what least restrictive means.

If you are worried about your daughter's other special needs being met in the general education setting, be assured that any of her specialists can "push in" to the general education classroom and deliver services there, or your daughter can still receive those services in a smaller specialized classroom. All of this can be included in the IEP. You may find it most beneficial to split where the services are delivered. In elementary school, Caroline usually had her speech sessions in the smaller speech room half of the time, and the other half of the time the speech teacher joined her in the general classroom, helping her to practice those skills. Never did anyone question why the speech teacher was there or Caroline's time spent in the smaller setting. She was a member of that class, same as everyone else.

In conclusion, whatever form your daughter's program eventually takes, be aware of her rights and all of the options that should be offered to her by law. I would strongly encourage allowing your daughter to spend as much of her day with her typical peers because she is not so different as the school or the world might have you think. You are ultimately the architect of your daughter's program, and you will have to decide what program best suits her needs. However, in case you are hesitant about putting your daughter in with her typical peers, or if you meet with resistance from the school in requesting an inclusive model, allow me to offer some perspectives which support inclusion.

Four reasons to support inclusion
Reason number one: Empathy is essential

There are several arguments against inclusion, and I would like to address those now. First of all, parents often think their kids are "safer" in the self-contained room. Let me assure you, typical kids are nicer than you think. If you explain special needs to them in a way they can understand, they will be empathic and willing to help. Sometimes other parents may resist, but it is not their choice. The children will take their cue from the teacher in school. When typical children are with developmentally challenged peers from a young age, kindergarten and up, they are accepting, protective, and kind to them right through high school. In the high school in which I teach, some of the children with most significant special needs are in a life skills class, a self-contained program focusing on basic living skills such as cooking and shopping and fostering self-advocacy. I have children in my classes, typical kids, who still stop by one of the life skills classes in high school to visit with their former elementary school classmates. Even though kids in the life skills class have left inclusive academic programming by high school to focus on more functional skills, they are not forgotten by their typical peers. The typical kids still feel connected to these special peers because they knew them as young children. Spending their young years with these kids changes how they view all people with special needs, and thus has the potential to change the way the people with special needs are viewed in our society in general. Unfortunately, not enough people have this shared experience that engenders such tenderness. This kind of empathy can only happen if we insist on inclusion for all kids with special needs, in the elementary and primary years at least. Bonds are forged there that age and developmental differences cannot break down. Friendships we make as children have a loyalty and sweetness that last forever.

Reason number two: Education is an experience, not a product

Second, there is a worry that the work will be too hard in the general education classroom. It need not be so. Let the teachers modify it, break it down, make it doable. Let your daughter learn what she can in the atmosphere of others learning, amid high expectations and achievement. You will never know what is too hard until you let her try. If her grades are poor, who cares? Is she learning? Is she trying? Is she happy? Is she lively? These are the only questions that matter. If Caroline scores poorly on a test, I tell Caroline's teachers not to write the grade on her paper, just "Nice job!" or "Good effort!" She is having the opportunity and the experience, and that is what helps. The teachers may resist because initially it may be more work for them. You must push back. You must tell them your goals for your daughter. It is the experience of school, not the grades, that matters for children with special needs. This is the only way to find their talents, discover their gifts. Reframe what you expect, leave it open-ended, and help the teachers do the same. If you approach the teachers and school staff, offering your help and asking for theirs, and you are polite but firm in your position, you will succeed. At some point when your daughter is older, it may make more sense to have her enter a vocational program, a program that focuses on more basic life skills, but don't give up on her academics too soon. And always insist your daughter be included for physical education, art, music, health; those classes will provide role-modeling and mental stimulation right through high school. And those typical peers still need to see our children, help them, and remember they are there. Our daughters' typical peers will make the laws that affect their lives. Let's keep their hearts open all through high school.

Reason number three: Money well spent

Another concern you may hear from other parents is the argument that inclusion takes funds away from the typical kids. The financial argument centers on the idea that it is too expensive to integrate children with special needs. On average in the US nationally, 50 percent of special education expenses are paid by federal and state funding allocated for this purpose. You can check the financial figures for your local school online at Federal Education Budget Project (http://febp. newamerica.net). Families aren't moving to districts to get funding; the funding follows the kids. The funds are there because the kids are there, not the other way around. It is true that schools do spend a lot of money on special education, but they also routinely spend a good deal of money on enrichment activities such as competitive sports and programming for the gifted, which are largely not options for our kids. So should taxpayers begrudge the money spent on our daughters just to allow them to participate in the basics of school with dignity? Finally, to those who say schools must spend far more per student on students with special needs than on the regular education student, think of your health insurance policy. Surely healthy people don't get as much money out of their health insurance as those with chronic or life-threatening illnesses. Yet do we begrudge ill people health care for those conditions? So ask those parents of typical kids: Would you rather have your child be the one acing the math test without help and then trotting off to baseball practice, or the one who needs extra funds spent on the expensive wheelchair, or the computer-assisted communication, or the one-to-one aide? Pretty easy to answer, huh?

Reason number four: Symbiotic success

> *"It is one of the most beautiful compensations of this life that no man can sincerely try to help another without helping himself."*
>
> —*Ralph Waldo Emerson*

Finally, I'd like to address the common objection that the presence of special education students in the general education setting takes away from the curriculum and instruction of typical kids. I have to take a breath before I address this one. In a world where some children are at such a natural advantage, it is hard to understand why anyone would begrudge a developmentally challenged child a chance to learn. However, all parents are most concerned with what is best for their child. So here goes… If the classroom is structured with the appropriate support staff—aides, teaching assistants, and so on—there is no reason why any student, challenged or gifted, should be neglected. By reducing the number of children in day-long, self-contained special education classrooms, you reduce the need for staffing there. Those members of staff are therefore able to be present in the general education setting. More staff means greater opportunity for all children to receive help and learn.

Additionally, typical children learn many vital skills when they work with their peers who are developmentally challenged. As teachers, we are constantly hearing that the skills required for success in the world are not strictly academic. The Partnership for 21st Century Skills is a national, non-profit, educational organization that "advocates for 21st century readiness for every student." They define readiness as having mastered the following skills: "critical thinking and problem solving, communication, collaboration, and creativity and innovation" (Partnership for 21st Century Skills 2011). Children need to learn to work in a team: to negotiate, share, compromise, and understand others' points of view. Therefore, typical students do not suffer from having peers with special needs in the classroom; on the contrary, the presence of those students provides them unique and meaningful opportunities to develop these essential skills. Working with classmates of varying abilities is a challenge to their creativity, problem solving, and communication skills. Sometimes the typical peers can even be mentors, helping to build both their self-esteem and empathy. As teachers, we know that we learn best when we teach. Gifted children learn an abundant amount when they are allowed to instruct their less capable peers. Done under the appropriately wise guidance of a teacher, this can be a wonderful opportunity for all children. Finally, when typical kids see the joy and struggles of their friends with special needs, it engenders gratitude, empathy, and love. There is no more meaningful or enriching experience for them than to know they have helped another child who is less fortunate.

We're all in this together

Inclusion is simply the best chance your daughter has to learn how to be a part of the world. If you feel unsure how to approach this with your daughter's school district, call your local Autism Society office (or local branch of the National Autistic Society in the UK) and ask about attending an educational conference on autism or special education. This will arm you with the knowledge you need to advocate for your daughter. If you truly feel after giving your daughter the experience in the general education setting that the class is too challenging academically, you can place her in a smaller class. But make sure that your daughter is still challenged academically in those smaller classes. And while I realize by secondary or high school our daughters may need to attend more practically based, vocational classes, continue to advocate for them to receive some academic instruction. Despite the fact that there are crucial developmental windows in early childhood, it doesn't mean that great strides are not made in the later years. Our daughters will keep learning and growing if they are provided with opportunities.

I was recently reminded of a story that illustrates the need to never give up on our daughters in school. A dear friend of mine has a young adult daughter with autism who is an avid reader. However, this young lady didn't start to comprehend what she was reading until she was 17 years old. Like so many kids with autism, she could decode written words, but their contextual meanings eluded her. In ninth grade, this girl's teachers told her mother, a psychiatrist, that reading comprehension was a skill beyond her daughter's level of ability, that although she could decode written language, she would never comprehend it. The school wanted her to be taken out of her English and reading courses. But the mother insisted her English and reading instruction continue. And at 17, something finally came into focus and the young lady started to absorb the content of what she was reading. She is now 21, and reading is one of her favorite activities and has provided her with much joy and solace. What an invaluable skill and glorious pastime she may have missed out on because her teachers judged too quickly, forgetting that learning is part of being alive and that the window never closes completely unless we slam it shut.

So, remember, just because a window doesn't open in elementary school doesn't mean it never will. Learning is a lifelong process, so ensure, no matter what setting you choose, that your daughter's school challenges her to keep learning throughout her education. And always insist that your daughter is included in the general education setting for art, physical education, and music classes, as well as lunch and recess. Those are times of the day when there is the greatest opportunity for social interaction. The beauty of physical education and the arts is that everyone can participate at his or her level of ability, and the classes are active and engaging by their very nature. So be sure your daughter is seen and has the chance to be part of her school throughout her entire school career. Trust me: the general education students need your daughter as much as she needs them. Our girls have much to learn from all the facets of school, and much to teach as well.

Lizzie

"Ability is of little account without opportunity."
—*Henry Wadsworth Longfellow*

Both of my girls have had successes in school in their own ways. As I mentioned earlier, Lizzie was one of those very compliant, quiet little girls on the spectrum. When she entered kindergarten, the school district wanted to place her in a program for children with special needs, specifically for kids on the spectrum. These children spent half of the day in a self-contained model, and the other half with their typical peers. I visited the self-contained classroom and saw a group of very active boys, all fighting over the same red square of carpet. When I inquired, I was told the population of the class would be largely the same the next year. I then followed the kids as they transitioned to the general education classroom where I was able to speak with both the special and general education teachers. I could see that even when "integrated," the children in this program remained a separate entity from the typical kids in the general education classroom, and their inclusion as a group seemed to be viewed more as an intrusion by their typical peers. Therefore, I politely declined, and told the district I wanted Lizzie to have a one-to-one aide in the regular kindergarten so she could benefit from being with her typical peers all day and be accepted as one of them. It was not easy, but I won. Lizzie had a great year, and the aide made sure she was not neglected or forgotten, and also facilitated social connections between Lizzie and her peers. The lesson from Lizzie's experiences is to make sure that you find a place and a program where your daughter's good behavior is rewarded, not ignored. In a world populated by high-flying boys, you must advocate for your timid little girl to be seen and heard.

For several subsequent years of elementary school, Lizzie had an aide to assist her in social situations because she was painfully shy and had some fears about new situations. Over time, Lizzie has grown tremendously and really opened up as a person. At this point, her only special education support is one period of academic support (resource room) during the day. Lizzie has been blessed with a great deal of natural intelligence, so she has always been in general education classes and earns high grades. She does struggle with processing information at times, but she is extremely bright. She is a fine writer, meticulous worker, and creative artist and singer. The academics of school, while challenging for her, are well within her abilities thus far. When Lizzie graduated from eighth grade, she won a prestigious award, voted on by both her teachers and peers, for personifying courage, compassion, and conscientiousness. Lizzie has made great progress in her maturity and academic skills. At this point, Lizzie's diagnosis is clearly Asperger's, so her challenges have been more social, and I will share those later.

Caroline

"What lies behind us and what lies before us are tiny matters compared to what lies within us."

—*Ralph Waldo Emerson*

Caroline's path in school has not been quite so smooth, but it has ultimately been pretty miraculous. When Caroline was first diagnosed at almost three years old, the next step was to have her evaluated by an educational psychologist to prepare her IEP for preschool. This educational psychological evaluation was done at a center for preschoolers with special needs. I was very nervous at what the outcome would be, given what I had already been told by the development pediatrician, whose pronouncement at Caroline's appointment had been fairly grim. Caroline was less than cooperative during the testing, and the results were terrible. She tested years behind in her language development. Her attention span was non-existent. She barely even glanced at the people administering the tests. I was told that Caroline was "mentally retarded"—they still used that awful term, instead of the current "mentally disabled" or "intellectually disabled." I was also told that Caroline's autism was severe. They told me she would most likely not be able to attend a regular public school for elementary school, and that her future was very limited. I was devastated by the news. Still, in my heart I didn't quite believe it. How could they possibly know that about her at three years old? Caroline always had this mischievous smile before she did anything naughty, and she was sneaky as can be. Surely these were signs of intelligence. And she loved to laugh! A sense of humor is a definite sign of intelligence. I knew there was a lot inside of her, and I wanted to help her get it out. I think that was the first time I got really angry at someone for claiming to know more about my daughter than I did, and I took it as a kind of challenge.

Preschool paradise

Caroline began attending Helping Hands Preschool that spring. It was a sweet place with lovely, patient teachers who were determined to help Caroline learn. Her program included a teacher who came to the house in the morning for one-on-one teaching, and then in the afternoon she attended a nursery school program with other children with a variety of special needs. The one-to-one sessions in the morning were ABA—applied behavior analysis. ABA involves reinforcing concepts through repetition; it is a well-respected, well-established method for teaching kids on the spectrum. Caroline learned quickly and was delighted to do so. She worked for bubbles—blowing bubbles when she mastered a word or color or letter. We also used PECS (Picture Exchange Communication System—a learning method that allows children with little or no verbal ability to communicate using pictures) to reinforce ideas and provide communication for the words she had not yet mastered. Through PECS she even began to initiate communication with us. She learned in leaps and bounds, and I started to feel hopeful. Please don't imagine it was a quick miracle, because it was not. She was three, not close to being potty-trained, still incredibly willful, her eye contact was fleeting at best, and at times she would refuse to work. However, I could see the intelligence inside of her starting to emerge.

By the time Caroline finished her second year at Helping Hands, her language had increased tremendously. She still confused her pronouns—"you" instead of "I"—but she could talk to me now, tell me what she wanted, if she was tired or hungry or cold. And her behavior had improved remarkably. She was always sweet-natured, but getting her to follow rules had been a struggle. School seemed to change all that. She loved the routines of school, following the rules and being with the other kids. She knew all their first and last names, and often named toys of hers after them. She had this one wooden drumstick she named William for a boy at school. Quirky, yes, but she carried that stick around all summer because she loved William so much. I could see how much these social connections meant to her, and how they were pulling her out of her own world and much more into our world. I cried when Caroline graduated from nursery school because Helping Hands had been such a safe, nurturing place where she was loved just as she was. She had learned so much there and from the home visits with the special education teacher; I wondered if public kindergarten would ever be able to compete.

Grade school greatness

The first hurdle I faced with Caroline's elementary (primary) school was at the CSE (Committee on Special Education) meeting to create her program. The committee wanted to put her in a self-contained special education class in another district elementary school. I visited the classroom and saw what I had feared: a small room, removed from the rest of the school, where a dozen children with varying developmental challenges were working quietly and individually. It was not a well-designed self-contained model, and I refused to allow them to place Caroline there. In fact, I wished I could have removed all those kids from that stifling quarantine of a classroom. What I had seen at Helping Hands Preschool was that Caroline could learn. She had an amazing memory, a great sight vocabulary, and an affinity for anything learned with music. I was determined that she have the chance to be in a general education classroom. Luckily, that year her elementary school was offering a program that combined the two—a special education program in the morning, and general education kindergarten in the afternoon. The committee considered Caroline "too disabled" for that program, but I would not budge. I got out my copy of the Individuals with Disabilities Education Act of 2004. I was able to convince them to let Caroline try the combination program in her home school. Caroline needed, and still needs, a one-to-one aide to participate in the general education classroom. I was able to fight for that, and win as well. It was not easy, but I stood my ground, politely and resolutely. That year the school used a combination of ABA (applied behavior analysis) and other more traditional educational methods to teach Caroline. She did extremely well, and her progress continued to surprise even me. She even mastered using the bathroom that year!

Caroline and the spelling bee

Every year in elementary school that followed for Caroline was the same thing. There would be a meeting at the beginning of the year, in which several people would try to convince me that it was time for Caroline to leave the inclusive program and be in a self-contained program. They would always tell me that the curriculum was getting too difficult, that the discrepancy between Caroline and her peers was too great. What amazed me was anyone thinking that discrepancy could be helped by removing her from these more gifted peers! The motivation for the school's desire to put her in self-containment was twofold. First, it definitely requires work on the part of the regular education teacher and the special education teacher to modify the curriculum for an exceptional student such as Caroline. Also, in order to help Caroline succeed and not require too much on the part of the general education teacher or take away from the instruction of the typical students, Caroline needs a one-to-one special education aide in the classroom with her to direct and assist her. That is expensive for the district. As I mentioned earlier, the job of the special education administrators is to provide the best program they can for the least cost. It would be cheaper for the school to put her in an existing self-contained class. Therefore, making sure Caroline keeps her one-to-one aide has been a yearly battle. The battle has always been worth it in the end.

Every year of elementary school I managed to convince the school that Caroline belonged in the general education classroom with a one-to-one aide. Every year the regular education teacher came to love her. Her second grade teacher, an absolute sweetheart, told me teaching Caroline had been the most fulfilling experience of her career. The kids have always accepted and loved Caroline. Most importantly, she has learned far more than I ever could have hoped. During her time in elementary school, she learned how to read with amazing fluency and expression. Comprehension is still hard, but she is making strides there slowly. I was once told she would never understand the one-to-one correspondence in math: that the number one stands for one apple. Now she can do long division by herself. By fifth grade, she labeled all 50 states in a map of the United States, and she was her class's representative in the school-wide spelling bee. In the gym on the day of the spelling bee, I watched in amazement as she competed alongside her classmates, spelling tough words; no one ever would have thought there was anything different about Caroline. I could tell every teacher in the gym was rooting for my special little girl to win. She lasted pretty far into it, and I have never been prouder in my life. I knew I had been right to demand she be included, to have her be challenged and recognized as a valuable student at her school. So never let an early grim prognosis stop you from fighting for your daughter. Don't let someone else tell you who she can be. You will never know until you let her try.

When Caroline graduated from elementary school the following June, she won a music award for her participation in the school's chorus, and a special award for being in the spelling bee. The principal came up to me and apologized for all the times she recommended Caroline be moved to a self-contained class. She said Caroline was a success story, and the school now had several significantly challenged students participating in inclusive models. Caroline did it, not me. I simply advocated for her to be given the chance. This year Caroline is in her first year of middle school, again in an inclusive class. I realize that at some point she may have to be in an alternate program, but right now, as long as she is learning, I want her to stay where she is. Her classroom behavior is perfect. She has lovely manners, a strong work ethic, and a deep desire to learn. She adores the other kids, and because many of them know her from elementary school, they accept her just as she is, and even watch out for her. Of course, part of her success is due to her natural charm, but most of it is due to the opportunities she was given by just being with the other kids.

Inclusion is imperative

Simply put, inclusion is not just advantageous, it is necessary. Please advocate for your daughter to spend at least part of the day with her typical peers. Our exceptional daughters need the best we can offer, not the least. The typical kids need the sensitivity, humility, and understanding that develop from being with our children. Don't worry about test scores or grades; just give your daughter the exposure to knowledge and the stimulation of learning. Remember the three S's—socialization, stimulation, and structure. If you have to fight for it, do so. I had some staunch supporters and some very critical opponents when I made the decision to have Caroline included in the general education class. However, nearly all of them eventually agreed that if she was their daughter, they would have done just the same. She still has autism, but her teachers know her now as a smart, creative, musical, sweet girl, and one heck of a speller. If we want our daughters to realize the full potential of their many gifts, we have to give them the chance. And if we want to change the way the world sees our kids, we have to *let* them see our kids.

The heart of the matter about education

1. Educational testing is just an estimate—a starting point from which to create a plan. It is not an absolute truth about your daughter's abilities or her potential.

2. Both the US and UK must provide, by law, free and appropriate education for students with special needs.

3. Be polite but firm when advocating for what is best for your daughter.

4. Remember that your daughter needs the stimulation and role-modeling of typical peers; advocate for her to spend as much time in the general education setting as possible.

5. Keep the faith, and your daughter will have many wonderful accomplishments because learning is a lifelong process.

Chapter 5

Friends

"Friendship is a sheltering tree."

—Samuel Taylor Coleridge

This is one of the toughest subjects for parents of kids on the autism spectrum. Believe me, I have cried for both of my girls when they have been left off birthday party lists and not invited to sleepovers. As I mentioned earlier, girls can be especially hard on each other because they are attuned to social nuances. They notice earlier when someone is different. I know in the early years I would try to encourage play-dates, and often during a scheduled play-date, one of my girls would wander absent-mindedly away, leaving me playing Candy Land with some bewildered five-year-old who wondered what she was doing there. Or I would take Caroline to someone's house, and she would destroy whatever Lego architecture someone else's visionary child had constructed. I wish now I had not taken those things so hard. Always, of course, I would apologize to the child and parent, but I wish I had just understood that my kids weren't "there" yet. The thing about kids with special needs is that their timetable may not be yours. The road to making friends may be a long one, and making progress takes a lot of effort. You need to be patient with your daughter and keep giving her opportunities to socialize. However, there are some things you can do to help prepare your daughter for a friend when she is finally ready.

Getting to know you: Speech class

One of the best resources school should provide for your daughter to help with friendships is the speech teacher. Make sure you have speech services on your daughter's IEP, and include social goals on her IEP as well. My daughters have both learned an enormous amount from their speech teachers. It is an absolutely essential part of any school program for kids on the spectrum. These are not speech sessions to help with fluency or pronunciation, although those issues may be addressed as well. Speech sessions for kids on the spectrum should focus on pragmatic language skills. Pragmatic language skills involve basic things such as knowing how to answer a question, how to ask a question, how to listen and have a conversation. Usually these sessions are done in a group, which offers your daughter a perfect chance to practice her skills and develop friendships. You can even ask the speech teacher or class teacher to choose one or two typical kids, if their parents are willing, to participate in your daughter's speech group. Kids generally like the opportunity to leave the classroom and have some fun playing games in the speech room, and this provides a less intimidating opportunity for your daughter to make a friend. Some of Lizzie's best friends are kids she met through her speech class. When your daughter's school program is developed, insist on speech services and specify that you want pragmatic speech therapy to help her develop social skills. I plan on insisting that it be a part of my girls' programs right through high school, and I would encourage you to do the same. Speech therapy is an invaluable tool to help our daughters learn how to build appropriate and meaningful social relationships.

What to say and not to say: Social Stories™

Another terrific way to help your daughter with friendships and many other social situations is through story-based interventions. In general, story-based interventions are short, written sketches that illustrate appropriate behavior in social scenarios. The most famous method for doing this is Social Stories™. Developed by Carol Gray, a Social Story is a short vignette which describes "a situation, skill, or concept in terms of relevant social cues, perspectives, and common responses in a specifically defined style and format" (Gray 2011). Ms. Gray's Social Stories follow a very distinct model, and you can access many of them at her website, www.thegraycenter.org. Through Social Stories, appropriate behavior is modeled and reinforced. Since these simple social exchanges do not always come naturally to our kids, it is vital that you review "how to"s with them on a regular basis. This will allow your daughter to initiate and maintain friendships.

You can find books of Social Stories at most large bookstores; there are many to help kids of all ages. Social Story books reinforce good social behavior in the simplest of ways. If you can't find one for an occasion, you can always create your own version of a story to show your daughter how to handle a situation: "Visiting Grandma in the hospital after her surgery," subtitled "Don't ask Grandma to show her scar!" It is not as much work as it seems. Just a piece of paper, some stick figures, and some comic strip bubbles. You can write a helpful story about anything: how to greet a friend, how to talk with your teacher, how to order a meal at a restaurant. These stories should include how to ask a question, wait for and listen to an answer, and make eye contact. Quite frankly, a lot of adults need a crash course in appropriate social behavior! My daughters look forward to these "scripts," and many of them do become internalized after a time. It is not that our girls are intentionally inconsiderate; it is just at times it doesn't naturally occur to them. Stories about how to handle social situations can give them some friendly guidance and preparation. All of these lessons are helpful when it comes to making and keeping friends.

Creative play: What Piglet taught my girls

Another way to help your daughter socially is through play. Often the toys our children like are not terribly social; they tend to prefer solitary activities that are repetitive and systematic. I really encouraged my girls to play with dolls or stuffed animals when they were younger. Dolls and stuffed animals present an opportunity for storytelling through toys, and they are an open-ended, creative way to play. I love dolls, so I always enjoyed playing dolls with my girls. It took some effort to get them involved because at first dolls didn't really interest them. However, with persistence, both of my girls came to love playing dolls, and it was a bonding activity for us. Not only did we have fun together, but it became a way to instruct them about social skills, and later an outlet for them to practice what they had learned. Through dolls, we were able to act out many important social situations in fun and silly ways. Lizzie and I have spent many hours playing dolls, helping Baby Brother or Maxy Muffins or Piglet navigate the complicated waters of the "Halfmoon School for Dolls"— her imaginative creation! When she was younger, Lizzie had her dolls put on epic theatrical productions, full of pathos and joy and calamity. Baby Brother was often the villain, and Piglet the downtrodden hero. I could see her imagination sparking and often heard her rehearsing social lessons through her dolls.

It took Caroline a long time to play imaginatively with dolls, and she was never as interested in following a long doll drama to its conclusion. However, she would make her dolls talk to me, and today she reminds them to brush their teeth, pay attention in school, and mediates "arguments" between them. In fact, Caroline often makes her dolls imitate behaviors of kids in school, which gives me a glimpse inside her day and a chance to talk to her about things that happened at school. I feel as if it gives her another way to communicate what she has seen. When doing my research for this book, I found it surprising and affirming that researchers have used puppets and dolls to teach empathy and social awareness to children on the spectrum (Schrandt, Townsend, and Poulson 2009). You may feel silly making the toys talk to your daughter at first, but I swear it works. So have some fun using your daughter's toys to help her recognize and adapt to social norms. This will help her with friendships. Your daughter may not want to tell you about her day, but she may be eager to tell Dora the Explorer!

Good grief: What television can teach

Television can be helpful when it comes to friendships and all social relationships. If you allow your children to watch quality, popular television (yes, it does exist), such as the Disney Channel and Nickelodeon, they can learn social norms and rules for friendship. The important thing is to watch *with them* and discuss with them what is happening in the program, pointing out how characters treat each other and affirm each other's feelings. Caroline often doesn't understand feelings unless they are obvious. She needs really overt social cues. She loved my Richard Simmons exercise videos when she was a toddler because his over-the-top expressions made sense to her. The characters in children's shows are usually exaggerated and Caroline gets that, and she can learn from it. SpongeBob is not subtle, and, in this case, that is a good thing! Television can provide an instructive window on ordinary life, plus it gives your kids common points of interest from which to draw when making conversation. It is something they can share with their typical peers. Our kids can learn to connect with and "read" people, but we have to teach them how to do that, and television can help. I always found Charlie Brown a great teacher because the characters talk and move more slowly, and the stories focus on feelings and relationships rather than action. The jazz music in the background is calming and always seems to help Caroline focus. I think Caroline started to experience real empathy while watching Charlie Brown go "Arghhh" when mean old Lucy kept swiping that football. She would say, "Poor Charlie Brown. Charlie Brown is sad." And we all know that empathy is so important to a meaningful friendship.

What not to wear: Dressing for social success

One other important piece of advice about our girls and friendships has to do with hygiene and appearance. It is generally hard for our daughters to "fit in" with their peers, as we know all too well. So please help your daughter to look as similar to the typical kids as she can. This may seem superficial, but, in the world in which we live, it is essential. I am not talking about beauty; I am talking about hygiene and grooming. I have seen too many special needs kids in my classes whose parents seem to have dropped the ball on this one, thinking their child's appearance doesn't matter because they are not typical kids. Not true! I know this can be hard. Caroline still hates the way the water feels on her head and face in the shower. I still have to stick my hand in the shower every day and wash her hair. It is a daily frustration. But I refuse to have her go to school with dirty hair. I make sure her teeth are brushed, her hair is clean, and her fingernails are trimmed and clean. Now that my girls are in the middle school years, there are even more hygiene issues, related to shaving and menstruation, for example. Lizzie has learned over time to be independent in these areas, but I am still helping Caroline manage these needs.

Another issue for teens is care of their skin. Sometimes it is too difficult for our girls to carry out a complicated skin routine. I have talked with parents whose kids are really suffering with acne, and I think the best thing to do is just take them to a dermatologist and get an oral medication. No child with special needs should be further ostracized because of terrible acne or body odor. I know our kids can be stubborn at times, but you must persist. These are life skills that make a huge difference to how people are received by the world. I have seen girls like ours shunned by their peers, not because of their developmental challenges but because of poor hygiene and appearance.

I also try very hard to help my girls dress as nicely as possible. Your daughter does not need to wear expensive clothes or dress like a supermodel, but she does need to dress like the other kids. Her clothes need to be clean and neat, and reasonably stylish. There have been times when Caroline has managed to sneak some crazy outfit by me, but usually she and I choose her clothes together the night before school. I know that teachers and kids respond better to a clean, neatly dressed child with special needs than to one whose appearance screams "I am different!" I know our kids can have peculiar clothing preferences. A friend of mine has a daughter with autism who dislikes anything other than elastic waistbands and long-sleeved t-shirts. So she dresses her in pink sweats, and her hair is styled in a ponytail with a matching ribbon every day. She always looks great.

Appearance is one area in which we can really help our girls, no matter what their level of special needs. This is something we can control! And I think it is an insult to our daughters to think they don't care how they look. Many of them care much more about their appearance than we think. They want to fit in and look like the other kids, but they are not sure how to do it. It may be harder and take longer to teach them how to groom themselves, but it is well worth it to help them be accepted in the world and cultivate friendships.

I am what I am

One of the best things you can do for your daughter with regard to all relationships is to talk honestly with her about her challenges. Keeping it a secret makes it seem like something shameful, and leaves a child bewildered and frustrated about why she can't make friends as easily. I have even seen some high school students full of self-loathing for what they perceive to be their innate inadequacies, and their parents insist they never be told they have autism or Asperger's. Clearly, they are suffering because they are struggling to understand themselves and a vital piece of information is being withheld from them. There is nothing wrong with being different, and not telling your daughter the truth only hurts them. I told Lizzie and Caroline pretty much as soon as they could understand. Caroline only says, "Autism makes me special." I don't harp on it or focus on it because it is only part of who she is, but if it comes up, we talk about it. Lizzie can understand what her Asperger's means and I think she finds it comforting to know there is a reason why she is so shy at times. As an adolescent, she asks more questions about what Asperger's means. I always reassure her, and I am sincere, that she is perfectly normal and fine. Asperger's may make her different from her peers at times, but it is not something wrong with her. She is exceptionally bright, has a remarkable memory, and is musically talented, and in many ways these gifts are part of Asperger's. I think it is so important to help your daughter understand why she struggles at times, just as you continue to remind her of her many gifts. This is especially important when it comes to forging friendships.

Dealing with bullies

Finally, I would be remiss if I did not mention the bullying that can sometimes happen with kids on the spectrum. First, it is the school's responsibility to keep your daughter safe. For too long schools have ignored the serious consequences of bullying and dismissed it as a normal part of growing up. There is nothing normal or trivial about harassment and torment. You must keep in touch with your daughter's teachers and classmates as best you can. Ask every year at your daughter's parent conference and IEP annual review if there have been any incidents of bullying. Bullying is most likely to happen during lunch, in the halls, in the bathrooms and locker rooms, or on the playground. These are the places where you have to make sure your daughter is safe. Teachers and school administrators may be unaware what goes on during these unstructured times, so you have to request that they check what is happening there. Be direct and make sure the school knows you are concerned about the possibility of bullying. If you get even one hint of bullying, demand a meeting in person at the school with the administrator. Make it clear that you will not tolerate this, and the school must be proactive in stopping the bullying. Do not let them downplay it. They should have a clear policy and a clear plan of action to keep your daughter safe.

The school may want one of their social workers or counselors to talk with the bully. If you feel it is appropriate, you may wish for them to explain to the bully your daughter's special needs. Sometimes educating a bully can help remedy the situation if ignorance is the cause. However, if your daughter wishes to keep that information private, respect her wishes. Don't be afraid to use your rights under the law to protect your daughter. As a teacher and parent, I have seen situations go too far before intervention took place. Stop it as soon as you hear about it with swift and firm action. All of us must have a no-tolerance policy towards bullies.

Caroline was the victim of other children's unkindness during her fifth grade year. On the playground some boys were teaching her graphic sexual words to say and laughing when she would do it. In her innocence she was doing what they asked because she saw that it made them laugh and thought they were her friends. I had no idea this was happening. A little girl who has known Caroline for many years in school alerted a teacher that this was happening. The little girl felt so upset that anyone would take advantage of Caroline in this way. The principal called me to apologize, explaining that when she informed the mother of the one of the culprits, the mother's first words were, "Not Caroline, please tell me he wasn't teasing Caroline." This is because all the kids and parents have known and loved Caroline since kindergarten. The boys apologized and were punished, and, according to the teacher, many of the other kids let them know what a rotten thing it was to tease Caroline. Because Caroline had always been in class with these kids, most of them felt protective of her and took her side. This episode made me profoundly sad at the time, but I was also able to see the silver lining: a child stood up for my Caroline, took her side, and did the right thing. And other children were glad she did. I hope those boys learned a lesson, if not about kindness, about how unpopular you can be if you hurt someone innocent.

Companions for Sweet Caroline

Friendships for Caroline have not always been an easy endeavor. Caroline has always loved other children even when she had no real idea how to make friends. Still, the desire has always been there. In Helping Hands, her preschool, it was easy because they were all little and all friends. In elementary school, Caroline made it a point to know the name and birthday of every child in school. Throughout the years of elementary school, there were always little girls who were sweet to Caroline. Again, having her included in the general education classroom has given her the chance to make those connections. Often, for Caroline, friendships with peers have been more of a mentoring relationship. Sometimes it has just been as simple as sharing laughter or lunch, but this has meant the world to her. She smiles and greets all her classmates, and they respond positively. I think much of her social success has been because she is such a happy and sweet child.

Middle school has been tougher for Caroline in terms of friendships. The social gap between Caroline and her peers has increased, and so her social invitations have decreased. Additionally, most of the children with special needs in her school are boys and Caroline really wants girlfriends, just as her peers have. Her social calendar has not been full, and at times that has been hard. I find the best thing to do is host a night at my house, and have both Caroline and Lizzie invite friends to have pizza and watch a movie, or play Mario Kart on the Wii. There are not usually reciprocal invitations for Caroline, but at least she is getting that opportunity to be with other girls and feel included. You may have to be the one always hosting, and no, that's not fair, but think of it as a chance to oversee what happens and be sure your daughter is having a positive experience. Also, encourage siblings to spend time with your daughter as much as is reasonable. Siblings are built-in friends, even if they argue, and provide a sense of connection and belonging. I am always grateful that Caroline has her sister.

In addition, when we do things as a family, I try to invite a couple of kids along to give Caroline some social experiences.

I have learned to be grateful for kind kids and believe they are out there. When Caroline was in fifth grade, one of her classmates just adored her. This sweet little girl insisted Caroline be invited to her birthday party, despite the hesitation of the girl's mother. That little girl will always be a hero of mine because she saw all that was good in Caroline and was drawn to it. Caroline wants friends so much, so I do my best to provide her with chances to be with other children. Through my friendships with other parents of special kids, I am also able to make connections for Caroline. There are a couple of families with whom we are close, and I know those children will always be her friends. I also know as long as she is a joyous child, loved and accepted, she will project that into the world, and good people will respond.

Finding friends for Lizzie

Friendship for Lizzie has been a more hopeful and yet a more complicated endeavor. Caroline's autism is obvious to her peers. This has created a distance between Caroline and her peers; however, the flipside is that they have generally responded with kindness. In some ways, Lizzie has struggled more socially because her peers are not as forgiving of her. Her real struggle is social, as it is with any person with Asperger's. She is shy by nature, and during puberty she developed a significant stutter which makes social interactions even more stilted. When she was younger, she watched more than participated in social relationships. I remember, when she finally adjusted to nursery school, I would ask her every day what she did. She would provide me with a long narrative of the day's events. After several weeks, feeling quite proud of her progress, I consulted with her teacher, only to discover she had never spoken to or interacted with anyone; she would just watch and report to me what other children had done. I cried for a long time about that one.

However, over time, in *her* time, she did reach out and make some friends in elementary school. In middle school, she found some really true friends, some of whom have their own struggles and challenges. Together they have camaraderie and support. I know the parents of her friends, and we are all supporting them in their friendships. We were able to work with the guidance counselor to ensure that three of them have lunch together. She works with the speech teacher and the school psychologist on social skills, and she has made huge progress. For her thirteenth birthday, Lizzie had a party at our house with a group of ten boys and girls. It was a bit like a middle-school episode of *Glee*, with all the kids singing to the Wii Karaoke game; they were so happy. I realize with Lizzie I had to be patient, provide her with opportunities, and wait for her to be ready. One of the great things with Lizzie has been the positive attention she has received from peers for her academic skills, her ability to draw, and her singing voice. Many kids with Asperger's have talents, and if they develop them, other kids will be impressed with their successes and be drawn to them. This creates a respect which can be an authentic foundation for a friendship.

The sun really will come out tomorrow!

I would like to share a story about my Lizzie that may give you hope. Lizzie loves musicals. She has since I showed her *Singing in the Rain* when she was four years old. At five she begged for the Frank Sinatra Barbie doll, and wouldn't go to bed without him for two years! She can tell you who wrote *La Cage Aux Folles* and who collaborated with Stephen Sondheim on his first Broadway show. For the past three years, she has been in her middle school's musical productions. During her seventh grade year, the show was a retrospective of previous year's shows. She had a small speaking part and a brief solo line in "Hard Knock Life" from *Annie*. On opening night, the number began, and, up on stage, Lizzie couldn't find her mop, her prop for the number. I could see her searching, and then her tears began. I was dying in the audience, my worst nightmare: she was finally on stage with a part and she was visibly falling apart. She stayed onstage for the number intermittently looking back and forth, and crying; it was torturous. As soon as the number was over, I ran backstage to help her. When I found her, she was surrounded by a huge group of girls who were comforting her—stroking her hair, fetching her water, telling her it wasn't that bad. I couldn't believe the outpouring of kindness. A little girl who had one of the leading roles came up to me and told me she was going to keep Lizzie's mop with her props, and she would be sure Lizzie would have it for the following two nights of the performance. What a sweet child—one of the stars of the production making sure her friend Lizzie was taken care of! Well, the next two nights Lizzie did a superb job with her lines and her songs. Even better, she made some new friends. Never underestimate the kindness of kids.

With a little help from my friends

Sometimes, our girls just need a little direction to find great friends. I teach a diverse group of kids in my job. For several of my classes, I co-teach with a special education teacher a junior level (16-year-olds) English class. Some of these kids have fairly significant special needs, everything from autism to ADHD to fairly low-functioning IQ scores. I love having them in class, and, like my own children, they are learning far more being included in general education classes than they would in self-containment. The first day of school last year, I ventured into the cafeteria to buy lunch, and I found one of my students very upset because she couldn't find anyone to sit with during lunch: a sweet girl with autism who tends to stress out about social situations. Our school is monstrously large (we graduate around 800–900 students a year), so the cafeteria experience can be daunting. I spent the next ten minutes walking around the cafeteria with her, looking for a good lunch match for her. Suddenly I recognized a sweet girl whom I had taught in ninth grade. She was sitting with her quirky little group of equally sweet friends. I introduced my lonely student, and she was immediately welcomed into their group.

I checked on her a few days later and found her sitting at that table as if she had always been there, laughing and chatting. Sure they were an unusual little group, but they were friends! They were happily munching on their food, drawing cartoon pictures, and laughing, oblivious to the heady drama of cheerleaders and football stars and class council presidents around them. They had each other, and isn't that all you really need in life—just your own group of friends to see you through? They were happy with each other, and that made all the difference. Since that day, I always make sure that my special kids never eat lunch alone. I check the cafeteria at the beginning of the year and find lunch matches. Ask your daughter's teacher to do that. The teachers may not think of it, but I am sure they will comply if asked. Teachers need to be your eyes and ears in this area, and can often help more subtly than we can as parents. Chances are there are kids more than willing to be your daughter's friends, kids who are looking for friends as well. Sometimes you just have to ask.

Furry friends

One final thought that may seem silly at first, but has been wonderful for my girls, is to get a pet for your daughter. While obviously nothing can replace friends and human interaction, I have found my kids, especially Lizzie, extremely responsive to animals. Many girls I have known on the spectrum seem to have a special affinity for animals. If you think about the fact that animals sense feelings rather than articulate them, you can see why it is a perfect relationship. There can be a wonderfully sweet, unspoken connection. I was hesitant to adopt a pet at first because I have asthma and allergies, and my girls seemed a bit afraid of animals. However, with the addition of allergy meds for me, we adopted a cat three years ago. She is called Juliet, and Lizzie absolutely loves her. I can hear Lizzie talking to Juliet the cat about her day, sharing her feelings. The next year we adopted another cat, Hena, to add to our household. Caroline has slowly warmed to the cats, and now occasionally allows Juliet to sleep on her bed. I am not sure what it is, but there is something truly healing about pets. This past April, I finally gave in and got a puppy. Scooter the Wonder Dog is a little rescue puppy, a Bichon Frise/Lhasa Apso mix. He is an absolute delight, and both of the girls love playing fetch with him. Lizzie loves cuddling with him on the couch while reading a book. I realize some people may advise you not to adopt because of the potential for allergies, but there are hypoallergenic animals available. Sadly, loneliness can sometimes be part of life with autism, and a loving, furry companion can provide tremendous comfort, as well as help provide our children with another opportunity to connect with the world around them.

Just a few good friends

"The most I can do for my friend is simply be his friend."

—Henry David Thoreau

I know that friendships for children on the spectrum can be one of the most painful and problematic issues parents or children confront. Don't despair. All your daughter really needs is one or two good friends. It may take patience and extra encouragement on your part. Obviously, if you can find a friend who has similar issues, that may be helpful, but don't feel you have to quarantine your daughter away from typical kids. And don't be too choosy. Don't be a friend snob yourself; welcome any child who wants to play with yours. Don't waste time or energy on parents or kids who aren't kind and don't get it. It truly is their loss. Despite the possible bullies and mean girls, there are plenty of nice kids out there who will want to help and befriend your daughter. Children are generally sweet if you give them guidance and affirmation. I have found many kids over the years who have been godsends to other children. Many times it has been the open hearts of other children that have kept me going when adults have been disappointments.

Try to be flexible about the form these friendships may take and who these friends may be. Kids need social interactions with other kids, so be open to how that may happen. You may have to work hard to facilitate it, or you may have to accept the pace at which your daughter is comfortable with making friends. Also, don't overestimate your daughter's differences. I have been teaching for many years, and I can attest to the fact that all kids are quirky, whether they have special needs or not! The world is full of individuals, all of whom don't fit in at one time or another. Eventually, all kids find some friends to whom they can relate, friends who make them happy. Your job is to provide opportunities and accept the friends your daughter finds. It is her happiness that counts, and it will work in time. As with all things, it takes patience, endurance, and an open heart, so keep the faith.

The heart of the matter about friendships

1. Our girls need and want friends very much. Helping your daughter find a few good friends is just as important as any therapy out there.

2. Speech class can help your daughter establish friendships and learn how to communicate with her peers. Be sure she is working with other children in her speech sessions at least part of the time.

3. Social Stories, creative play, television, and attention to grooming can help your daughter learn social norms that will support her friendships.

4. Be honest with your daughter about her autism, so she can understand why she struggles, but reassure her that she is perfectly fine and normal as she is.

5. Be patient and accept the friends your daughter does find. They give her something she needs very much—a sense of belonging.

Chapter 6
Siblings

"She ain't heavy; she's my sister."

Having addressed some of the social and emotional issues our girls with special challenges face, I want to take a moment to talk about the siblings of daughters with special needs. Our daughters' siblings face unique challenges as well, and we must address their needs with equal thought, care, and sensitivity. The key idea here is balance. We must be sure we are balancing the needs of all the children in our families, and acknowledging each child's unique contributions and personality. When things get out of balance, we not only damage the relationships we have with our children but also their feelings about each other. While we are raising our children as individuals, we are also shaping their relationships as siblings. Sibling relationships are some of the most significant relationships we have; they are emotionally intimate, unique in their nature, and, we hope, lifelong.

For our daughters with special needs in particular, sibling relationships may be the most significant and important ones of our children's lives. Our girls on the spectrum can learn so much from their siblings about personal relationships and all the negotiating, sharing, and even fighting that these relationships can involve. In turn, our typical children have the chance to learn empathy, patience, and gratitude from witnessing the struggles of their special siblings. They often grow up to be the best advocates for our special needs population and can be role models through their compassionate treatment of our more challenged citizens. Finally, most of us hope that, down the road when they are adults, our typical children will help guide our special needs children when we are no longer able or there to do that. However, we must remember that during childhood, our daughters' siblings are not extra parents but children themselves. In order to preserve the sweetness and joy of their sibling relationships, we must allow them to be brothers and sisters, before we ask them to be teachers, role models, or protectors.

When families lose their balance

"A happy family is but an earlier heaven."

—*Sir John Bowring*

Balance seems to be the key in so many of the issues we face as parents of children with special needs, and yet it remains a constant challenge. How do you balance work and home, your sanity with your responsibilities, and the competing needs of your family members? However difficult it may seem, keeping your life in balance is essential for everyone involved. I have seen two unfortunate dynamics that can develop in our families when parents overcompensate in one way or another as a reaction to their children's autism, and throw the whole family structure off kilter.

The "woe-is-we" family

First, I have seen families where the focus on being a "special needs family" has overtaken all other family dynamics, to the point where the parents' misery has become the greatest challenge they face. I know it can be difficult, but your perspective on the situation sets the tone for the entire family. It is essential that you get the support and counseling you need to remain as positive as you can about the situation. I have seen parents grab on to the mantle of "long-suffering parent of a disabled child" and turn it into their singular identity. They see everything through the filter of this identity, and rather than make the best of the situation, make it far worse for everyone involved. The typical siblings are enlisted as co-parents, with everyone's time and energy focused solely on the treatments and therapies of their special needs sibling. Obviously, this creates tremendous frustration and resentment in the siblings.

It is additionally a burden to the special needs child who feels the pressure and guilt, even if she cannot verbalize it, of being the resented center of attention. She also loses the comfort and joy of a happy family dynamic. Often in these families, the typical children go as far away as possible, as soon as possible. And the best hope for continued lifetime guidance for their special needs siblings goes with them. By forcing our typical kids to be adults long before they are ready, all we really do is alienate them from their siblings. And if we make the job of caring for our children seem like such a dreary burden, how can their siblings not feel the same? How will they ever want any part in overseeing their sister's life after we are gone? That is why our outlook is what shapes the lives of all of our children. We must find positive coping strategies, so we can teach them to our children, their siblings, their teachers, and the world. And we must be sure we allow all our children to be children.

The not-so-golden child

The other unfortunate dynamic I have seen at times in our families is the exaggerated "worship" of the typical sibling. I have encountered parents who are so thrilled to have a typical child in the family that they end up spoiling him or her. Underlying this excitement is a hidden or not-so-hidden disappointment at having a special needs child—a disappointment which is all too obvious to both children, and devastating to the child with special needs. I have seen parents who are actually apologetic to their typical child for having a child with special needs. Because of this, instead of creating an empathic advocate for their special needs child, they create a callous self-centered individual who has no interest in helping his or her sibling. I knew a family at school who felt their typical son should never have to acknowledge his autistic brother at school for fear that he would be embarrassed by him. They actually requested that their schedules be designed so that they would never cross paths. Far from asking him to help with his brother, they insisted his life should not be affected at all by his brother. Not surprisingly, this boy was downright mean about his brother.

What these parents failed to see was that having a brother with autism is a blessing, not a curse. It brings with it challenges, but also tremendous opportunities to learn empathy, compassion, humility, and gratitude. The nicest kids I teach are often the brothers and sisters of children with special needs. However, when parents cannot accept their child's autism, neither will their siblings. This family described above was a mess. The child with autism was meek and terribly insecure. The brother was exceptionally arrogant and self-absorbed. The irony was the brother with autism had far better manners and social skills than his idolized sibling! Teachers loved working with the boy with autism, but the other boy was a trial for every teacher who encountered him. Remember, being born typical is a gift, not an accomplishment. Make sure what you celebrate about all of your children is the good they do, not the advantages with which they were born.

Four simple ways to keep your family centered

Since both of my girls are on the spectrum, you may think this chapter doesn't apply to me, but it does. Lizzie is really becoming a very typical girl, and Caroline is still very affected by autism in many ways. So Lizzie does struggle with being Caroline's big sister at times. Lizzie can become very frustrated with her sister's persistence and rituals. When I remind her that Caroline is dealing with more challenges than she is, she usually reflects on this and is patient. I don't expect her to be a saint, just a nice older sister. Negotiating the relationships between your kids can be challenging. For my family, it is a work in constant progress, but I am trying to make sure we stay on track. I have discovered a few easy, yet essential, things to remember to help keep our special families in balance.

Number one: Listen

> "It is the province of knowledge to speak, and the privilege of wisdom to listen."
>
> —*Oliver Wendell Holmes*

First of all, siblings of children with special needs also have some special emotional needs of their own to consider. Perhaps the most important need they have is to be free to talk about how it feels to have a special sibling. They may be frustrated and perhaps even embarrassed at times by their sibling with autism. All kids just want to fit in, and siblings may have conflicting feelings about protecting their siblings and trying to fit in socially themselves. Try not to become too defensive or judgmental about how they feel. Many times, their feelings are similar to our own. They may even give voice to feelings we would rather not acknowledge, and this can be difficult. However, the best way to get over something is to talk it out and release it. Just the ability to vent frustration can be cathartic and help anyone feel less pressure. Keeping communication open also presents you with the opportunity to provide framework and put their sibling's struggles and their own in the appropriate perspective. Of course, always encourage empathy and understanding, but do not shame them because this will only cause them to shut down. We can't help the way we feel at times, but we can choose how to deal with our feelings constructively. The most important thing you can do for them is just listen as they tell you how they are feeling. You may be surprised how much less frustrated and resentful they will be after they have been really heard.

Sometimes, when I can see Lizzie's patience wearing thin with her sister, I will take a moment to talk to her alone. Often Lizzie will tell me that she feels lonely because she cannot have the kind of conversations with Caroline she would like. She also sometimes resents how responsible she feels for Caroline. I know the special circumstances of their lives can be overwhelming for her. At times she has cried about this, partly from grief and partly from feeling guilty about it. I tell her that her feelings are natural and normal and that I understand. I reassure her that we all feel frustrated with the people we love at times, and talking about it can help. Mostly I just listen. Usually, after unburdening herself, she feels better and she can approach her sister with renewed patience. I know she loves Caroline, but I also know that being Caroline's sister can be demanding at times. It means so much to her to know that I acknowledge her struggles and her efforts. My daughters love each other very much, and by recognizing their individual needs, I support their relationship. Our daughter's siblings will be with them, watching out for them, we hope, for their entire lifetimes, so be attentive to their feelings. It is in the best interest of all of your children to look at things from everyone's perspective and keep the lines of communication open.

Number two: Celebrate everyone

"Appreciation is a wonderful thing: It makes what is excellent in others belong to us as well."

—*Voltaire*

It is also important to encourage your typical children to have activities of their own which are celebrated as well. It is easy for all of your time to be consumed by the efforts to help your special daughter. I know what it's like to have that constant feeling that you should be doing more. However, that is too much stress to put on your special child, and it leaves the other children feeling left out. One of the best things all of our children can learn from being part of a family is that it isn't all about any one person. As a family, you must take turns being the center of attention. Having your children all support each other in their interests and endeavors will help to create a sense of family that is balanced and unified. Remember, we chose to become parents, but our kids didn't choose anything about their lives, neither their parents nor their siblings. It is our job to make sure every child in the family feels validated and included. Providing our children with a variety of outlets will help them develop their own identities and offer needed respites from the responsibilities at home. I try to make sure Lizzie has her own things to do, such as drama and music, so she is not always her sister's keeper. Don't be afraid to celebrate your typical child's accomplishments for fear of hurting their special sibling. They deserve to develop their talents as much as their sibling does. Try to play down the competition as much as possible. Remind your children we all have gifts and we all have struggles. The chances are good that your special daughter will feel pride in her sibling's accomplishments. I know Caroline was thrilled to see Lizzie on stage in the school play. And I watched Lizzie applaud enthusiastically as Caroline performed in the school band. As each child's individual happiness grows, so too does the happiness in the family. Again, the spirit you bring to it is everything.

Number three: Share the work
HI, HO, HI, HO: WHY SNOW WHITE IS BETTER THAN CINDERELLA

If there's one thing all children are obsessed with, it is fairness. As adults, we know that life is not fair, but it is important to try to make family life as fair as possible. Therefore, to whatever extent possible, try to make sure all members of the family contribute in any way they can. I am guilty of chronically making the mistake of doing too much for my kids. And if I do ask someone for help, it is most often Lizzie because she is more capable. Even though Lizzie doesn't usually complain, I realize that I am not helping Caroline by doing this. Caroline also needs to learn life skills, such as doing laundry and cleaning her room. So I am making more of an effort to organize and assign their chores, so each girl can contribute what she is able to. Sometimes we baby our child with special needs (or all our children), and we actually limit them further, rather foster their independence. There is often so much guilt that arises when a child has special needs, but that is our issue, and it should not become our kids' issue. So, as much as possible, dole out chores for everyone; that will help everyone grow more independent, and no one will feel unduly burdened or "unfairly" expected to compensate for their sibling. Even if your daughter can only do the smallest task, that is better than not being asked to do anything. I find that everyone is happier or at least equally unhappy when we all pitch in. Even though they won't admit it, I think both of my kids are proud when they make their own beds and clear up their own rooms. At least that's what I am telling myself! You don't want any child to feel like Cinderella scrubbing the floors. Better to be Snow White's charming companions, sharing the toil, even if somebody is "Grumpy" about it.

Number four: Special time
BEING AN ONLY CHILD FOR THE DAY

Another important thing you can do for your typical children is to spend some individual time with each child. Even just taking a walk with your child can provide him or her with the chance to talk with you and open up to you, without the distraction of the sibling. I have found with my girls that just a break from each other can do the world of good for their relationship. I know it can seem hard at times to find the time, but it is so worthwhile. Lizzie likes to have some time just with me once in a while, so we can talk and laugh, and she can have my full attention. Often we will go shopping; then we go out for lunch at Friendly's. If I buy Lizzie something, she always makes sure we choose something for Caroline as well. At the end of the day, she is always so happy and eager to see her sister, as am I. It is amazing how much just a little undivided attention can do for a child.

I know I ask a lot from Lizzie in terms of patience and understanding with her sister, so it is only fair to give her an opportunity to have a special day once in a while. As for Caroline, now that Lizzie is participating in more activities, such as drama club, I have opportunities to spend time just with Caroline. She loves to play dolls, play Wii, or just go shopping. Caroline loves to pick out pink accessories at Target. As far as she is concerned, a girl can never have too many pink berets, pink boa scarves, or bejeweled tiaras. Truth be told, however, Caroline would always rather have Lizzie along. Caroline worships her sister and loves her more than anyone on earth. I am definitely second choice to her beloved sister. Still, having one-on-one time with each of my daughters gives me a chance to really focus on each of them, and also gives them some needed time apart. Sometimes absence really does make the heart grow fonder.

Sibling support groups

Because at times all of this seems overwhelming for you to accomplish on your own, there are many organizations for the siblings of special kids. Many of them have support groups and social groups for siblings, providing chances to have fun with other kids in similar families. You may want to offer this to your child. It can be incredibly validating and comforting for your child to know he or she is not alone in feeling overwhelmed and frustrated at times with his or her family. One of the best websites I have found to introduce the topic is the Sibling Support Project (www.siblingsupport.org). You may want to print out their list of "What Siblings Would Like Parents to Know" (www.siblingsupport.org/publications/what-siblings-would-like-parents-and-service-providers-to-know) and discuss it with your child. Most local chapters of the Autism Society of America have sibling groups, as do many schools. In the UK, the National Autistic Society has a very useful page devoted to supporting siblings along with links to local resources (www.autism.org.uk/living-with-autism/parents-relatives-and-carers/siblings/support-for-siblings-of-people-with-autism.aspx). Finding ways for all of your children to feel less alone and unusual in their circumstances is always encouraging and reassuring. There are lots of us out there facing the unique challenges of raising a child with autism. One of the things I love best about spending time with my friends who have special kids is the laughter we share. Our typical kids need to feel that same connection with their counterparts and have the chance to share their stories with kids who "get it." There are times when the best therapy of all is simply feeling that you belong.

Sibling joy

"Delight and liberty, the simple creed of childhood."

—*William Wordsworth*

Simply put, the best way to support your children's relationships is to allow them to be ordinary brothers and sisters as much as possible, and that includes playing, fighting, annoying each other, and, best of all, laughing together. In fact, the single greatest thing you can do for your children's sibling relationships is to provide them with opportunities to have fun together. It doesn't have to be anything outrageous or expensive, just ordinary sibling fun. It could be baking cookies, sledding, riding bikes, playing a board game, or anything else your family enjoys. It may take more effort and planning than usual, but giving your children chances to have fun together can really cement their relationships. These are the memories you want your kids to have of their childhoods. The best activities are ones that give them a chance to laugh together. I realize that sometimes that seems impossible. But even cuddling together under a blanket and watching a favorite movie can be a moment to bond without the pressure of teaching or learning something.

Nothing makes me happier than when I hear my girls playing together in the next room. I know that those moments, fleeting and sweet, are building one of the most important relationships and support systems for both of their lives. As ambitious as we may be at times for our children's progress, we have to remember that this is their one and only childhood. Don't focus so much on interventions that you forget to give your daughter a chance just to be a kid with her siblings. Siblings need time to play, to goof around, and to figure out how to get along. Their relationships with each other will, we hope, outlast our relationships with them. Try to make time for joy and affection and natural sibling bonding. Their shared childhood will be what bonds them together as adults, so cultivate happiness as much as you can. I hope when my girls think of each other, they always smile.

Lifetime friends

"What greater thing is there for human souls than to feel that they are joined for life—to be with each other in silent unspeakable memories."

—*George Eliot*

The most important thing to remember is that your children are siblings first, and special needs and typical children second. The relationships of siblings are so special; there is no bond comparable in life to the one we share with our brothers and sisters. It is even more important that your children have good sibling relationships when one of them has special needs. Your daughter with special needs will need her brothers and sisters to be there for her throughout her life, after you are gone. It is essential for you to balance your family, so that your children can enjoy their sibling relationships. Typical siblings have the right to enjoy all the activities and milestones and celebrations that all kids do. They also have the unique opportunity to develop greater empathy, patience, and gratitude through their relationships with their special siblings. As with everything in this journey, your children's relationship will depend on your outlook. If you look at all your children and see miracles, so will they.

At times, your typical kids may think it isn't fair that their family has been given this challenge. They may become frustrated with their siblings, as all siblings do. However, with your guidance, they can work through it and come out with an enlightened understanding of the unique value of each human life. If you are sure to give all your children special attention, applause for their accomplishments, and chances to build their own identities, I think positive sibling relationships will naturally follow. And, in time, we hope that our more capable kids will become amazing advocates for their special siblings. Personally, I hope Lizzie will be there for Caroline throughout her life, at least to oversee the architecture of her life and make sure she is okay. However, I know it is essential and right for Lizzie to feel free to have her own life as well. I have to help her find the balance because the reality is that Caroline is her sister, and that carries with it a responsibility. I am hoping, with time and a deep enough bond, that responsibility will not seem like such a burden, but more of a labor of love.

The heart of the matter about siblings

1. It is important for everyone in a family to stay in balance and celebrate all members of the family for their unique contributions.

2. Try not to idealize the typical peers of your special daughter, nor focus obsessively on your special daughter. All children deserve attention and praise for their accomplishments.

3. Do not force your daughter's typical siblings to co-parent; it only creates resentment and interferes with the normal, healthy sibling bond you want to foster.

4. Remember that you set the tone for the family. If you face your daughter's challenges with confidence and optimism, so too will her siblings.

5. Your daughter's sibling relationships may well be the most important of her life. Make sure you let your children be kids together, so they can create a bond to last a lifetime.

Chapter 7

Causes, Treatments, and Acceptance

How to Help Your Daughter and How to Accept Your Daughter

"I am different, not less."

—*Temple Grandin*

To date there has not been a single, definitive scientific explanation for the cause of autism. As a result, a multitude of theories about the cause of autism have been espoused and debated in the media. Theories range from brain inflammation, to toxic metal poisoning, to immune system failures. However, most scientists and physicians firmly believe, based on years of research, that there is an underlying genetic basis for autism. In 2009, leading Cambridge University autism expert Simon Baron-Cohen remarked that autism researchers had by that time identified 133 genes linked to autism (BBC News 2009). A year later in 2010, a research team working for the international Autism Genome Project Consortium published the results of a large-scale study comparing the genes of nearly 1000 children on the spectrum with the genes of a comparable number of children without autism. The study focused on copy number variations (CNV), which are parts of DNA that are disrupted or irregular in some way. The researchers found that the children with autism were 20 percent more likely to have these copy number variations, and they also discovered more affected genes in those individuals with autism than were previously identified (Harmon 2010). This specific discovery could eventually lead to an understanding of how the genetics of autism affect the brain. The researchers further reported this specific research "might eventually find up to 300 genes which are involved" in autism (Ghosh 2010). And in June 2011, the journal *Neuron* published three studies that found that "autism is not caused by one or two gene defects but probably hundreds of different mutations" (Roan 2011). Research continues to uncover new genetic markers linked to autism, and it is likely that genetics will eventually be able to explain the fundamental roots of autism.

Many researchers also believe that it is probable that environmental factors, most likely during prenatal development, contribute to autism. As mentioned in Chapter 1, these prenatal factors may include "parental age, maternal genotype, maternal-fetal immunoreactivity, in vitro fertilization, maternal ingestion of drugs, toxic chemicals in the environment during pregnancy, and maternal illnesses during pregnancy such as maternal diabetes or infections" (Szatmari 2011, pp.1091–2). And this is just the beginning of the list of potential "environmental" factors that researchers are investigating as possible contributors to autism. Although the way in which these factors affect fetal development is not understood, recent studies make it clear that autism is caused, at least in part, by the environment in the womb.

A study published in 2011, which focused on the concordance of autism in fraternal twins, highlighted how influential prenatal factors may be in the development of autism. The study found that in the case of fraternal twins, if one twin is diagnosed with autism, the second twin is 31 percent more likely to have autism (Zarembo 2011), as compared to 10–20 percent found in earlier studies of non-twin siblings (Johnson 2011). Fraternal twins do not share any more genetics than regular siblings. However, fraternal twins do share a common prenatal environment or womb. The heightened tendency of both fraternal twins to have autism would seem to indicate that something in the prenatal environment may also contribute to autism. Of course, this study does not rule out the tremendous influence of genetics, evidenced by the fact that repeated studies have concluded that if an identical twin has autism, his or her twin has a 90 percent chance of also being diagnosed with autism (Szatmari 2011). However, this study does indicate that there could be specific environmental factors that may augment a genetic predisposition for autism.

In light of recent scientific discoveries, most scientists now believe that it is likely that both genetics and prenatal conditions are contributing factors to autism. Unfortunately, the specific processes involved in how genetics and the prenatal environment contribute to autism, as well as the possible interaction between them, are still unknown, leaving scientists and physicians unsure how best to prevent or treat autism. And until there is conclusive proof about what causes autism, there will remain a variety of conflicting theories about the causes, resulting in competing approaches to treatment. And that is where it gets mighty tricky for parents, all of whom want to do what's best for their children.

One of the difficulties when a condition has no definitive cause is that it likewise has no definitive treatment. Over time, researchers have found that certain behavioral and educational therapies are effective in helping people on the spectrum to connect with the world and overcome some of the more challenging aspects of autism. However, there is no treatment that can "remove autism" from a person. That fact has not prevented people from marketing an overwhelming number of treatments and therapies to parents, each based on a specific "theory" about the cause of autism. In truth, one of the most difficult parts of having a child with autism is the dizzying array of therapies and treatments advocated by national organizations, special schools, alternative doctors, and other parents. Adding to the confusion is the fact that too often mainstream physicians offer little in the way of answers or direction to parents. I believe physicians, specifically pediatricians, need to be more positive and proactive in their knowledge of autism and interventions with children on the spectrum. However, as it stands today, with many pediatricians not well versed about autism therapies and treatments, parents are left to navigate these murky waters alone. Feeling frustrated and hopeless, parents often turn to the internet. This can be a confusing, scary, and downright dangerous journey at times.

Although I am not an expert in autism, I have spent hours, days, and months reading and researching; I hope to save you some time here by condensing what I have learned and sharing the tentative peace I have made with the entire subject of treatment. I hope that this brief overview of some of the therapies will help make it a bit less confusing for you, or at least give you a place from which to start your own research. Some autism therapies seek to decrease or eliminate the more troublesome behaviors of autism, while others claim to treat the cause, and a few even promise to "recover" or "cure" children. In general, the more traditional therapies, such as applied behavioral analysis (ABA) and speech therapy, should all be options at your daughter's school and therefore be of no cost to you. Counseling and medications, if necessary, should be accessible through your health insurance. The alternative therapies are not typically covered by any insurance company. The descriptions are the therapies as I have researched them and as I see them. You may come to different conclusions about what is most helpful, but at least you will have a sense of what's out there.

Treatments and therapies
Developmental-relational therapies
FLOORTIME™

There are many developmental-relational therapies out there to investigate. One of the best established is Floortime™. Floortime is a therapy that involves a parent or teacher literally getting down on the floor and engaging the child at his or her developmental level. Developed by Dr. Stanley Greenspan, the Floortime method believes: "From a mutually shared engagement, the parent is instructed how to move the child toward more increasingly complex interactions, a process known as 'opening and closing circles of communication'" (Autism Speaks 2011b). By meeting with the child at her level, in an activity of her choice, you can guide her to a more advanced level of interaction. The basis for the therapy seems to be respect for the child and a willingness to understand the child. It makes sense to me that if you want to draw your daughter out, you first need to meet her where she is. I did find if I joined my kids in the types of play they liked, it helped me communicate with them. Eventually I was able to expand the way they played with certain toys as well as teach them. As I mentioned before, imaginative play was extremely helpful in encouraging my girls to engage in spontaneous conversation. There were times when my girls wouldn't talk to me, but they would talk to Winnie the Pooh or Scrooge McDuck! You can visit Dr. Greenspan's website for more specific details and a complete description of Floortime (http://stanleygreenspan.com).

RELATIONSHIP DEVELOPMENT INTERVENTION (RDI)

Another developmental therapy is Relationship Development Intervention or RDI. Developed by Steven Guststein, RDI trains a parent to encourage and reward social skills. The basic premise is that relationships are a symbiotic situation, especially parent–child relationships. A parent teaches a child social skills, and a child teaches a parent what he or she needs and wants. When the child is unable to teach due to a development challenge, the parent is unable to learn from the child, and a breakdown in the relationship occurs. The child becomes fearful and frustrated in the relationship and shuts down further. RDI proposes a way to reconnect, thus drawing the child out and re-establishing a functioning symbiotic relationship that allows for social growth. This is done through interaction at the child's level and positive reinforcement. According to the RDI website, "Parents learn to re-think their daily lifestyle, restructuring routine activities, to provide safe but challenging opportunities for mental growth" (RDIconnect 2011). As I have not gone through RDI training, I cannot comment on its process or effectiveness. According to a report published in *Pediatrics* in 2007, "The evidence of the efficacy of RDI is anecdotal; published empirical scientific research is lacking at this time" (Myers and Johnson 2007, p.1165). I cannot say if its theoretical premise is completely solid, but I can certainly see how spending time thoughtfully encouraging our children's curiosity and nurturing their needs would be therapeutic and helpful to their development.

SON-RISE PROGRAM®

The Son-Rise Program® is another developmentally based therapy you may hear discussed, especially if you are surfing the net. Son-Rise was named after Raun Kaufman, the son of authors/teachers Barry Neil Kaufman and Samahria Lyte Kaufman. According to his parents, when Raun was 18 months old, he was diagnosed with severe autism. The Kaufmans claimed to have transformed their son from a non-verbal toddler to a highly social adolescent. Eventually Raun Kaufman graduated from an Ivy League university and he is now a motivational speaker for their program. As with RDI, the parent is the teacher in the Son-Rise program. The basic idea is to join your child in her pursuits. If your daughter has Asperger's, you are encouraged to learn about whatever her interests are, and rather than trying to discourage an obsessive interest, you are to embrace it as a way of connecting with your child. Similarly, if your daughter has autism and is engaging in a self-stimulatory behavior such as spinning or rocking, you are told to join her in the stimming activity as a way to meet her at her comfort level. The Son-Rise website states that participating with a child in these behaviors "facilitates eye contact, social development and the inclusion of others in play" (Autism Treatment Center of America 2011a). Unlike other programs, the Son-Rise program discourages parents from using other developmental programs at the same time, including Floortime. And the website makes a point of saying that it is not the repetition of skills but motivation that holds the key to success with children with autism, thereby denouncing ABA (applied behavioral analysis), the most widely used and time-tested behavioral program for kids on the spectrum.

The program is expensive and, as with most therapies claiming to "rescue" children from autism, the reports of success are only anecdotal. I haven't tried the Son-Rise program with my daughters, due to its expense and intensity. Also, I am skeptical of the Kaufmans' claims on their website that their son had severe autism and is now "cured" or, in their words, "[b]earing no traces of his former condition" (Autism Treatment Center of America 2011b). If that were so, certainly there would have been other cases like that by now, and we would all know the cure for autism. Additionally, the Son-Rise program is affiliated with Defeat Autism Now (DAN), the biomedical movement which likewise claims to potentially "cure" autism through questionable alternative treatments. This also makes me wary of the cost and claims of cure.

Developmental-relational therapies in general

What all developmental-relational therapies have in common is time spent trying to connect with your child, and that is a good thing. I can see how any of these therapies could help support a child's social development because parents are devoting enormous amounts of time and effort into playing with their children and talking to their children, and just plain loving their children. That kind of positive attention and encouragement will always yield some results and rewards. As far as the particular developmental-relational therapy you choose, I am not sure that matters nearly as much as the dedication and love you are giving to your daughter.

ABA (applied behavior analysis)

Without question, the therapy that was most helpful for Caroline was the behavioral therapy ABA (applied behavior analysis). ABA is a well-respected and proven effective teaching method which breaks learning down into manageable steps and reinforces through repetition. A teacher will sit with your daughter and practice a skill, such as learning the meaning of a word, until it is mastered. The method is the same every time with every skill. Since kids with autism seem to work best in routines, it teaches to their strengths. Caroline loved the predictability of ABA. Since the routine of teaching was the same every time, once she was familiar with it, she could focus on learning the skills. Our kids are so often overwhelmed by stimuli that it is almost impossible for them to focus enough to listen and learn. ABA gives them a comfortable groove in which they can then process new information.

ABA also involves positive reinforcement for a skill mastered. Caroline's favorite reward was blowing bubbles. I know there are a variety of other philosophies out there, and I would encourage you to visit a few schools, especially in the preschool years, to see what fit is right for your daughter. The preschool Caroline attended offered a combination of ABA, Floortime, and other strategies which seemed to provide balance and variety. I visited one school that only implemented ABA all day, and it seemed too rigid for Caroline's free-spirited personality. You want your daughter to learn, but you also want her to be happy. I think moderation and balance is the key in any program you pursue. And, of course, contact your local school district and social service agency to see what help they can provide, both with financial assistance and their expertise in navigating the local schools. You can learn more about ABA at the Autism Speaks website (www.autismspeaks.org).

Speech therapy

As I have mentioned several times already, speech therapy is an essential part of educating a child on the autism spectrum. In early intervention, a speech therapist may use PECS (Picture Exchange Communication System—a learning method that allows children with little or no verbal ability to communicate using pictures) to reinforce ideas and provide communication for the words your daughter has not yet mastered. If your daughter is able to acquire language, speech teachers can help to increase fluency and vocabulary. They also teach pragmatic language skills that focus on conversation, reading facial expressions, and taking social cues. One technique used in speech therapy to develop pragmatic language is Social Stories. Developed by Carol Gray, Social Stories describe "a situation, skill, or concept in terms of relevant social cues, perspectives, and common responses in a specifically defined style and format" (Gray 2011). Ms. Gray's Social Stories follow a very distinct pattern and you can access many of them at her website (thegraycenter.org) which provides step-by-step guidance for implementing Social Stories.

Your daughter's speech therapist may use the Social Stories model or more general story-based interventions. The speech therapist will provide short instructional sketches that describe common social situations; they include how to interpret social cues and illustrate appropriate social behavior. Social Stories are not trying to change your daughter's behavior, but to model and reinforce appropriate behavior. If you are interested in reinforcing this at home, books of these simple stories can be purchased at most bookstores, or you can write your own stories. Through stories such as "Sally goes to the doctor" you can prepare your daughter for common social situations and guide her through the appropriate behaviors. These stories teach the basics of social interactions in a fun and straightforward manner. Also, since speech services are often provided in small groups, your daughter will have the opportunity to practice her skills and form friendships. From preschool through high school, kids with autism should receive consistent speech instruction. My daughters have learned enormous amounts from their speech classes, and I often find that speech class provides the most effective and practical instruction in my children's school days.

For children who really struggle with learning any language, sign language can be a viable option. Many children with autism learn signing first (Caroline did for many words), and it gives them the opportunity to communicate. It is often easier for our kids to recognize a visual cue than to process a verbal one. Sometimes a child who does not speak at all can develop an extensive vocabulary in sign language. This has always mystified me, but I know it can be true. The goal is communication, even if what we would most love is to hear our daughters' voices. So ask your speech therapist about signing. There are many methods for bringing about communication in non-verbal people with autism.

Occupational and physical therapy

In addition to speech therapy, your daughter may also receive physical and occupational therapy to assist with gross and fine motor skills. Many children on the spectrum have issues with coordination, balance, strength, and muscle tone. Physical therapy can help with all these issues. Occupational therapists may help your daughter with fine motor skills, such as eating, grooming, and other self-help tasks. These therapists can also provide sensory integration therapy which can address some of the more limiting sensory issues our kids can face: aversions to smells and sounds and sensations. The goal of sensory integration therapy is to "identify disruptions in the way the individual's brain processes movement, touch, smell, sight and sound and help them process these senses in a more productive way" (Autism Speaks 2011c). The idea is that with controlled exposure, kids with autism can learn to handle and process the sensory overloads they sometimes experience. This therapy is enormously helpful because we all know how quickly things can go downhill if our kids get overstimulated or have an aversion to a sight, smell, or sound. You and your daughter will learn what to do when she is in the midst of a sensory overload.

I know when Caroline was younger, she loved to swing on the swing set. The motion would soothe her, and she would sing until she felt better. She also loved to be squished between two big bean bags when she was stressed. The deep pressure would calm her nervous system and give her a feeling of security and peace. Both of my girls love to have their arms and legs massaged. When Caroline was in elementary school, she had sensory breaks built into her IEP. At certain intervals she would be allowed to jump on a mini-trampoline or go on the swings to relieve her stress. It helped tremendously with her spirit and her focus when in school. When you think of the kaleidoscope of sensory input to our kids' neurologically challenged brains, it is no wonder that they sometimes need a good massage! Of course, it would be nice if their parents could have a nice spa treatment too!

The GFCF diet

One of the more widely discussed treatments for autism on the internet is the gluten-free/casein-free (GFCF) diet. The GFCF diet is based on the theory that children with autism may have a deficiency that makes it difficult for their bodies to metabolize gluten (protein from wheat, barley, rye, and oats) and casein (milk). According to this theory, when these proteins are not properly metabolized, peptides (small proteins) rise in the bloodstream, creating an opiate-like effect. Proponents of this theory believe when children with autism eat these foods, they become numb to their environment as if they were under the influence of an opiate (stoned). This creates isolation and detachment. According to the theory, when you remove the foods, the child is no longer "doped" from the peptides and has fewer autistic behaviors. Despite years of research, the effectiveness of the diet has never been established in a well-controlled study. The results of a recent study, published in May 2010, show that "The so-called autism diet—a gluten-free, casein-free eating plan—does not appear to improve the symptoms of children with the group of neurodevelopmental disorders known as autism spectrum disorder or ASD" (Doheny 2010). Furthermore, repeated studies show that children with autism do not have greater levels of peptides in their blood (Autism Science Foundation 2011).

However, despite the lack of scientific evidence, the fact remains that some parents feel the GFCF diet has really helped improve their children's behavior. This may happen because some children on the spectrum have food allergies which adversely affect their behavior. Therefore, if you are interested in pursuing the diet, the first step is to talk with your daughter's pediatrician about testing for food allergies. Obviously, gluten and dairy are two of the more common food allergens. If your daughter has major acting-out behaviors and her sleep and health are compromised, I certainly think that food allergies could be worth investigating. It makes sense to me that a child who is feeling major discomfort because of food intolerances, and who does not have the language to tell you how lousy she feels, would exhibit poor behavior. I would tantrum if I had chronic stomach aches; wouldn't you? So, if your daughter seems to have problems with irritable bowel, constipation, or eczema, for example, she may have food allergies, and trying a GFCF diet may help alleviate discomfort and therefore improve behavior. However, this is not a cure for autism but a treatment of food allergies. I do not personally know anyone whose child was "cured" of autism by the GCFC diet, and I have known many children on the diet. One thing to make sure of when implementing the diet is that your daughter is getting enough protein and vitamins. For most kids, milk and cheese are their main sources of both protein and calcium. Without milk and cheese, children on the GFCF diet could also be at risk for lower bone density, so it is important to be sure your daughter receives all the nutritional building blocks needed to grow up healthy (Childs, Salahi, and Mazzeo 2010).

I cannot provide a personal perspective on the GFCF diet because I only tried it briefly with my girls when they were younger. I had read so much about it that I decided to give it a try, even though my girls have no food allergies at all. However, I quickly found the diet too restrictive; they were eating very little on the diet, and I started to worry about their nutritional health. Furthermore, my girls were already "different enough" without eliminating most typical food from their diets. The diet became one more thing isolating my kids from their peers. I did not want them to be the kids who couldn't even eat the cupcakes at the birthday party the times when they did get invited! Luckily for me, neither of my children ever had any real digestive issues after early infancy when they both had reflux. They do not suffer from constipation or diarrhea. They are both regular as the sunrise, and right as rain in that area. I have also been lucky with them as eaters. When they were younger, they had healthy, if somewhat limited, diets, and as they have matured, they have both been willing to try most foods at least once. Caroline loves fruit and Lizzie loves vegetables, and they both readily eat lean protein such as fish and chicken. Because of their good health and eating habits, I decided against eliminating so many foods from their lives. I just try to be sure they are eating as healthily as possible.

Any treatments for autism should be ways to potentially help improve your daughter's quality of life and expand her potential. Therefore, I see the GFCF diet as a tool to improve your child's health if food allergies or gastrointestinal issues are present. I do not believe it is a requirement for all children with autism, nor do I believe it is a cure. However, I certainly am supportive and understanding of parents who choose to try it when their children are struggling with stomach issues. In fact, as rigorous as it is, I admire parents who are willing to make that commitment.

Neurofeedback or EEG biofeedback therapy

One very intriguing and safe therapy is EEG biofeedback therapy, also called neurofeedback therapy (NFT). I had a brief chance to explore neurofeedback therapy with both myself and my daughter Lizzie. We were fortunate to have the opportunity to try it with a psychiatrist who specializes in autism. This progressive doctor has since moved on to work at a hospital, and I have not been able to find another practitioner in our area whom our insurance will accept. Neurofeedback is definitely calming and pretty amazing for anxiety. Simply explained, the brain waves are monitored and calmed through a non-invasive EEG type procedure. It is neither scary nor harmful. It has even been recognized by the American Academy of Child and Adolescent Psychiatry as a treatment for attention deficit hyperactivity disorder (ADHD). As defined by the International Society for Neurofeedback and Research on their website:

> NFT uses monitoring devices to provide moment-to-moment information to an individual on the state of their physiological functioning... During training, sensors are placed on the scalp and then connected to sensitive electronics and computer software that detect, amplify, and record specific brain activity. Resulting information is fed back to the trainee virtually instantaneously with the conceptual understanding that changes in the feedback signal indicate whether or not the trainee's brain activity is within the designated range. Based on this feedback, various principles of learning, and practitioner guidance, changes in brain patterns occur and are associated with positive changes in physical,

emotional, and cognitive states. (International Society
for Neurofeedback and Research 2011)

In my sessions, as I was monitored, I watched a screen of changing abstract images. My frenetic, anxious brain waves were discouraged with less feedback, and my calm, soothing brain waves were "rewarded," and thereby positively reinforced. I truly felt relaxed for a few hours after my first session. It is not a cure for autism or ADHD, but rather a non-medicinal therapy which helps to soothe the sometimes erratic brain activity of people with autism, and may help in improving behavior and alleviating anxiety. If widely and readily available, I think it could be a fantastic alternative to taking an ADHD or antidepressant medication. Unfortunately, like too many treatments, it is hard to find a practitioner near you and treatment sessions you can afford. And, of course, most insurance companies will not cover it. Also, according to all I have read, it would take many sessions—a costly endeavor—to make a substantial long-term change. I am presently searching for another neurofeedback provider to help Lizzie with her stutter. As with anything else, consult your daughter's pediatrician before beginning any treatment. If your daughter's pediatrician is not knowledgeable about the treatment, ask him or her to research it for you.

Common medications

As far as medications go, this is definitely a topic for discussion with your daughter's pediatrician. There are *no* medications for autism, but some are prescribed to help with the other issues that can affect people with autism. The classes of drugs that are sometimes used for children with autism are:

- SSRIs (selective serotonin reuptake inhibitors) such as Prozac and Zoloft, taken for depression and anxiety

- anti-psychotics such as risperidone or Zyprexa, prescribed for behavioral issues

- anti-seizure medications, such as Depakote

- ADHD drugs, such as Strattera and Ritalin.

(National Institute of Mental Health 2011)

Most of these medications can have serious, and sometimes permanent, side effects. When Caroline was around four years old, she was having trouble focusing at school and sleeping at home. Her pediatrician prescribed risperidone in an attempt to even out her behavior, a drug commonly prescribed for behavior problems in autism. It was a disaster. Almost immediately, Caroline developed Parkinsonian tremors, a side effect of the medication, which can be permanent even if the medication is stopped. Her pediatrician immediately took her off the risperidone, and the tremors stopped. However, I learned a valuable lesson about the potential risks of medication.

A few years ago, when Lizzie entered puberty, she began experiencing anxiety attacks. Her pediatrician prescribed an SSRI which helped alleviate her anxiety, but she was taken off the medication when she developed a stutter. Presently my girls are not on any medication because they are doing well without any. At this point, I would rather deal with the issues they do have through counseling, rather than have them take medication. Medications can help, but often there are unwanted side effects. The important thing to remember is that *there is no medication for autism itself.* It is really a matter of whether certain behaviors or conditions can be improved with medication. And, as with all things, the benefits and risks may be not be fully evident until you try. Sometimes that is a scary proposition, so make a fully informed decision with your daughter's pediatrician.

Vitamins and supplements

There are some safe, healthy supplements I do give to each of my children daily. I am not recommending them here, as only your daughter's pediatrician can do that. However, I feel comfortable giving them to my girls and consider them safe. Daily, both of my girls take a multivitamin and an Omega-3/fish oil chewable supplement, along with a magnesium/B6 supplement, which has been shown to help with anxiety. They also both take sublingual B12 vitamins daily; B12 is extremely helpful according to pretty much every autism expert, and it is very hard to absorb through the stomach in vitamin pill form. Recently, I began giving both of them an acidophilus supplement to help with general digestive health. All of these vitamins and supplements are easily available, and the safe, appropriate doses can be discussed with your daughter's pediatrician. It is important to note that vitamins can be very dangerous if you exceed recommended doses, so always talk with your daughter's pediatrician first. Beyond these supplements, I just make sure my daughters eat right, go to the pediatrician and dentist regularly, play in the sunshine, laugh a lot, and get plenty of hugs.

Counseling

As far as treatments and therapies go, perhaps the most important thing you can do is find a family therapist for you, your spouse, and eventually your daughter; this is an absolute must. You will need someone to whom you can vent, and at some point your daughter may need to talk about the many complicated feelings she has being "different" and struggling with social connections. You would be surprised how even significantly autistic people benefit from therapy. I am always amazed at the unexpected eloquence both my daughters express when given the opportunity with the therapist to share their feelings. And, for me, the therapist has been a blessing. So often, as a parent of an exceptional child, you neglect or avoid your own feelings. It is important to remember you are a person too, and you need a chance to vent your feelings of anger, frustration, and fear in a safe environment. Otherwise these very natural feelings can seep out like toxic waste at all the wrong times. I have met some parents who are so heartbroken at their children's plights that they become very angry. And that anger becomes directed at spouses, family members, teachers, physicians, and anyone who could be a resource or support. At times, the anger is even directed at their own children. Bitterness and isolation are not good for you or your daughter. So seek counseling early and continue to seek it because solid emotional support is the best thing for you as a parent and a person.

Mercury, vaccinations, and alternative treatments

Before I describe what some of the alternative treatments are, I need to explain the theory behind a good many of them. In recent years, many media stories have focused on autism and vaccinations, and whether or not vaccines or the mercury in vaccines cause autism. Vaccines first came under scrutiny because the rise in autism in the last 25 years occurred at the same time as the number of vaccinations given to children increased. In addition, the MMR (measles/mumps/rubella) vaccine is given between 12 and 18 months, the age at which the first signs of autism may first be observed by parents and physician. Whether this is just a matter of unfortunate timing or actual cause and effect is at the heart of the controversy. As many physicians and scientists will tell you, correlation is not causation: just because two things happen at the same time does not mean one caused the other.

Initially, the focus of concern was on thimerosal, a preservative which contains mercury and was used for years in many vaccinations. Some physicians and parents worried that the mercury in the vaccinations may have caused brain damage, resulting in the behaviors of autism. Essentially this theory claimed that autism was a form of mercury poisoning. The revelation that many childhood vaccinations contained thimerosal, an ethyl mercury derivative, caused tremendous controversy. Due to the concerns of the public and the CDC, by 2002, thimerosal was removed from nearly all vaccines given to children, except for trace amounts in a few (CDC 2011c). If the theory linking thimerosal and mercury was true, in the years that followed the removal of thimerosal from vaccines, the autism rates should have begun to decrease. Instead, the autism rates continued to climb (FDA 2011). At that point, most experts concluded that mercury could not be the culprit in the rising rates, and many proponents of the mercury theory (though not all) reluctantly agreed (Schechter and Grether 2008). With mercury removed from vaccines and the rates continuing to climb, the search for a cause continued.

Soon after the thimerosal theory was disproved, certain members of the autism community wondered if the vaccines themselves were the culprit, specifically the MMR vaccine. A theory developed based on a premise that children with autism have vulnerable immune systems that cannot effectively manage vaccinations. This theory describes the progression of events that then lead to autism as follows: when a the child's immune system cannot handle the vaccination, the child's gut becomes the dumping ground for the overflow; toxic changes then occur in the intestinal flora, and proteins are released from the intestine; these proteins travel to the brain, and the neurological result of this chain reaction is autism. Susan Dominus of *The New York Times* describes the theory this way: "the three vaccines, given together, can alter a child's immune system, allowing the measles virus in the vaccine to infiltrate the intestines; certain proteins, escaping from the intestines, could then reach and harm neurons in the brain" (Dominus 2011). Some parents who believe their children's autism presented after the MMR shot found this theory convincing, especially if their children also suffered from gastroenterological issues.

Wakefield/Lancet controversy

The issue of the MMR vaccine and autism first took the autism world by storm in 1998, when the *Lancet*, a highly respected British medical journal, published a study led by Dr. Andrew Wakefield, a British gastroenterologist, which appeared to show a connection between the MMR vaccine and autism (Wakefield *et al.* 1998). The study focused on 12 children whose autism, the authors suggested, had been caused by the MMR vaccine. Wakefield's study indicated a possible connection between gastrointestinal issues in these young patients and vaccines, when the MMR virus was reportedly found in their intestines. This would have supported the theory that their immune systems could not handle the vaccine, and that the virus collected toxically in the gut, affected their brains, and caused their autism. Although the study did not outright claim a connection between autism and the MMR vaccine, it "identified associated gastrointestinal disease and developmental regression in a group of previously normal children, which was generally associated in time with possible environmental triggers" (Wakefield *et al.* 1998, p.1). The environmental triggers referenced were the vaccines combined in the MMR shot. This potential discovery had enormous implications. For many years, people made decisions about whether or not to vaccinate based on this study.

Twelve years later, however, in 2010, the theory connecting autism and vaccinations was dealt a major blow when that same study was formally retracted by the *Lancet*. The retraction was a monumental move by the *Lancet* which has only retracted, "'10 or 15' studies in its 186-year history" (Denoon 2010). The retraction came after it was revealed that the study was deeply flawed, and its results were therefore deemed invalid. Even more damning, the flaws in the study have been characterized not as oversights or mistakes, but as "elaborate fraud" by the *British Journal of Medicine* (Salahi 2011). The *British Journal of Medicine* also asserts that Dr. Andrew Wakefield, who headed the study, made "a deliberate attempt to create an impression that there was a link by falsifying the data" (Knowles 2011). Furthermore, in May 2010, Dr. Wakefield had his medical license revoked for "ethical lapses, including conducting invasive medical procedures on children that they did not need" (Burns 2010). According to reports, Dr. Wakefield performed medically unnecessary colonoscopies on children to collect data. In addition, Britain's General Medical Council reported that Dr. Wakefield neglected to reveal that while he was publishing research to discredit the current MMR vaccine, "he was developing a vaccine that would have been very profitable if the MMR vaccine was discarded" (Maugh 2010). Dr. Wakefield has denied any wrongdoing, stating in an email to the *Los Angeles Times*, "The allegations against me and my colleagues are both unfounded and unjust" (Maugh 2010). Both the study and the subsequent retraction continue to cause tremendous controversy. There are parents who still believe fervently in Dr. Wakefield's work despite the fact that he has had his medical license revoked for his actions. And there are still people who believe vaccines caused their children's autism despite the fact that the mainstream medical community has concluded vaccines are safe.

What to believe

Choosing which side to believe can be hard for a parent, especially when vaccines can be scary for parents anyway. I remember how uneasy I felt receiving the warning pamphlets that accompanied my girls' vaccinations. First, the scary stuff. It is true that some children are injured by vaccines, as is evidenced by the National Vaccine Injury Compensation Program, which reviews cases of adverse vaccine reaction and awards damages. These cases are usually incredibly severe, with children suffering from a devastating array of disabilities: brain damage, severe intellectual impairment, cerebral palsy, severe seizure disorder, and more. Although these cases are statistically very rare, any injury is one too many. Further work needs to be done to make sure vaccines are as safe as they can possibly be with no collateral damage for the public good.

Now for the reassuring facts. The vast majority of children who receive childhood vaccinations remain healthy and fine. Furthermore, studies continue to show that vaccines do not increase the risk of being diagnosed with autism spectrum disorders (CDC 2011d). To date there have been at least 18 controlled epidemiological studies which have found no link between autism and vaccines (Rope 2010). And in August 2011, the American Institute of Medicine (IOM) issued a report after a close review of over 1000 vaccine studies, and found *no* evidence that the eight common childhood vaccines contribute to autism (Stein 2011). The eight vaccines in the study were: measles/mumps/rubella, varicella (chicken pox), influenza, hepatitis A, hepatitis B, human papillomavirus (HPV), diptheria/tetanus/acellular pertussis, and meningococcal (Kotz 2011). The IOM is "an independent, nonprofit organization that works outside of government to provide unbiased and authoritative advice to decision makers and the public" (IOM 2011); therefore, the results of this study should reassure even the most skeptical of parents. In addition, the American Medical Association, the American Academy of Pediatrics, and the National Institutes of Health are among the many public health agencies that state emphatically that there is no link between vaccines and autism. Furthermore, pediatricians, who administer vaccines daily and watch for reactions in patients, do not believe there is a link between vaccines and autism. If anyone could see a pattern of correlation, it would be pediatricians. I believe in the integrity of our children's physicians; if they saw such a correlation, they would be very concerned about the safety of vaccines. Instead, pediatricians continue to advocate for vaccines to protect children from dangerous diseases.

When you take a closer look at the hypothesized link between autism and vaccines, it may well be a matter of unfortunate timing, rather than cause and effect. Autism is typically diagnosed in the first three years of life, when vaccines are given regularly; therefore, it is likely that your daughter's diagnosis happened around the time of a vaccination. But that does not mean that the vaccine caused the autism. It is also important to note that the MMR vaccine has been given routinely to American children since 1971, nearly 20 years before the dramatic rise in the autism rate began; therefore, it seems unlikely that the MMR vaccine would be the cause of the recent rise in autism rates (Baker and Clements 2010). With the MMR vaccine removed as a likely cause, some people have hypothesized that it is the sheer number of vaccines that overwhelms the immune systems of children susceptible to autism. However, a closer look at vaccines reveals that while the number of vaccines in recent years has increased, children are actually exposed to fewer antigens than in the past. The "antigen" is the part of the vaccine that provokes the immune system reaction. The American Academy of Pediatrics explains it this way:

> Although we now give children more vaccines, the actual number of antigens they receive has declined. Whereas previously 1 vaccine, smallpox, contained about 200 proteins, now the 11 routinely recommended vaccines contain fewer than 130 proteins in total. Two factors account for this decline: first, the worldwide eradication of smallpox obviated the need for that vaccine, and second, advances in protein chemistry have resulted in vaccines containing fewer antigens (e.g., replacement of whole-cell with acellular pertussis vaccine). (Offit *et al.* 2002, pp. 126–7)

This report indicates that the challenges vaccines present to a child's immune system have actually decreased over the past 100 years. Therefore, if autism was caused by the sheer number of vaccine antigens overloading the immune system, the rate should have decreased, not increased, over the past 100 years. As for the immune system in general, scientists are presently studying the role the immune system may play in autism, but have yet to determine how it may contribute to the condition. There are certainly children with autism who have physical illnesses, such as gastrointestinal problems and seizures; however, there is no proof those symptoms and illnesses are due to vaccines. In addition, there are many children with autism who are very healthy. As with so many things about autism, there is not one definitive profile of the health of a child with autism.

A final fact that would seem to cast doubt upon vaccines as the cause of autism is that autism seems to run in families, with the condition repeating in younger siblings of children on the spectrum (Rochman 2011). A study in 2011 concluded that siblings of children on the spectrum had a 20 percent greater risk of being diagnosed on the spectrum (Szabo 2011). In addition, there are many accounts of families who, having older children diagnosed with autism, declined to vaccinate the younger ones, and the younger ones were still diagnosed with autism despite never having had one vaccination.

With regard to the toxins in vaccines, the truth is we live in an extremely polluted world, and the majority of the toxins to which babies are exposed come from our food, air, and water. And as far as the toxins in vaccines go, Immunize.org, a national website devoted to vaccine information points out, "If you assume that a baby is breast-fed exclusively up until six months of age, that baby will consume about 360 micrograms of methyl mercury. That's twice the amount of mercury that was ever contained in vaccines and 25 times the quantity of mercury contained in the influenza vaccine" (Brown 2011, p.3). From exposures in our environment, we all have mercury in our bodies; therefore, so too does breast milk. Understanding how much mercury a baby ingests from the mother puts into perspective the amount of mercury that was in vaccines. Obviously, vaccines should be as safe and clean as possible, but I also understand that certain elements are there for a reason, to preserve the integrity of the medicine in the vaccines.

Keeping it in perspective

Despite the studies and arguments of scientists, there are parents who are convinced that vaccines caused their children's autism, and swear that their children regressed after vaccination. And although the research says no, I respect other parents' feelings about their children. I would not tell other parents what they did or didn't see. I would not presume to know their children better than they do, and I would expect that they would not presume to know what is true for my children. However, it is important to remember, in the midst of this controversy, that before childhood vaccinations, children suffered and died from these diseases. The prospect of polio or whooping cough making a comeback is extremely scary. And if someone chooses not to vaccinate their child, they are presuming that the rest of us will vaccinate our children, so that their child is never exposed to those diseases. And in doing so, that parent is risking not only their own child's health but the health of any child with whom their child comes in contact. There are babies who are too young for certain vaccinations and children who cannot be vaccinated due to illnesses such as cancer; those children and their families must rely on the rest of us in order to stay healthy. In light of those facts, choosing not to vaccinate seems like a dangerous choice to me. You should raise your concerns about the vaccines to your child's physician, but always remember choosing not to vaccinate leaves your child vulnerable to far worse fates than autism.

My girls and vaccinations

I learned about the vaccine controversy well after both of my girls were both diagnosed and all of their infant vaccinations were already given. Furthermore, my girls were given nearly all of their big vaccinations before the thimerosal was removed from vaccines. I never saw any kind of short- or long-term behavioral change in my girls after they were vaccinated. Like my nieces, who do not have autism, as infants both of my girls were a bit sleepy and slightly feverish for a day after big vaccines, then quickly returned to normal. There were no prolonged fevers or illnesses or signs of a compromised immune system. In fact, both of my girls are quite healthy and have been so throughout their lives with the exception of ear infections and some typical childhood sicknesses when they were younger. Their early signs of autism, which I missed, such as feeding issues and hypersensitivity, were there before vaccines and after them. Therefore, I have continued having my girls receive their vaccinations. My primary concern is always my girls' health and well-being, so I am relieved that vaccines can protect them from so many serious illnesses.

Vaccine theory/"biomedical" treatments

The following treatments are based in large part on the belief that vaccines cause or at least worsen autism. They are generally not recommended by mainstream physicians and are not covered by most insurance plans and therefore tend to be very expensive.

Chelation

Since mercury (thimerosal) from vaccinations is a theory about the possible cause of autism, chelation—the attempt to rid the body of mercury and other heavy metals—is an autism treatment often promoted on the internet. This has continued despite the fact that the mercury–autism link has taken some serious hits the past several years. To date, there is no scientific proof that children with autism have excess mercury or other heavy metals in their bodies. Chelation is typically used to remove lead from the body, and it is most successful when done soon after exposure. As an autism treatment, chelation seeks to remove mercury and other toxic metals from the body intravenously, orally, or by applying the chelating agent to the skin. However, chelation cannot reverse damage already caused by heavy metal poisoning; it can only remove heavy metals from the body. Therefore, I am not sure how it could remedy mercury poisoning and reverse autism if mercury from vaccinations years earlier was a cause of autism. If you are interested, you should ask your daughter's pediatrician to test her for heavy metal poisoning, and see what he or she recommends.

It is very important, however, to mention that chelation is a potentially risky treatment because it can damage the liver or cause kidney failure (Hoecker 2010). As with so many treatments for autism, the information supporting the practice of chelation is anecdotal at best. Furthermore, there are at least as many stories about the dangers and damages of chelation as there are about the benefits. One possible negative side effect is that chelation can free up mercury stored dormant in the body's soft tissues which can then travel to the brain, actually *causing* neurological damage (Stratton, Gable, and McCormick 2004). Another risk is that if the child's mercury level is not high enough to absorb the chelating agent, certain chelating agents can actually attack the brain itself, also causing brain damage (Coplan 2010, p.285). And, to date, there has been one death of a child with autism during a chelation procedure at a physician's office (Kane 2006). I caution against any at-home chelation method; there are just too many unknowns. To even consider chelation, you would need a hospital and qualified physician. Chelation is not something I have tried with my daughters, nor do I plan to. To me, the marginal, hypothetical benefits just don't outweigh the considerable risks.

IVIG

Since some people believe that vaccines damage or overwhelm the immune system and cause autism, they likewise recommend treatment that seeks to heal a person's immune system in order to alleviate the behaviors of autism. Intravenous immunoglobulin therapy (IVIG) is a treatment that seeks to restore a patient's immune system through injecting proteins into the blood. These proteins come from thousands of blood donors, so there is a risk of infection from the treatment. Very rarely, a child can go into anaphylactic shock due to the treatment (Tsouderos and Callahan 2009). IVIG is a treatment usually reserved for those whose immune systems are seriously compromised from illnesses such as AIDS. IVIG must be done in a hospital under the careful supervision of a physician. It is a serious medical procedure, and certainly not without trauma for the child. Treating patients with autism with IVIG is very controversial, and even the most ardent proponents admit that not all patients show improvement after treatments. Measuring improvement can be a very subjective process. As with the many other alternative treatments out there, it has not been proven through scientific analysis to be an effective treatment for autism. Because of this, most insurance companies will not cover IVIG for the treatment of autism. It is not something I have tried or plan to try with my daughters. Again, I cannot see how a theoretical benefit, not proven through scientific study, could be worth the considerable risks.

Hyperbaric oxygen chamber

One therapy you may read about for children with autism is treatment in a hyperbaric oxygen chamber. It is based on the theory that autism is caused by brain inflammation. The brain inflammation is attributed to a variety of factors depending on which theory you read, although many theories again blame vaccines. Proponents say these treatments can help reduce the behaviors of autism by increasing oxygen in the blood (known as hyperoxia) in an attempt to decrease brain inflammation. There are anecdotal reports by parents of improved behavior. However, too much oxygen can actually be toxic. As renowned autism expect Dr. James Coplan explains, "Hyperoxia triggers cell death by a process known as apoptosis...

and can lead to Alzheimer's disease-related changes in the brain" (Coplan 2010, p.286). With potential for harm and only anecdotal testimonies of benefit, hyperbaric oxygen treatment is a very risky proposition. Consult your daughter's physician and do your research before embarking on such a treatment for your daughter. I have read nothing about hyperbaric oxygen chamber treatments that would ever convince me to put my girls in one; the trauma and weirdness of the experience alone would undo any marginal benefit in my opinion.

More vitamins and supplements

Another major component of most biomedical/alternative approaches to autism is supplementing your child's diet with a wide assortment of vitamins, mineral supplements, and digestive enzymes. These include high doses of vitamin B12 and magnesium, as well as amino acids, fatty acids, and glutathione, an antioxidant. Many alternative doctors also recommend thyroid medication, antifungal treatment, and a course of probiotics. I believe in basic vitamins, but, as you can imagine, administering all these supplements to your daughter would be difficult and costly. Furthermore, the doses must be carefully monitored by repeated blood tests. Vitamins can be toxic in high doses. Most mainstream physicians do not believe this course of treatment to be necessary or effective.

What is "recovery" and what should we hope for when we "treat" our children?

> *"Most of the shadows of this life are caused by standing in one's own sunshine."*
>
> —*Ralph Waldo Emerson*

I wanted to share some thoughts on treatments, "recovery," "cures," and just coming to a peaceful acceptance of who your daughter is. I know how incredibly frustrating it is when a self-appointed "expert" comes on television, telling you that if you just do all of these unproven, incredibly expensive, not covered-by-insurance treatments, you can "cure" your child. And because he or she is a wealthy celebrity, with access to everything from a private chef to a personal tutor to a monogrammed hyperbaric oxygen chamber, he or she can do that. Most of us cannot. I am not sure we should. Every parent must make his or her own decision about treatments and therapy, but my advice would be to read all you can and proceed with caution. Our children are not science experiments to be put through any and every "treatment," hoping to change who they are. They are bright, sensitive, and *soulful* human beings who trust us to protect them and guide them, even if they cannot tell us so in words. Our first rule must be to do no harm.

As for parental testimonies, I believe they are generally sincere. However, I also believe people who want their children to improve, and who are going to extraordinary lengths in an attempt to force that to happen, will desperately want to see results. This is especially true when they put their children through difficult ordeals, take questionable risks, and spend exorbitant amounts of money. Also kids with ASD tend to improve in spurts of growth and progress, followed by periods when progress slows to a crawl. I have seen this with my girls and many of my students. It is easy, therefore, to see why a parent might believe a sudden spurt of progress is the result of a treatment of some kind. The Autism Speaks organization wisely explains the multiple stories of "recovery" this way:

> Growing evidence suggests that a small minority of children with autism have progressed to the point where they no longer meet the criteria for a diagnosis. The theories behind the recovery of some children range from the assertion that the child was misdiagnosed to the belief that the child had a form of autism that may resolve as he matures to the opinion that the child benefited from successful treatment. You may also hear about children who reach "best outcome" status, which means they score normally on tests for IQ, language, adaptive functioning, school placement, and personality, but have mild symptoms on some personality and diagnostic tests.
>
> Some children who no longer meet the criteria for an autism diagnosis are later diagnosed as having ADHD, Anxiety or even Asperger's Syndrome.

We don't yet know what percentage of children with autism will recover, or what genetic, physiological or developmental factors can predict which ones will. Recovery from autism is usually reported in connection with intensive early intervention, but we do not know how much or which type of intervention works best, or whether the recovery can be fully credited to the intervention. Presently, there is no way of predicting which children will have the best outcomes.

In the absence of a cure or even an accurate prognosis of a child's future, do not be afraid to believe in a child's potential. Most children with autism will benefit from intervention. Many, if not most, will make very significant, meaningful progress. (Autism Speaks 2011d)

"Recovery" can mean anything from a child's natural developmental growth over time, to progress made through early intervention, to a child who was over-diagnosed or misdiagnosed in the first place. There is no one definition. Therefore, when you see the words "cure" or "recovery," remember they are extremely subjective terms in the context of autism. That is not to say there isn't great reason for hope. Our children are not static in their development; with love and support they will grow and mature over time. Many of the more troublesome challenges of autism can be helped with proven treatments: early intervention programs in education such as ABA, speech therapy, and peer role-modeling offered through inclusion, to name a few. However, as of today, there is no proven cure. That fact has not stopped people from touting "miracle cures." Nor has it stopped other self-appointed experts from selling books claiming that certain experimental treatments have cured autism, and exerting pressure on loving, devoted parents to follow their protocols. The truth is these books frequently lack solid scientific evidence for their claims and often do more harm than good. The other truth is that there are a lot of people making money from our children's autism. I have seen families suffer as they chase "cure" after "cure" with no positive result, spending tens of thousands of dollars, devoting hours and hours of time, only to cause distress and potential risk to the child, and a rollercoaster of hope and devastation for the parents.

There are people ready to do *anything* to drive the autism from their child, almost as if it is a demonic possession. One of the most devastating things I read recently was an article about parents "chemically castrating" their children through use of a drug intended for extreme cases of precocious puberty. Parents were injecting their children with this hormone drug because of a gross misinterpretation and misuse of a scholarly article on the effect of testosterone on autism by renowned autism researcher Dr. Simon Baron-Cohen. Upon hearing about this, Dr. Baron-Cohen said the use of the drug on children with autism "filled me with horror" (cited in Tsouderos and Callahan 2009). There are no clinical trials to indicate this would be an effective treatment for autism. This use of the drug for autism is not medically sanctioned, and the health risks for the child are unknown but can include sterility and osteoporosis (Tsouderos and Callahan 2009). Can you imagine how poorly a parent would have to regard their child to try a bungee-jump of an experimental treatment like that?

I do not see my children as deficient or inadequate or damaged, so I will not take chances with their health. Constantly putting our children through experimental medical treatments sends them the message that they are sick. We must consider the emotional effects of invasive treatments as well as the physical risks. Believe me, there are times when I cry for what may not be possible for Caroline. I understand the desire to help your child in any way you can. I am always researching and reading and investigating. But I always measure the promise of the therapy against the trauma, danger, or pain it could cause. The risk must be worth not just the possible benefit but the *knowable* benefit. I would not put my children through something risky in a blind attempt to fix them.

Furthermore, if the illusion of an available "cure" is projected into the world, there will only be more rejection from the world when our children are unable to "recover." An even greater stigma will be placed on those who remain significantly challenged by autism. Parents of children with severe autism will be regarded as failures who have not tried hard enough to heal their children. If we begin to claim that a "cure" can be had if parents just spend enough money and work hard enough at it, we are further ostracizing those parents and children for whom great change may not be possible.

> *"Temple is not cured. Temple is fulfilled."*
>
> —*Eustacia Cutler, Temple Grandin's mother*

I love this quotation because it describes what we, as parents, should hope to accomplish for our daughters through therapy and treatment: to be fulfilled, happy, and loved for who they are. Treatment should help our daughters to improve their daily quality of life, not experiment on them in hopes of changing them into what we need them to be. If you do choose to explore alternative treatments, do it to improve your daughter's health, not because you want to rid her of autism. It must be about who she is and what is best for her. Human beings are all on a continuum of abilities and struggles. We should not segregate people into two groups—developmentally challenged and "normal." We all have gifts and we all have limitations. The greatest "disability" I have ever encountered is a cold heart, one that judges, limits, excludes, and defines people by cruel and dismissive words. I believe all children, no matter what their level of autism, know if we love them and accept them as they are. The anger and angst present when any parent cannot accept a child is felt in every cell of that child. If, every time you look at your daughter, you only see a "disability," your vision of your daughter will become her greatest obstacle of all. You must love and accept your daughter first; only then you can truly help her fulfill all her miraculous potential.

The heart of the matter about causes, treatments, and acceptance

1. Most research indicates that autism is a genetic condition, perhaps augmented by prenatal environmental factors. However, since there is no one definitive cause, there is no one definitive treatment.

2. Applied behavioral analysis, a behavioral therapy, and Floortime, a developmental-relational therapy, are two well-established treatments with a reliable history of positive results. When choosing treatments, it is best to start with one that has a long and proven track record of helping children.

3. Most major medical organizations, including the National Institutes of Health, American Academy of Pediatrics, and the American Medical Association, do not believe vaccines cause autism. To date, there have been 18 controlled epidemiological studies which have found *no* link between autism and vaccines.

4. Always consult with your daughter's pediatrician and do your research before beginning any therapy, especially an alternative or experimental therapy. Be very skeptical of treatments that promise to "cure" children, are not accepted by the medical establishment, are extremely expensive and not covered by insurance, or involve risk to your daughter's health.

5. The single most important treatment for your daughter is your unconditional love. No matter what course of treatment you choose, she will make the most progress when she is loved and accepted just as she is.

Chapter 8

The World Wide Web

> "It would be so nice if something made sense for
> a change." Alice in Wonderland

> —Lewis Carroll

After your daughter is diagnosed on the autism spectrum, no doubt one of the first things you will do is turn to your computer and dive through its portal into the World Wide Web. I know I did that. Well, there is indeed a plethora of hypothetical "answers" out there to all your questions, but the world of autism online is a very confusing and complicated place. There are many sites sponsored by government organizations, hospitals, and other medical facilities. Then there are those sponsored by charitable organizations, activist groups, and a variety of treatment centers. There are also thousands of blogs, offered by parents, therapists, and adults on the spectrum, sharing testimonies, opinions, and advice. Finally, there are also the salesmen of all shapes and kinds, peddling their "cure" potions and procedures, like Professor Marvel in *The Wizard of Oz* before the tornado. It is bewildering to know what to think. You start off just looking at symptoms and hoping to find some guidance about basic treatment, and by the time you know it, three hours have passed and you have wandered, link by link, 20 websites off course, until you are wearily looking at the blog of some person who believes autism is related to alien activity in Area 51. Just then, one of your kids pops up like the gopher in *Caddyshack*, and any hope of sleep you had has been squandered. And what have you learned? That there are lots of crazy people in the world with lots of crazy opinions on your daughter.

I will be very honest with you about what I have found in my ten years of researching autism and the autism community online. I will also be very candid and upfront about my impressions and opinions of these websites. I am not trying to convince you to believe any particular theory or philosophy, but to save you some time by explaining the various positions and the websites that promote them. I would just encourage you to exercise caution, and remember that truth can be a very tricky thing with a condition that has no proven cause and no proven cure.

There are very distinct divisions within the autism community. So you have to know that whatever you read is fueled by an underlying position or philosophy about autism: what it is, what causes it, and how to best treat it. The major schism is between those who believe autism is fundamentally a genetic condition, possibly augmented by prenatal conditions, and best treated by traditional methods, such as developmental-relational, behavioral, and educational therapies; and those who believe it is a physical illness, likely caused by vaccines and best treated by biomedical treatments. And, unfortunately, there is very little middle ground in between.

Mainstream medical websites

First, there are the mainstream medical websites and government-sponsored websites. These websites provide detailed information about what autism is and the ways in which it may affect a person. They are parent-friendly and comprehensive. Generally, they only endorse treatments that have been studied, tested, and passed the stringent requirements of the scientific method. These are the sites to which your daughter's pediatrician will most likely direct you.

Duke Health
www.dukehealth.org/health_library/advice_from_doctors/your_childs_health/autism
This is the website sponsored by Duke University School of Medicine. There is an entire section devoted to autism, which is super user-friendly and answers the most common questions about causes and treatments, along with easy to read explanations about studies and research. Duke also has a well-respected autism program affiliated with the site, so they not just providing information, but are deeply involved in and committed to helping individuals with autism.

Mayo Clinic
www.mayoclinic.com/health/autism/DS00348
From one of the most renowned medical centers on the planet, this well-respected website provides reliable information and links to scientifically credible articles about autism. It is an excellent place to begin to learn about autism and the most reliable treatments available.

Centers for Disease Control and Prevention
www.cdc.gov/media/subtopic/asdResources.htm
Obviously this is the main government-sponsored medical website of the US. It provides not only excellent information about autism, but also plenty of links to studies and research currently being conducted about autism causes and treatments. Again, it is an excellent place to learn about autism.

National Institute of Neurological Disorders and Stroke
www.ninds.nih.gov/disorders/autism/autism.htm
This website is part of the National Institutes of Health and provides an overview of autism from a neurological perspective, with information about seizures and possible genetic predispositions. Again, it cautions parents to take a conservative approach to treatment. I like this website because it provides more specific information about the brain and the neurological impact of autism. Learning about the brain differences in autism helped me to better understand some of my girls' behaviors which stemmed from their differing sensory and cognitive experiences.

Children's Hospital Boston
www.childrenshospital.org
This is the hospital associated with Harvard Medical School, so I believe I can safely call it a very reputable and solid source of information. It provides pretty extensive information on autism and the latest in research and treatments, with links to many interesting articles and websites. Even if you don't live near Boston, the website can give you a sense of how an excellent treatment center or program should look.

PubMed
www.ncbi.nlm.nih.gov/pubmed

This is the database of medical articles and studies maintained by the US National Library of Medicine and the National Institutes of Health. There are over 20 million citations from MEDLINE, life science journals, and online books. It is obviously a great website for finding articles and studies on autism. However, a warning: not all studies are equally credible, nor are all articles sound. You must look for studies and articles that have been peer-reviewed, cited in other research, and whose results have been replicated in other studies by other researchers. It is the preponderance of results that gives certain ideas credibility. Also, look for researchers who are educated and skilled in the area they are researching. I have found some pretty crazy studies published on PubMed by people with no credentials in the subject area of their "study." So remember that not all studies are of equal value or credibility. Still, PubMed is the most complete source of information on medical research available.

There are obviously many other websites sponsored by medical centers and government agencies. These are just the ones I find easiest to navigate and with the most complete information and links.

Autism groups, societies, and associations

After you search the medical websites, you will probably want to check out the various societies and associations dedicated solely to autism. These websites can often be a great help in finding local support and resources. Most try to offer information as objectively as possible about all the possible causes and treatments of autism. I find it admirable that many organizations try to be deferential to both schools of thought; however, it can be confusing for a parent who is just seeking a straightforward answer.

Autism Speaks
www.autismspeaks.org

This is the largest autism advocacy organization in the US, providing reliable, solid information on treatments as well as ongoing studies and initiatives, both local and national. Autism Speaks explains very well how the currently available therapies work, and it has links to many articles. It also has information on local and national charity events, and links to find services in your area. I would say Autism Speaks is more conservative in its approach because it stands by the medical establishment's conviction that vaccines have not been shown to cause autism. However, it is sympathetic to the concerns of parents who wonder about vaccine safety for certain children, and is continuing to promote further research about vaccine safety. I visit this website a couple of times a week to see what is new in the world of autism.

Autism Society of America
www.autism-society.org

This is the original autism organization, founded by autism doctor and researcher Dr. Bernard Rimland in 1965. It offers a wealth of information and advice, along with links to your local chapter, so you can get involved on a personal level. I find the Autism Society tries nobly to offer all points of view, including information on genetic research and the possibility of environmental causes of autism. They do a good job explaining dietary interventions, which to me are a pretty safe way to try to help your child feel better and just might help. Conversely, they also offer information about chelation and IVIG therapy, which have not been proven to be effective treatments for autism and involve considerable risks. It should be noted that Dr. Rimland went on to form the Autism Research Institute, which is the original biomedical autism organization, so there are more than a few links to that website in the biomedical section. Generally speaking, the Autism Society tries to represent everyone's perspectives and concerns.

The National Autistic Society (UK)
www.autism.org.uk

This is the equivalent organization in the UK to the Autism Society of America. It has very comprehensive information about the way services are delivered in the UK to people with autism and their families. The treatments discussed are generally those that have been proven to work. Additionally, there is a very specific position statement on the MMR vaccine and autism, which acknowledges that the studies at this point indicate no link between the two. However, the society also recognizes the ongoing concerns of parents and the need for further research into the causes of autism. This website focuses on the help that is available to parents and gives very specific information about how to access it.

Autism Education Trust
www.autismeducationtrust.org.uk

This is an enormously helpful website for those in the UK. It was established in 2007 with financial assistance from the Department for Children, Schools, and Families. It explains in detail and plain language how services for children with autism in the UK operate and are accessed. The AET is an incredible resource that provides information on both public and private support systems, and how parents can find the best help for their child and themselves.

The more conservative websites

These are the websites that demand autism treatments go through the scientific process of rigorous research before they are recommended to parents. Obviously, these sites will fall in line more with the medical establishment's philosophy. I feel more comfortable with these websites because it is important to be sure that, while helping our children, we do not harm them in the process. These websites advocate giving people with autism opportunities to reach their full potential, but do not believe in fundamentally changing who they are. That is how I see my girls, so I am comfortable with websites that are based on that premise.

Association for Science in Autism Treatment
www.asatonline.org

This website is dedicated to helping families by providing well-researched information on autism causes and treatments. The home page states eloquently:

> As you know, there are many websites about autism
> treatments and interventions. In many ways ASAT is

unique. We are not a business with a particular agenda. We are not trying to promote any particular treatment. We are not selling anything.

Our mission is to share accurate, scientifically sound information about autism and treatments for autism because we believe individuals with autism and their families deserve nothing less.

I decided not to summarize or paraphrase here because this expresses so well how I feel about autism treatments. I want to offer my children only what has been proven effective and safe through rigorous testing and multiple studies. The website includes the common questions about autism with lots of well-respected research to support their answers. The tone of the ASAT website is calm and hopeful, not at all the frenzied panic you find at some of the other websites. After the standard medical websites, I would tell a parent to turn here for advice and guidance.

Research Autism
www.researchautism.net/pages/welcome/home.ikml

This is a very impressive UK website devoted to "research into interventions in autism." Its mission is to improve the quality of life for people with autism. It provides loads of information about every possible treatment and intervention, and even rates them for efficacy and safety based on high-quality research studies. It is a terrific place to go to find all the facts and statistics about treatments before you begin them. They have done the work of evaluating studies and research for you. I highly recommend this website.

Autism Digest Magazine
www.autismdigest.com

This is an excellent online and print magazine which focuses on the daily living challenges of people with autism and their families, and also includes articles about research and treatment. The magazine includes contributors such as Temple Grandin, a famous adult with autism, and Tony Attwood, one of the leading experts on girls and autism. I put it in this conservative category because it takes a grounded, positive approach, and encourages proven treatments over experimental ones. And, most importantly, the magazine has tremendous respect and empathy for people with autism. It says in its vision statement: "We believe in the ability, rather than the disability of individuals with Autism Spectrum Disorders."

Autism Digest does include information on all sorts of treatment options, but cautions parents to beware of things that seem too good to be true, and to do their research before embarking on any course of treatment. Reading this magazine is comforting, uplifting, and incredibly informative about the day-to-day issues that are important to parents of kids on the spectrum.

Important note: don't confuse the *Autism Digest* with the *Autism Science Digest*, which is the biomedical magazine of AutismOne.

Autism Spectrum Quarterly
www.asquarterly.com

This is a great magazine, both online and in print, which discusses lots of practical issues faced by parents of kids on the spectrum, and offers great tips and strategies to manage those issues. It has also an amazing advisory board, including Simon Baron-Cohen (prominent Cambridge University autism researcher), Tony Attwood (expert on girls and autism), Carol Gray (Social Stories), and Temple Grandin (accomplished adult with autism). It is a first-rate magazine with tons of credible, helpful, and uplifting information.

Autism Science Foundation
www.autismsciencefoundation.org/aboutasf.html

This site is devoted to scientific research into the causes and treatments of autism. It is based on the premise that individuals with autism are best served by science when it can offer proof, not theory.

The Foundation's mission is "to support autism research by providing funding and other assistance to scientists and organizations conducting, facilitating, publicizing and disseminating autism research."

If you are looking for answers about why autism occurs, then this site is part of where that discussion is happening.

TempleGrandin.com
www.templegrandin.com

This is Temple Grandin's own website. As I have mentioned and you may already know, Temple Grandin is arguably the most famous person with autism in the world today. She is accomplished, brilliant, and spunky. Temple's website is full of informational and inspirational material. There are links to video clips of Temple, her speaking schedule, and her professional accomplishments. Temple also regularly answers questions posted by visitors, so you can send her a question through the website, and she may answer it on the site's home page. When I visit the site, I always find a new and enlightening way to look at autism through Temple's eyes. She is truly an ambassador to the wider world for people with autism. I find it kind of prophetic that her mother named her Temple because her website is exactly where I go when I need to feel hope.

Neurodiversity.com
www.neurodiversity.com/main.html

This is a website created by Kathleen Seidel, a woman who has a son with autism. She created this site as a way to honor the gifts of people whose brains work differently, thus the name. Neurodiversity provides a wealth of information and inspiring writing by people who see all the inherent good in our children. Ms. Seidel is a beautiful writer, and she advocates so passionately and eloquently for our children to be not just accepted but valued and embraced. I always find something new and worthwhile when I visit this website. As Ms. Seidel states: "Genetic research indicates that at least twenty different genes can signal a predisposition to autistic development; autism is pervasively embedded in the deep structure of humanity… Autism is as much a part of humanity as is the capacity to dream."

I rejoice at her belief that those with autism are, as Temple Grandin said, "Not less, but different."

The Vaccine Education Center of the Children's Hospital of Philadelphia
www.chop.edu/service/vaccine-education-center/home.html

I include this only because so many parents of children with autism are bombarded with vaccine stories and become so fearful of vaccinations. I am not telling you what to do with regard to your child's vaccinations; that is your decision. This website does explain a lot of the history of the controversy and cites the studies that have largely disproved the connection between autism and vaccines. It helped me understand the issue and put many of my fears to rest.

Biomedical/alternative websites

In general, the underlying belief of these sites is that autism is a physical injury caused in large part by vaccinations, and therefore the treatment needs to remedy the physical effects of that injury. Most of these sites regard autism as a disease, and some refer to children and adults with autism as "injured" and "damaged." Generally, these websites will recommend that you seek the help of a doctor affiliated with Defeat Autism Now (DAN), a group of alternative doctors who advocate biomedical treatments such as chelation and IVIG therapy. In the spirit of full disclosure, these are generally not websites that I turn to for information or inspiration.

Autism Research Institute (ARI)
www.autism.com

This is the original biomedical website for autism, and it has been the catalyst for many more radical offshoots in the biomedical realm. There is a lot of information on here if you choose this route. I personally find the information about vitamins helpful. However, the ARI does encourage parents to delay or decline vaccinations, and the basic premise of this website is that autism is an illness that needs biomedical treatment. Nevertheless, as far as biomedical websites go, the ARI is more cautious about the treatments it will endorse and encourages parents to seek the personal care of a physician. If you are interested in exploring biomedical treatments, this is the best place to begin your research.

By the way, DAN (Defeat Autism Now) is also the Autism Research Institute, and it will lead you back to the same place if you do an online search.

Treating Autism
www.treatingautism.co.uk

This UK site is exactly what its name states, which is refreshing as it seems so many of the US organizations are not so transparent about their purpose. Here you will find all of the biomedical interventions offered to parents. There are also testimonials from parents about what they believed worked with their children, but they are often more confusing than convincing, with many treatments tried simultaneously. However, you can certainly check it out for yourself.

National Autism Association
www.nationalautismassociation.org

Despite the all-encompassing name of this US organization, it does *not* represent all points of view about autism; it is a site devoted to biomedical approaches to autism. It does include some good general information about autism. However, a good deal of the website is devoted to recommending biomedical interventions, and Dr. Andrew Wakefield is on its Board of Scientific Advisors. Dr. Wakefield was the physician involved in the now discredited *Lancet* MMR/vaccine study. Offering a biomedical approach is fine, but continuing to support Dr. Wakefield seems an unwise decision for an organization that seeks to advocate for all people with autism and their families. Also, the National Autism Association advertises biomedical supplements for sale on its website; I am always skeptical of support organizations that promote and sell commercial products. Finally, the NAA provides a link to the National Vaccine Information Center, the foremost organization in the US devoted to questioning the safety of vaccines, which makes the National Autism Association's position on autism and vaccines fairly clear.

Global Autism Collaboration
www.autism.org

This is a sort of clearing house site started by Dr. Stephen M. Edelson, PhD, who is affiliated with the Autism Research Institute. It provides links to many other autism organizations that offer information and support. However, only organizations that are supportive of biomedical approaches to treating autism seem to be included.

Generation Rescue
www.generationrescue.org

This is the website with which celebrity Jenny McCarthy is affiliated. I find the attitude towards autism to be very negative on this site. The website suggests your child may "recover" if follow their protocol, and it puts forth theories about vaccines causing autism and the alternative treatments that can "rescue" your child from the "clutches" of autism. If you choose this route, Generation Rescue can put you in touch with a "Rescue Angel" in your area, who will initiate you in all things biomedical. You can also shop online there for the many supplements recommended, the books written by Ms. McCarthy, as well as her new line of non-toxic baby bedding, window treatments, and mobiles. There is a lot of stuff for sale at Generation Rescue.

AutismOne
www.autismone.org

This website is very similar to Generation Rescue. It advocates the same philosophy and sells many comparable products.

National Vaccine Information Center
www.nvic.org

Despite the fact that its name sounds like some government department, this is actually an independent organization that calls itself the watchdog group for vaccines. Their motto is "Your Health. Your Family. Your Choice." Most of the information on this website is devoted to questioning the safety of all vaccines. The National Vaccine Information Center does provide assistance for the families whose children are truly injured by vaccines, but its primary purpose seems to be opposing vaccines as a public health requirement. For me, this is hard to understand when vaccines have done so much good for humanity.

The Autism File
www.autismfile.com

This is an online magazine, also available in print form. It provides mostly biomedical information about autism, and Dr. Wakefield is one of its major contributors. I am not a subscriber.

Talk About Curing Autism
www.tacanow.org

This is another biomedical site. They offer for sale the same supplements and products as AutismOne and Generation Rescue, and they recommend chelation and other alternative treatments.

The "conspiracy" websites

I do not list these separately because I do not want to promote them, but I want to make you aware they are out there and to recommend that you proceed with caution. In doing research for this book, I realized there is a host of websites that believe some mighty strange things about the causes of autism—everything from ultrasounds to toxic rain to watching too much television to excessive hygiene. Then there are the conspiracy sites that offer dark plots, such as pharmaceutical cover-ups about medications that cause autism, physicians knowingly injecting children with poison through vaccines, and government plots to control the population through inducing autism. I have not found one of these conspiracy theories to be the least bit credible. Most upsetting to me is the unfounded mistrust and vilification of pediatricians who care for our children by recommending vaccines. I find pediatricians to be some of the most humble and empathic physicians out there. They work long hours, being screamed at by toddlers, puked on by babies, and trying to soothe parents, as they cajole the children into cooperating with examinations. I do not believe pediatricians would ever knowingly hurt children.

If you do visit these websites, be careful about commenting, and if you do, do not use your real name. Unfortunately, some of these conspiracy websites have even stooped to the level of personal attacks and character assassination of those who disagree with them, in attempts to further their cause. I have been shocked and upset by some of the things I have read, and some of the things people have written to me and about me, when I have voiced my opinion. I stopped visiting these websites when I realized there was no real discussion, just angry people raging against a mythical machine.

Keep moving
Don't get caught in the web of anger

> *"The last of the human freedoms is to choose one's attitudes."*
>
> —*Victor Frankl*

One of the most important pieces of advice I can give you is not to spend too much time online searching for answers. I spent a ton of time online to research this book, and it was overwhelming and confusing. It is easy to get lost and have hours evaporate as you read one person's argument and theory, and then an opposing one, and then another, like a never-ending tennis game where no one wins. And there is plenty of anger and blaming and dwelling on the unknowable and unchangeable out there. It can change who you are and how you see your children. I know there are hard times, but when people only focus on the hard times, I think it becomes a self-fulfilling prophecy. Instead of seeing potential, they see only limitations. If you spend your time online with people who focus on the negative, who call their children soulless and damaged, who harp continually about how hard it is, your world will darken. Lost in that maelstrom of negativity, how can you or your daughter overcome anything? Angry people seem to feed off of each other, and pretty soon your commiserating turns into co-misery.

Remember the web is a public forum
Furthermore, when people speak publicly about our children in online forums, they are shaping not just the way *we* see autism, but

the way the *world* sees autism. When parents depict raising children with autism as a heartbreak or nightmare, they are disparaging every person with autism in the process. How can we expect the world to see our children as whole people if we ourselves see them only as a shadow of what we wanted them to be? That's why I become so upset when parents refer to their children as "injured" and "damaged." How will the world care about programs and therapies for children whose parents describe them as damaged? Why would the world want to invest money and time when parents make their own children sound so empty and hopeless? I believe my job as a parent is to love, accept, and celebrate my daughters, so that I might show the world how to do the same.

Be wary of the web and its promises

As parents of children with autism, we need to exercise caution and skepticism when entering the crazy web. Be especially wary of websites that claim to "cure" autism. The sad reality is that people are making an awful lot of money off our children's autism. I know how heartbreaking it can be to have your child struggle with the ordinary skills that other kids master effortlessly. As parents, we would do anything to help our children. But that very devotion and desperation to help our children can be dangerous if we put our faith in the wrong people. And with most of these "cures," there is no proof and no rigorous studies, just moving anecdotes which tug at your heart strings, play on your hope, weigh heavily on your conscience, and drain your bank account.

Trust people you know

Limit your time online to a few websites that stick to the proven facts and offer you hope, humor, and comfort. Spend time with people online and in life who encourage you and give you hope. If you stay positive, you will make it, and so will your daughter. I know it sounds like a cliché, but there is a choice in how you deal with autism, just as with everything else. Our perspective is a large part of what creates our children's realities. Rather than trusting a physician online, find a good physician in your area and a local positive parent group, and put your faith in good people you know, rather than anonymous personalities pontificating in cyberspace. Your daughter's physicians, therapists, and teachers are your best resource for treatments, information, and support. The best people to help your daughter are those who know her and you personally. I hope you will continue to see all the ability in your child, and let faith and optimism guide your mouse and your mind. Because your daughter is already perfect, no matter what those websites say.

The heart of the matter about the web

1. Be sure to educate yourself about autism in general before you embark on researching specific treatments for your daughter. Visit the established medical websites first.

2. There is a tremendous schism in the autism community with regard to the theorized link between vaccines and autism. Many websites are based on a belief that vaccines cause autism, a belief for which there is no scientific proof to date. Be sure you know the position of the website and your own opinion before you take their advice.

3. Be very skeptical of websites full of advertisements selling supplements and treatments. Sadly, there are a lot of people out there making money by exploiting the desperation of parents of children with autism. Many promise the moon and just leave you broke. Always consult with your daughter's pediatrician before buying or beginning any treatment.

4. Beware the crazy people out there. Some people thrive on anger, conspiracy theories, and blame. Avoid them; they offer neither hope nor help.

5. The internet is a great place for information, but nothing can replace real people you know and trust. So when it comes to making big decisions about your daughter's treatment, stick with those who love her and have an investment in her well-being: your family, your friends, and your daughter's physicians.

Chapter 9

Milestones

"Patience and fortitude conquer all things."

—*Ralph Waldo Emerson*

Oh, the baby books and the toddler books, telling you when your little girl should accomplish important things! They were the bane of my existence when my girls were toddlers. The baby years weren't so bad, but by toddlerhood we never did anything on time! Even before I knew they were on the autism spectrum, milestones came late. Neither of my girls walked until almost 14 months; talking came later than usual; toilet training, not until four and five! My best advice is to stop looking at those books. Trust me; your daughter will accomplish many milestones in her life, just not on your timetable, and certainly not on the timetable of those pesky, chiding books! So graciously bow out of the neighborhood "When did your child potty-train?" race, and be glad to be done with all those petty competitions in which so many other moms seem to revel.

Once I finally embraced our new normal, I actually found it kind of liberating. No longer did I hang out with the other moms on the street, chatting about how brilliant their kids were as they flew by on bikes, while mine were still riding Big Wheels around in their own orbits. Instead, I found other moms like myself and we supported each other. The most important thing to remember is that your daughter will continue to improve and grow. My girls are so much easier now, so much more civilized and rational than they were as toddlers and young children. Every year it gets better. Learning is a lifelong process for everyone. So take heart: your daughter will mature and master many things, just not necessarily when you thought she would, or when those annoying books decreed it to be so.

Milestone number one: Sleep
The elusive dream

It doesn't seem fair that our kids can require so much extra effort during the day and then not sleep at night, but, alas, that is the way many of them are. I have always cherished my sleep; my mom says I slept through the night the first night home from the hospital. So the sleep deprivation of motherhood hit me hard, and I wasn't prepared for it to be never-ending. My girls, especially Lizzie, had erratic sleep patterns from birth. As an infant, Lizzie never slept for more than an hour or two at a time, and that was usually during the day! I spent many days and nights just walking around the house, singing to her. I was so tired sometimes that the only songs I could think to sing were old TV theme songs. It exhausts me now to remember wandering around sleepily in my pajamas, singing "The Facts of Life" and the theme from *Family Ties*. And forget about letting her cry it out. Even if I had the stomach for that, and you can probably tell I don't, Lizzie was so high-strung that she could have screamed for days.

Once Caroline came along, sleep was even more elusive. She slept great as a baby, but once the toddler years set in, she was reluctant to call it a day. For many years, I spent the night wandering like a zombie back and forth between cribs and gliders and toddler beds, trying to get people to fall asleep. It was as if I was enduring some cruel and endless fraternity initiation! After a long series of trial and error, I found a few key components to getting my whirling dervishes to go to sleep. Now they both sleep all night, and I couldn't be happier. Uninterrupted sleep is like manna from the heavens. So take heart: these things will happen, sometimes just much more slowly than seems merciful. As a formerly weary night-time wanderer, I have a few suggestions.

Sleepytime suggestions

First of all, a lot of the inability to settle down comes from their overstimulated nervous systems. So I found doing some deep pressure on my kids would help. Squishing between beanbag chairs before bed time, rubbing their feet, and generally soothing their circuitry through sensory pressure helps a ton. I know you are tired at the end of the day, but a little extra effort before bedtime may just pay off in some uninterrupted sleep.

Second, our kids tend to have super-sensitive awareness to sounds and other sensory stimuli. I swear by white noise. Neither of my girls would sleep if there is the hint of a breeze blowing a leaf. I remember years ago insanely begging neighbors having a Memorial Day barbecue to whisper so Lizzie would sleep as a baby. This was at seven o'clock at night! How much of a loon did they think I was? Eventually, I invested in one of those little sound machines, which made just enough of a steady rain sound to drown out other noises. Now I have fans in both of my girls' rooms. It helps enormously, as long as it isn't too loud. Just the steady, repetitive whirr of those noises seems to calm them down. I just pray that the power never goes out, or Caroline pops up like a jack-in-the-box!

Third, some kids need weighted blankets to make them feel secure and settled. Caroline needs heavy blankets lying on top of her even when it is warm, so I keep her room cool enough to allow her to swaddle herself in blankets. And I usually tuck her blankets in all around her, so she feels cocooned. I never thought about it before, but maybe that's why she emerges like a butterfly every morning, flittering around the house!

Fourth, the room must be reasonably dark. I invested in room-darkening shades, pretty pink on the inside for the room, but heavy metallic on the outside to keep the 5 a.m. light out. Keeping the room dark accomplishes two important things. It makes the room seem sleepy and peaceful when you want them to go to bed, and it keeps them in bed longer because they don't wake up with the farmers at dawn. Ironically, if you make the room dark enough at bedtime, you may have to employ a nightlight, but that is okay. Nightlights are gentle and reassuring, and they make such cool ones now. A friend of mine bought a large, high-tech one for her daughter that looks like fish swimming, complete with the sounds of the ocean—very soothing and sleepy.

Fifth, you need a good, regular bedtime routine. When my girls were younger, we had a chart. They liked looking at the chart and knowing what came next. This gave them time to adjust to the fact that daytime was over and it was time for sleep. First the PJs, then cups of tea or water, then the teeth brushing, then foot rubs, then prayers, tucking in, and lights off. Make sure you don't make the bed-time routine too complicated, because once you establish the routine, it will not be easy to change it.

Sixth, encourage a lovey—a toy, preferably a stuffed animal or soft doll that can provide your daughter with comfort and companionship during the night. I know some children with autism don't choose comfort objects as readily as other children, but with encouragement your daughter will find one. I know I am probably starting to sound as if I have multiple personality disorder, but make the lovey talk to your daughter and offer reassurance about sleeping and night-time. I always found that Piglet from *Winnie the Pooh* and BJ from *Barney* had better luck convincing my kids to go to sleep than I did.

Last of all, your daughter's room has to be neat and orderly to sleep. Kids with autism need the calm and control of a neat room, without too much clutter to distract and lure them away from sleeping. My girls always had certain toys they held while they slept, but their rooms were always tidied up and clean at night. That meant that the day and playing were over, and it was time to sleep. Don't clean right before bedtime because you are just reminding them of their many toys and interests. Do it after dinner and before bath, so the room looks like bedtime when they enter it.

If your daughter is still struggling, ask your daughter's pediatrician to try melatonin. It is a natural way to induce a gentle sleep. I also found a great magnesium supplement that helps relax my girls before sleep. It's a powder you can mix in with juice. Magnesium has a naturally calming effect on the body. Again, consult with your daughter's pediatrician on its use. And there is always the time-trusted soothing cup of chamomile tea, which really does work. My girls will only drink the one called *Sleepytime* because there is a bear on the box wearing a nightcap. Hey, whatever it takes. As a last resort you can talk to your daughter's pediatrician about consulting a sleep specialist or taking prescription medication. Make the physician understand how tired you are, because in this parenting job, getting sleep isn't a luxury; it's a necessity.

Milestone number two: Using the bathroom
The potty predicament: To tinkle or not to tinkle

Getting your daughter to use the bathroom will probably be one of your greatest challenges and happiest accomplishments. I remember hating that old adage, "No child goes to kindergarten in diapers," because my Caroline did. Most kids on the spectrum will master this skill later, but they will master it. I like the way Dr. Brazelton, the famous pediatrician, calls it "toilet learning," rather than toilet training, because I think that points out an important distinction: it is a skill your daughter is mastering for herself, more than something you are training her to do (Brazelton and Sparrow 2006, p.193). If you think of it as something good for her, you will have more resolve in helping her accomplish it. The strategies that work with most other children will work here with one important addition: the patience and faith of Job.

The potty proficiency plan

First of all, make sure your daughter is ready. Can she control her bodily functions and does she know when she is going? When kids are aware that they are going, most will retreat to somewhere semi-private, such as their bedroom or behind a chair when they are going number two. If your daughter is ready, like all things with autism, you must be organized and systematic in your approach.

I heartily recommend a potty chart. I know a chart for everything! Buy one in an office supplies store. Our kids generally respond better to visual cues, so put a picture of a potty on the bathroom door, and use the chart to show the steps of the process. For consistency, you can use PECS (Picture Exchange Communication System) visuals if your daughter is using them in school. You should also have the days of the week and stickers, and reward her just for time spent sitting on the potty. Have your daughter help make the chart if she wants to. This is her learning process after all. Lizzie put Winnie the Pooh stickers all over hers, and for Caroline it was scented Strawberry Shortcake, which I found both amusing and helpful as it was in the bathroom.

Make the bathroom a safe and comfortable place. Our kids are put off by certain sensory things, so think it through before you start. Caroline hated the noise of the fan in the bathroom for a long time, so to reassure her that I wouldn't turn it on, I put a piece of electrical tape over that switch. Only then would she enter the bathroom. She would also freak, and still does, if a light bulb is out. I keep a stock of them now. If there is any toy that can hang out in the bathroom for a while, put it there. If it is a doll or stuffed animal, make it talk about how great the bathroom is. However, don't put too many toys in there, or it will become just another playroom. And you do *not* want poop and play in the same category!

You can start by just having your daughter go in the bathroom when she is peeing or pooping, even if she is still going in the diaper or pull-up. Then transfer the contents of the diaper into the toilet, showing her and telling her simply that this is where pee and poop goes. Try to do this cheerily, as if it is a lovely thing. Tell her that Mommy's and Daddy's goes too, and if there is a big brother or sister, they can also be mentioned. Don't linger; just stay long enough to get the job done.

If the regular toilet is not to your daughter's liking, then you may use a smaller potty, but keep it in the bathroom. However, I would avoid the smaller potty if possible and encourage you to start her with a soft seat on the regular toilet. Otherwise, you are adding one more transition to the process when she eventually has to switch to the regular toilet, and we all know how hard transitions are. Because most of our kids are older when they start, they tend not to fit really well on those little personal potties anyway. If your daughter will not sit on the seat with her pants down, let her start by sitting on it with her clothes on, just to get the feel. Reassure her with songs and smiles.

You have to keep visiting the potty at regular intervals and trying. Now, don't expect the old "Great Aunt Edna came and trained all the kids one weekend" story to work here. This transition takes a lot longer than that usually. Our kids are creatures of habit like no other. And diapers are one tradition that has been with them since birth. It will take time for their minds to make this adjustment. So just keep visiting the potty. Be positive and lighthearted, but determined.

Bribery works!

I used lots of rewards with my girls for using the potty. I am not talking about smiles and Smarties here. It got expensive, but, in the long run, it was a lot cheaper than diapers. Our girls love praise and positive reinforcement. Like an amusement park game, the little prizes were for just going in and sitting down, and the big ones were for actually going pee or poop in the toilet. I strung the prizes from the shower rod, so they could gaze up at them while they were trying to go. For the record, bribery does work.

It is also a good idea to offer lots of fluids during this process. Even ice cream, freeze pops, and popsicles will eventually turn to water, so let them have all the frozen treats they want. And during the intensive training, you have to stay home a bit more than usual. Getting your daughter to go in your bathroom is one thing; a public restroom is a whole different ballgame.

Once the peeing in the potty is mastered, you are on to the big guns—poop. Both of my girls were far more willing to pee in the potty than poop, although Caroline was pretty adamant about not wanting to do either. If you find your daughter is holding her poop and becoming constipated, ask your daughter's pediatrician about a senna laxative. Senna is a natural vegetable laxative that works gently, but effectively. There are brands that offer kid-friendly flavors, such as Fletcher's Laxative for Kids, Original Root Beer Taste. Senna was the saving grace with both of my girls because it made them unable to resist the urge when nature called.

There is a great video for kids, made by Duke University, called *It's Potty Time*. When I say great, I mean your daughter will like it, but it will probably drive you crazy. Still, it has catchy tunes (I think I can still sing "I use my potty when I have to pee") and my girls both really liked it. We watched it over and over again. It makes it all seem normal and not scary to use the bathroom. You can look for it at the Duke website or on ebay.

Lizzie also really liked her potty doll. This doll would sit in the bathroom with her on a little plastic pink potty, and sometimes the doll would tinkle sympathetically. It was just another way to make the bathroom a friendly place.

Will there be accidents? Yes. You have to just show them what to do when there is an accident. Don't freak out and make it a big deal; just clean it up and move on. If, however, your daughter smears her poop, that is another matter. My girls never did this, and certainly not all kids with autism do, but some do. It is most likely a sensory craving, which you can satisfy with something else such as

Play-Doh. Or it could be a play for attention or a reaction to stress or pressure. Either way, you need to have a candid talk with your daughter's pediatrician. Don't be embarrassed to bring it up; there are typical kids who go through a stage of doing this too. Your daughter's pediatrician will have heard this before and may have some excellent suggestions for you. You want to squash this habit (no pun intended) as soon as possible before it becomes some kind of ritual.

A word about night-time dryness: don't worry about it yet. Caroline finally learned to use the potty at five and was in pull-ups at night until she was nine because she was such a sound sleeper. That is not a matter of will, but just maturity. It will come in time. When you see that your daughter is dry the majority of the time in the morning, you can begin to tackle that by making sure she empties her bladder right before bed and immediately upon waking. Once she masters it in the day-time, the night-time will follow in due course.

Once your daughter is capable of controlling bodily functions, you must be determined to help your daughter learn to use the bathroom in order to meet with success. Be pleasant and calm, firm and patient. And when she does succeed, really celebrate her achievement.

Lizzie's passive potty resistance

Just so you know that it didn't go smoothly for me, I will share how the whole potty episodes went down in my house. As with most kids on the spectrum, my girls were "traditionalists," not keen on change. The tradition I speak of was, of course, the diaper. Their basic attitude seemed to be "This is working for me, so I am not changing; you just keep changing diapers, Mommy!" Lizzie took a more philosophical approach to her defiance. She would look over my head when I mentioned the potty, and say, "Not for me." People kept telling me she had to be ready. I would give up on the potty for a time and then try again. Finally, when she was around four, and I knew she was physically ready but would never be eager to make the transition, I decided to make it a goal for both of us. Lizzie and I made a potty chart; I put little gifts in bags and hung them up on the shower bar in the bathroom—kind of like a potty grab-bag. We visited the bathroom at regular intervals and read the same book, *The Little Kitten*, over and over, while she silently contemplated tinkling.

Some days I thought I would scream, but I kept my sunny smile and stayed determined. I could've strangled those "helpful" friends who told me their kids would use the bathroom for a mere M&M. For many weeks, I was reading, plying her with freeze-pops, bribing her with gifts, and decorating a chart with a picture of a big purple toilet on it. Just when I thought I couldn't take it anymore, after several *months* of quality time spent bonding in the bathroom, she allowed herself to pee. I could tell it was a really strange transition for her; she stared at me skeptically as she went. I tried not to get too excited because I was afraid she would her change her mind. I could almost see the methodical processing in her head, gears shifting stiffly as she evaluated the new routine. She held out on the poop for a couple more months, until senna and apple juice changed her mind. Slowly, over time, using the bathroom became the new normal. Hallelujah! She still doesn't like public restrooms, but she will very cautiously use them, but, then again, I am the same way.

Caroline versus the potty

Caroline was my real challenge. Whereas Lizzie was more of a quiet conscientious objector to the bathroom, Caroline was adamantly opposed to the idea. She would freak out if I even put her near the potty. It took months of coaxing and gifts to even get her to sit on the potty, but she still had no intention of using it. To her it was simply a chair of faulty design. She would sit down carefully on the edge, avoid the "hole" as she called it, and look at catalogues. Sometimes I thought maybe she needed privacy as she perused Sears appliances, so I would sneak away to empty the dishwasher. However, more than once, when left on her own, Caroline would amuse herself by making "snow," otherwise known as shredding toilet paper. Talk about speed; the child could shred an entire role in minutes. Several times upon my return, I found Caroline and the bathroom covered in a Scott tissue blizzard.

Everyone says not to worry, that no child goes to kindergarten in diapers; well, Caroline did—a Disney Princess pull-up. The amazing thing was she wouldn't actually pee in the pull-up at school. She would hold it all day long, from 8.30 a.m. when the bus picked her up, until 3.30 p.m. when it dropped her off. Then, as soon as she arrived at home, she would run to her room and pee voluminous amounts in the pull-up. The teachers would take her to the bathroom regularly at school. At first she wouldn't go near the toilet at school, but eventually she agreed to sit on the toilet briefly and then dashed away. One morning she woke up dry. She had last peed in her pull-up at about 8 o'clock the night before. I am not sure why, but she never peed in the pull-up before school that morning. I called school and told them to try the bathroom right away. Well, that stubborn little missy did not use the bathroom or the pull-up all day! Can you even imagine the iron will? I am sure, actually, that you can. Our kids are nothing if not willful about what they want.

As soon as she arrived home, I immediately took off the pull-up and led her to the toilet. At that point, she had been holding her urine for about 19 hours! She held it in, sitting on the toilet, for another hour! We had done months of trying, had done the gifts, the chart, the freeze-pops, the songs, the rewards. I didn't know what else to do. I was begging her to just let it go, and she started to whimper. I was about to give in and give her a pull-up when all of a sudden she let it go. Oh, what a glorious sound it was! She looked surprised—and mightily relieved. It was as if whatever wordless fear she had about using the bathroom suddenly just disappeared. A switch flipped in her, and after that she used the bathroom regularly. Caroline was almost six years old at that point, halfway through kindergarten. She still wore a pull-up at night until she was about nine years old for the occasional accident because she is such a deep sleeper, but now she doesn't even need that. She is completely self-sufficient in the bathroom. Sometimes small miracles are the most amazing and rewarding.

Milestone number three: Eating healthily

Food, glorious food: Basic nutrients

People may not typically think of eating as a milestone, but, with our girls, making sure they are eating nutritiously and incorporating variety into their diets can definitely be a challenge. First, there is the whole issue of food allergies, which is a topic for discussion with your daughter's pediatrician. Once you figure a way through that potential maze, there may still be an issue with your daughter's preference to eat only certain foods. Neither of my girls was ever easy to feed. Even as infants, they showed preferences for and aversions to certain textures and tastes. I spent many days trying to entice them into trying new foods when they were young, only to have them stonewall me completely. Toddlers as a rule are not adventurous eaters, and our kids mature more slowly, so those years of selective eating last much longer.

The first step in handling a finicky eater is to think in terms of essential nutrients—protein, carbohydrates, fiber, calcium, and so on—and work from there. When my girls were younger, I would figure out their daily diets that way. As long as I had those bases covered, I felt that my kids would be okay. If you are concerned that your daughter's fussy eating habits are not providing adequate nutrition, talk to her pediatrician. You can also visit the website for the Mayo Clinic which provides a great overview of nutritional needs of children by ages: www.mayoclinic.com/health/nutrition-for-kids/NU00606.

At the Mayo site, you can figure out the appropriate intake of calories and nutrients, and work from those basic necessities. You can also take reassurance from the fact that *Pediatrics*, the journal of the American Academy of Pediatricians, published a study in April of 2010, which found that despite irregular eating patterns, children on the autism spectrum showed "no differences in weight, height or BMI at 18 months and 7 years, or in hemoglobin concentrations at 7 years" (Emond *et al.* 2010, p.337). I find this fact encouraging because for years I worried that my girls were not getting enough of one or another vitamin or nutrient.

Obviously, it is also a good idea to give your daughter a multivitamin daily, which is easily accomplished now with the vast array of vitamins available—chewables and gummies that come in every shape and flavor from Disney Princesses to Buzz Lightyear. If your daughter doesn't like milk or cheese, or is allergic to those foods, you can also give her a chewable calcium supplement, with your physician's guidance. However, it is always better for your daughter to consume vitamins and nutrients in food when possible. And remember that vitamins cannot provide protein or calories, so although they may supplement a diet, they cannot replace a child's basic need for calories and fluids. Some kids with autism even resist drinking. One of the most important things to make sure of is that your daughter is getting enough fluids during the day, so you can offer freeze-pops and popsicles to keep her hydrated. Another option is the protein-packed milkshake drinks that are available which can offer vitamins, calories, and protein.

Trying a new food...otherwise known as anything but chicken tenders and French fries

When introducing a new food, it is better to tread lightly and gently. You can let your daughter touch the food, smell the food, and just taste it, but not consume it. You can put it on a separate plate if she doesn't want it touching a favorite food. Think about the textures of the foods your daughter does like, and try to find nutritious foods with similar textures. If pretzels are a favorite, maybe raw carrots would work. If hotdogs are the food du jour, maybe turkey sausage would make the grade. I also find with my girls that temperature makes all the difference. Caroline hates her food cold. She will even heat up a turkey sandwich to room temperature. Both of my girls reheat their dinners in the microwave mid-meal, sometimes multiple times in one sitting. Is it a stall tactic? Maybe. But usually they will finish their dinners if they are not cold.

One strategy that may help to encourage trying a new food is positive peer pressure. If your daughter has siblings or cousins or friends who are willing to eat more adventurously, they may be able to cajole your daughter into trying a new food. I find my girls are always much more willing to do something when their older cousins promote the idea than when I do. Holidays and family celebrations are always good opportunities to let someone see if they can convince your daughter to expand her palate. Make it lighthearted, so it seems fun to try a new taste or texture of food.

Keep in mind that it is never a good idea to force a food down, even with a reward, if your daughter doesn't like the look, smell, texture, or taste. My girls both had reflux as babies, and have retained the talent for regurgitating food they find distasteful. Many kids on the spectrum have sensitive gag reflexes, and if you push, it will backfire, sometimes all over the table. There is no sight more unappetizing than your child heaving like a cat with a hairball at the kitchen table. Your own dinner can certainly be a food they resist trying, and you can let them know how enjoyable it is, but don't try to make them eat it or like it. Sometimes it just takes maturity and consistent encouragement for a child to change her eating habits. So be patient, but continue to offer your daughter new food options. In time, she may surprise you by actually liking something different.

Sharing more than just food

I know many of us had visions of wonderful family dinners where everyone shared stories of their day and relished a fine, healthy dinner. Instead, dinner can turn into a stomach-churning battle over food. Try your best to remember that what you eat isn't necessarily as important as spending time together at the table, learning how to enjoy a meal, even if it only lasts for ten minutes. If your daughter starts to look forward to dinner as a nice time with her family, she may become more relaxed and eat better. We all know relaxation is important to digestion, and positive feelings about eating play a great part in developing a healthy relationship with food. In order to change our dinner dynamics, I learned I had to focus more on family time and less on what everyone ate or didn't eat. Over time, by shifting my focus, our family's dinner table has become a much more pleasant place. A surprising byproduct has been that both my girls usually finish their dinners now and have been more open to trying new foods. So try to enjoy sitting down with your children at night to share a meal. You may just find the relaxed atmosphere gives everyone a healthier appetite.

Manners count too

No matter what you and your daughter are eating, make teaching manners a part of every meal. I have met far too many kids with any number of developmental challenges whose parents must have decided that manners were low on the priority list when facing other challenges. I can understand that to some extent, but they are really doing a disservice to their children. Etiquette is actually something our girls can understand because it follows regular rules and patterns, and learning good manners helps them enormously when they are trying to be a part of the wider world. Temple Grandin devotes an entire chapter in her book *The Way I See It* to distinguishing between bad behaviors and the challenges of autism. It is interesting to read her perspective about how children on the spectrum have an even greater need to learn the rituals of common courtesy, and how very capable they are of learning those. So, don't forget, amid all the worry about what your daughter eats, that sharing a meal is also a wonderful opportunity to teach social skills and manners.

Nourishment or medicine

Finally, I know a huge part of the autism community is interested in dietary interventions. As I said earlier, that is not something I have tried in earnest with my girls, so I cannot speak from personal experience. I do know parents whose children have food allergies, so obviously that affects what foods they can safely offer their children. And I know other parents have tried various diets to try to lessen some of the behaviors of autism. For what it's worth, absent a physical ailment, I would encourage you to look at eating as a healthy and pleasurable thing for your daughter. I would not restrict mainstream, healthy food in an effort to change behavior unless you can really see it working in some tremendous way, which I have not seen in the families I know well who have tried restrictive diets. Our children are different in so many ways, and there are already so many limitations on their lives that it just seems a shame to me to make their diet another odd ritual. I know parents who view food as a kind of medicine for their child and strip it of all enjoyable qualities. Their kids can never have sugar or salt or chocolate or ice cream. As with all things, use common sense. If a food is causing your daughter digestive difficulty, remove it from the menu. But permit her to exercise some freedom of choice, and allow her to really enjoy some of life's simple pleasures, like pepperoni pizza or a soft ice-cream cone on a hot summer day.

Eating should be a healthy pleasure

The bottom line with food is that it should be both pleasurable and nutritious for your daughter. Establishing a healthy relationship with food is something that all parents should work on with their children. So try not to obsess about what your daughter is or is not eating. Never make food or eating a battle of wills or a punishment, or your daughter will use it as a way to exert some control. I found with my girls that, with time, maturity, and gentle but consistent encouragement, they have been willing to expand their diets. Dinner time in our house is now pretty pleasant. And rather than dread it as a battle, my girls look forward to it as a shared time to talk and laugh, which has made it a favorite time of the day for all of us.

Milestone number four: Dressing appropriately

Avoiding fashion nightmares

Dressing appropriately is also a kind of milestone for many of our girls because their sensory issues and desire for routine can make clothes a tricky issue. When Lizzie was a baby, I had to cut the tags out of all of her clothing because they bugged her so much. I know kids who can't stand jeans or turtlenecks, or who will only wear certain fabrics. Then there are the nudists. At the nursery school where I worked, one little boy would come back from the bathroom naked every time. Something about the feeling of clothes in general just bothered him. This is not an unusual sensory problem for kids on the spectrum. However, it is unacceptable to walk around naked most places. And, obviously, as kids get older it becomes less and less acceptable to walk around in your birthday suit. So you have to find a way to make the clothes stay on. Then there are the kids who will only wear the same thing day after day. So you scramble to find multiples of that item so it will always be readily available, or wash it daily so it will at least be clean. Here are some approaches to these quandaries.

Clothing is not optional

First of all, with regard to your little streaker, I think the answer is to be gentle but firm. Caroline loved to be "au naturel" from the time she was a baby. At any given moment as a toddler, she would strip off all her clothes and roll in blankets, or run around the house. In fact, Lizzie called it "naked time," and when she was little, she would sometimes join her sister, laughing all the way, shouting, "It's naked time!" Of course, this drove me crazy. As Caroline grew older, she would readily dress to leave the house, but as soon as we arrived home it was "naked time" again. No matter how much I pleaded and lectured, and redressed her, she would be naked again as soon as I turned my back. I understood the whole sensory thing with clothing and fabrics, but the fact is we live in a society that expects us to be fully dressed (although I think some of my high school students might have missed that memo as well). And for girls, it seems even more essential to instill a sense of modesty.

I decided to take an ABA approach with Caroline, just hand over hand: "This is how we stay dressed." She was really stubborn on this, but I became more stubborn. If she undressed, I helped her get dressed again. For a while, she would only wear a long shirt and underwear at home, but that was better than being naked. And though it was easier for her to take off, it was also easier for me to make her put it back on. A couple of times, she lost computer time or watching *Rugrats* for taking off her clothes. However, when she realized I was not backing down, she gave in, and eventually she realized she had to stay dressed. This is one problem you have to resolve early on before it becomes a way of life and your daughter is streaking around the house at 16, or making an appearance at the family barbecue wearing nothing but a baseball cap. That actually happened at my friend's house with her 14-year-old son with autism. If reinforcement doesn't work, there is always taking away a privilege. Even if your daughter isn't verbal, a PECS chart can reinforce the need for clothing and the consequences of not staying dressed.

New day, same outfit

Clothing choices are another issue. Our daughters tend to find certain items that are comfortable and stay with them. Again, this is an issue best addressed in the early years. Sticking with soft cotton and minimal decorations will yield the best results. Even if you just buy multiple colors of the same shirt or dress, you are making some headway towards variety and flexibility. Let your daughter exercise some choice and self-expression by giving her options, but just make sure she is trying different styles and colors of clothing. It is important not to let your daughter get too stuck in a clothing ritual because when she is older, you want her to dress in a way that helps her fit in with her peers. And what is cute at five might not be so cute at 15.

One of my students this year had been allowed for too long to stick to one clothing item, and, by high school, it was a big problem. He has autism, is pretty verbal, and is very bright. Unfortunately, he is also very stubborn and set in his ways. Ever since he was very young, he has insisted on wearing a bright canary yellow shirt. He absolutely refuses to wear any other color. And he is quite a big boy. Can you imagine how odd he looks day after day in a blazing yellow shirt? It really makes him stand out, and not in a good way. And the shirt is just the tip of the iceberg in his sea of stubbornness. I can't help but think that a change could have been effected when he was younger. But now it is so much a part of his security and identity that it would be nearly impossible. And unless he can find a place of employment where bright yellow shirts are the uniform, he will not work. This is so unfortunate because he is smart enough and has some very employable skills that could help him land a job. So when you are thinking that it's not a big deal to let your daughter wear the same thing every day, you might want to think about helping her change that now while she is younger. Believe me, I know it's hard, but in the end your daughter will be much better off if she is known for her smile and charm, and not the repetition of her wardrobe.

Caroline and the pink jumper: A cautionary tale

It's funny how a seemingly innocuous moment can be the start of an unyielding ritual. When Caroline was a little girl, she loved to walk around the mall and look in all the store windows. During one trip, just before Christmas the year she was six, she tugged my hand and led me into the Disney store. It was one of her favorite spots, and she usually begged for some toy, so I reluctantly entered under Mickey's smiling face. This trip she picked out a pink, corduroy *Aristocats* jumper. As she had never really shown an interest in clothes before, having spent much of her childhood resisting them, I bought it immediately. I was thrilled that she wanted an item of clothing. Be careful what you wish for. Every day for the next several months she insisted on wearing that jumper with Marie from the *Aristocats* on it to school. I washed it every night, so she could wear it to school the next day. And I had the opposite problem when she came home, tugging it off her squirmy little body. The bright spot was that Caroline was starting to see the appeal of clothing; the down side was it was only this one item.

By February of that year, I was so sick of that jumper, and it was becoming threadbare. I had let it go on for too long, and Caroline was actually becoming known by that jumper. So I enlisted the help of her speech teacher. We made a chart for both home and school, and the pink jumper was only to be worn three days a week, then we went to two, then to one, and so on. It was hard at first; Caroline cried a lot as I sent her off to school in other clothes. But I knew the speech teacher would be there at school to reinforce that she was proud Caroline was sticking to the chart. In time, she adjusted, and slowly she began to adjust to her expanding wardrobe. As a reward, I took Caroline shopping at Target and indulged her in ridiculous feather boas, tiaras, tutus, and all things pink, girly, and glamorous. Allowing Caroline to have a choice about her new clothing seemed to help her accept that the jumper was on its way out. For a while, she looked like some pageant child gone wrong. But, as time progressed, and her inner fashionista emerged, she began to have her own little style. We never phased the jumper out altogether, but eventually it lost its appeal. And when she hadn't mentioned it for some time, I clandestinely tossed it in the trash. For the next few years, she would only wear dresses with tights and Mary Jane shoes, but eventually she gave in to jeans and sweatshirts too.

I am proud to say that Caroline dresses quite appropriately for all occasions now. It took time and determination, but Caroline has acquired a sense of style. Maturity helps with these issues, and sometimes it only gets better when you decide you can't take it anymore and get tough. Other times, you just have to charge up your credit card and get some feather boas and tiaras!

Milestone number five: Mastering meltdowns
She's come undone

One of the biggest challenges to parents of children on the spectrum is meltdowns. It is even more difficult when it is your little girl who falls apart and acts like a feral cat. Somehow boys are allowed to become frustrated and then act out in a physical way. Even though meltdowns in boys are unpleasant, they don't seem to elicit the same reaction as a sweetly dressed little girl turning red, screeching, pulling her hair, and kicking you with her shiny patent leather shoes. People seem to react more judgmentally to a girl being out of control. That is not fair. However, because no one benefits from a child who has frequent meltdowns, it is crucial to find a way to handle these volcanoes early on in your daughter's life.

Caroline's worst meltdown

I can remember clearly Caroline's worst meltdown. Caroline was four and Lizzie was six. Lizzie had been invited to a birthday party at a local bowling alley. For the first time, she was actually willing to attend without me and get a ride home with another mom, who was a close friend of mine. This was huge progress for her. I had Caroline with me when I dropped Lizzie off. As Caroline and I started to leave, I was feeling really good about Lizzie's surprising spurt of independence. Then Caroline began to cry. She wanted to stay and bowl. I knew we couldn't stay without undermining Lizzie's progress. So I very firmly led her to the car and put her in her car seat. As we drove home, her crying started to escalate. Pretty soon, she was full blast. Caroline's crying used to start like a whine and slowly build to a five-alarm siren. Halfway home, Caroline wriggled out of her car seat and climbed up into the front passenger seat. She then attempted to turn the steering wheel around as we were whizzing down the interstate. The power in a four-year-old having a meltdown is staggering. She was beyond reason and full of will. Eventually, when we were nearly home, I pulled over and held her until she had cried it out. When we arrived home, she passed out on her bed. I was shaking for a long time after that.

Here's what I did wrong. First of all, I should not have brought her with me. Even though it would have been an effort, I should have made other arrangements. I should have anticipated her reaction. When she became upset at the bowling alley, I should have told her then about a concrete plan when we would go bowling another time. When she started crying in the car, I should have pulled over and intervened immediately, rather than thinking I could make it home while she was escalating. After her nap, I should have made it clear to her that she can never get out of her car seat while I am driving. And I should have tied that action to a very clear consequence. What I did right was not giving in to the bowling because she was just pitching a temper tantrum at that point, and you cannot reward temper tantrums. I did a better job after that of being proactive with regard to meltdowns, and I can say now that Caroline almost never loses it like that.

Meltdown or temper tantrum?

First of all, it is important to distinguish between a temper tantrum and a meltdown. Temper tantrums happen when kids want something they cannot have. They are pure manipulation and all kids throw tantrums to see if they can have their way. If it is a temper tantrum, you must use time-outs and loss of privileges, and be firm. A developmental challenge is not an excuse for simple bad behavior, and I have seen many kids who are still throwing tantrums in high school because their parents allowed them always to get their way. I know it's hard because they are all will and no reason at times, but it is much easier to curb this behavior in a small child than in an adult-size teenager.

A meltdown is just as it sounds: your daughter is losing complete control of herself in a maelstrom of tears, frustration, and even rage. Most often, a meltdown is an involuntary reaction to a neurological overload, and your daughter is not in control of herself. She may be feeling overwhelmed by sensory experiences: sights, sounds, smells. When the world is too much for the brain of a person with autism to process, that person can temporarily implode. You will know it is a meltdown if your daughter seems truly unable to control herself, and she does not respond to your words or a consequence.

To complicate things, there are times when a temper tantrum may *lead* to a meltdown. If you are unable to halt a temper tantrum quickly, your daughter may send herself into such a tizzy that she simply cannot calm down. Once a meltdown has begun, no matter what the cause, your goals are to keep your daughter safe and help her calm down as quickly as possible. This is when you need to employ all the sensory interventions you can. Here are some steps you can take.

Ten tips for managing a meltdown

1. If you are at home when the meltdown happens, lead your daughter to her room if possible or to another quiet place, and use low lights or a favorite toy to calm her. I have always had room-darkening shades in my girls' rooms and fans at all times of year, so I could take Caroline to her room where it was soothing and quiet if she was losing control. White noise can blur out other sensory input that may be overwhelming.

2. If you and your daughter are in a public place or crowded area, try to lead her somewhere quiet, away from public view if possible. If it is not possible to move her, just sit down with her where she is and try to hold her and comfort her. However, do not restrain her too firmly or her behavior may escalate. After a few minutes of holding her, try to lead her away again. People may stare or judge; that is not your problem. If you stay calm, people will recognize that you are just trying to control a difficult emotional situation. A few times Caroline lost it at the mall, and I had to just sit down in a store and hold her until she could control herself well enough to walk to the car.

3. If your daughter will let you hold her, hug her firmly but gently to calm her and anchor her. Renowned autism expert Dr. Stanley Greenspan recommends a subtle rocking motion, as you would do with an infant, to calm a child having a meltdown (Greenspan and Wieder 2006, p.363). Cuddling her this way may help her to feel centered and grounded, and thereby allow her brain to slow down.

4. Sometimes your daughter may just have to cry to calm her nervous system. Some studies indicate that crying actually

releases endorphins which calm and relax a person. My girls always seemed calmer after a cathartic cry.

5. You can also sing songs or whisper to her softly to calm her. Don't try to explain anything, but use some repetitive phrases of reassurance. I usually just say, "Mommy's got you; it's okay." Caroline always knows when I say this that she is safe. Sometimes now she will even say it to herself when I hug her.

6. Don't attempt to reason with your daughter during the meltdown; chances are she cannot process much of what you are saying when she is so upset. Whenever I tried to chastise Caroline during a meltdown, it only escalated things. She could hear the tension in my voice and it made her worse. Save the lecture about whatever caused the meltdown for after the meltdown has subsided. You and your daughter will be more able to focus and listen then.

7. If you are afraid your daughter is going to hurt herself, use pillows and blankets to make the area around her soft and safe. If you are afraid she will tumble down from a sofa or bed, you can make a bed on the floor (preferably carpeted), and that way if she kicks and flails, she will not get hurt. I found beanbags worked best with Caroline. We have two big beanbag chairs at home which Caroline loves squishing between for sensory input. When she would have a meltdown as a younger child, I would let her pummel and kick the beanbag; letting out her frustration that way was safe and usually tired her out pretty quickly.

8. As best as you can, remain calm yourself. Although your daughter may not be processing what you say, she will sense your feelings. Try not to take the meltdown personally. I know it is difficult. Keep in mind that this is not your fault, nor your daughter's. It is not about your parenting; it is about her overloaded nervous system.

9. Once the meltdown is over and your daughter is rested and recuperating, you can then talk to her about the trigger or behavior that caused the meltdown. If it was a trigger beyond her control, talk about ways to manage those feelings next

time, or ways to avoid the trigger. If a tantrum started it all, you must address that behavior. Although the meltdown was not her fault, the initial tantrum was within her control; therefore, that manipulative behavior needs to be dealt with firmly and clearly. As defeated as your little sweetie may look at the end of a meltdown, you must not give in to whatever the initial tantrum was an attempt to accomplish. Meltdowns resulting from tantrums should be understood and managed, but not rewarded. Otherwise you are encouraging them.

10.   Finally, you have to have a plan for yourself and your daughter—where to go and what to do in case of a meltdown at home, at school, or in public. Certain things should be reinforced at all times, such as not running from you or another adult when she is upset. Also, have a list of things that calm your daughter to share with her caregivers and teachers. They need to have a plan in place that your daughter is aware of, so she can be part of the solution and begin to internalize how to manage her own feelings. The ultimate goal is to help her learn to calm herself by employing some of these techniques on her own.

Strategic planning: Identifying and managing triggers

When your daughter is young, the best way to deal with meltdowns is to avoid things that trigger them. If you see a tantrum beginning, try immediately to redirect your daughter's attention on to something else. When your daughter first fixates on something, if you react calmly and casually by refocusing her attention, you can often avert the tantrum altogether. However, do not give in to the behavior out of fear of a meltdown, or you are just reinforcing bad behavior as a method by which your daughter can control you. All kids, autism or not, can learn how to manipulate their parents with tantrums. I know meltdowns can be scary, but allowing your daughter to manipulate you with her bad behavior will only worsen with time, and it is much harder to control a meltdown in a teenager or adult than a small child. That is why you need to set firm rules early. If your daughter learns that tantrums will cause her to lose privileges rather than reap rewards, she will be less likely to tantrum, and you can eliminate tantrum-induced meltdowns.

Another way to avoid meltdowns is to keep your expectations for your daughter reasonable. When my girls were younger, I tried to be cautious in making plans, taking into account the length of an activity, the ease with which we could leave if necessary, and the sensory implications of any place we would visit. Fatigue, hunger, and confusion will all lead to meltdowns. I never wanted to put my daughters in a situation in which they would be the object of unwanted stares and judgment. There were times I missed. I can remember one major freak-out because of a dirty bathroom at the county fair. Neither of my girls likes dirt or grime. They get that from their mommy. Anyway, we had to run to the car, which was quite a distance away. We definitely made a scene. However, in general, as long as I kept activities within reasonable bounds for us, I could manage occasional meltdowns. You simply cannot expect your daughter to handle what a typical girl her age can handle. Her brain is not operating the same way. So resist the urge to say, "We should be able to handle Six Flags amusement park because other families do." You are just setting yourself and your daughter up for disaster. And don't let relatives pressure you either. They don't understand. Don't put your daughter in a situation she can't handle just to please other people.

Unfortunately, some triggers are unavoidable, and for those you have to employ some exposure therapy. Your pediatrician or psychologist can help with this. It involves some controlled exposures to things that trigger a meltdown. Over time, a child will learn to tolerate the trigger and will be able to handle her reactions. Do not despair if it seems impossible. Learning coping skills takes time, but it is so important for your daughter's confidence and future independence. As she grows older, she will need to become aware of her triggers and how to handle them, so that she can begin to regulate her own emotions and feel less at the mercy of other people and her surroundings. When I think back to Caroline in the car that day, I am amazed at how fully civilized she is today. She still doesn't like certain things, but she will use words now and try to remove herself appropriately from things she doesn't like, just as the rest of us do. And if she does occasionally let out a yelp because she doesn't like something, such as an elephant on TV, she will apologize afterwards. She knows that such behavior is not acceptable. You don't have to work alone on helping your daughter learn to manage her triggers. Schools can also work with you on ways to help your daughter become accustomed to certain stimuli, so that in time those triggers don't cause a major meltdown. This is especially important if it is a trigger that is impossible to avoid.

It takes a village when the fire alarm sounds

When Caroline was in kindergarten, every time she heard the fire alarm she would scream like a maniac and attempt to run blindly out of the building. One time she made it out of the building on her own and she kept going. One of the gym teachers chased her down and caught up with her a half a mile from school. Her behavior was not only creating a huge scene which upset the other kids, but it was downright dangerous. Caroline's very devoted and patient special education teacher created a Social Story about the fire alarm, took Caroline on a "field trip" to visit the fire alarm, and had the principal tell her about it. Caroline would then be warned when it was about to ring so it didn't come as a shock. Over the course of the year, she was able to tolerate the noise more and more and, eventually, proceed calmly to the exit with all the other kids. This only happened because a thoughtful plan was put in place with my input, and Caroline was part of the learning process. It is important that you find ways to help your daughter cope with meltdowns early on as best you can.

Mastering meltdown mantra: Stay cool, calm, and consistent

So, while meltdowns are trying and exhausting, remember that your daughter is looking for guidance to deal with her sensations and feelings. As far as temper tantrums are concerned, make every effort to remedy behavioral problems in the early years when they are most correctable. Get the school involved as your ally. You want to use the school's resources to help you conquer meltdowns and temper tantrums for many reasons. First, it will make your life more livable and create continuity between school and home. Also, any child exhibiting acting-out behaviors is at risk of alienating her peers.

In addition, if behaviors are disruptive enough, no matter what the reason, your daughter's academic prospects can be limited as well. There may be general education classes in which your daughter could be successful right through high school, but her behavior could disqualify her from participating or at least diminish the value of her participation. Finally, throughout their lives, our daughters will experience the kind of discomforts that can trigger a meltdown, as well as the feelings of disappointment that cause a temper tantrum. Learning to manage those feelings in appropriate ways is one of the most indispensable life skills your daughter can master. The good news is your daughter will eventually outgrow meltdowns if you help her learn to regulate her feelings and give her tools to handle unpleasant stimuli, and if you are calm, consistent, and firm in your response to all of her behaviors.

An individual milestone:
Taming Caroline's crazy hair

This may seem like a silly milestone, but you will probably get it. One of Caroline's biggest milestones was letting me brush her hair. She has this crazy, naturally curly hair, and as a baby she hated to have her head touched. It would knot up after her bath, and especially after she slept because she burrows under her covers at night. I tried every detangler spray, every brush, comb, As-Seen-on-TV gadget, but her hair remained a wild mess. She even started to get baby dreadlocks at one point, which I had to cut out when she was sleeping. In fact, I used to have to cut both of my girls' hair and nails when they were asleep because when they were awake they would go berserk and scream so loud that I thought one of my neighbors would call Child Protective Services. Anyway, as with her clothing issues, Caroline's saving grace turned out to be her vanity.

When she was about nine, I took her to the salon for a haircut, and in a miraculous moment, she allowed the stylist to dry and straighten her hair with a flat iron. You should have seen her looking in the mirror, tossing her hair back and forth like a supermodel, saying, "Caroline is beautiful." She still hadn't gotten the hang of the "I" pronoun at that point. After that, our whole hair world changed. Every day after her bath she would half ask/half order me, "Mommy, you will blow dry and straighten my hair?" And she now withstands every tug and pull in the name of beauty. I must say, Caroline looks quite refined with her shiny, styled hair. Professor Henry Higgins would be proud of her transformation. Of course, now I have created another job for myself; Mommy's salon is open every night, blow-drying and straightening Caroline's hair, and now Lizzie's too, not one to be left out of any special treatment. Last month, we got Scooter, a little white dog with a penchant for rolling in mud puddles, and I am now blow-drying him as well. I am seriously thinking about shaving my own head to have one less thing to do. Still, it is an accomplishment that Caroline's hair is so coiffured now. If you had ever told me when Caroline was four that she would want her hair styled every night, I would have said you were crazy.

Many more miraculous milestones

The most important thing to remember when working on milestones is never to compare your daughter with other children, only with where she was in the past. Then you will surely see progress. Remember, autism is not a shame, nor a flaw. It is just a different way of being. I know it is embarrassing when your daughter acts up or does something very quirky or bizarre. You are human, and at times it will get the best of you. Let it go. And I know it's hard when other people's kids just seem to blossom sometimes in spite of their parents' mistakes. But, believe me, as someone who teaches high school students, all kids humble their parents at some point and burst that bubble. Kids are here to test our limits, and remind us that our hopes, dreams, and ego are not what their lives are about. So, drop the shame; you are doing your best and so is your daughter.

In writing this chapter, I have been amazed how far my girls have come. And I can smile about the ups and downs from a comfortable distance. Back then, however, I thought I would lose my mind trying to get my girls to sleep, eat, and use the bathroom. Such simple goals seemed like reaching for the stars. Our girls can be mighty willful, and at times that obstinacy can almost defeat you. When that happens, take a deep breath, take the pressure off yourself, and just know you will try again later. Eventually the time will come when you have enough conviction that something has to happen, and your daughter is finally ready. In the years since mastering sleeping and the potty, Lizzie and Caroline have learned many other things I wasn't sure they could. At end of fourth grade, Caroline finally mastered the "I" pronoun. For example, she had always said, "You are tired" when speaking of herself. Somehow in fourth grade, it just clicked for her. This summer, at 12 years old, she also finally learned to ride a bike without training wheels. Caroline is now whizzing around the neighborhood, and she couldn't be prouder. Lizzie had some delayed milestones as well. She was late to open up to friends, but she is doing so now and acting in many ways like a typical teenager. Heaven help me! So many of the things I thought they would never get, they finally did get. They learned things late, but they still learned, and they are still learning. So toss out the baby books and try again. Just because it doesn't happen when the book says it will, it doesn't mean it won't happen at all.

The heart of the matter about milestones

1. The most important thing you can do to help your daughter meet her milestones is be patient but persistent.

2. Our girls are usually visual learners, so get used to making charts! If they can visualize it, they can usually adjust to it.

3. It is perfectly normal for you to become frustrated, tired, and crabby at times. Just take a break and try again at a later date.

4. Never compare your daughter to her peers; it will just frustrate you. Just reflect on all her progress thus far, and know she can do it.

5. I promise you that some of the things that may seem impossible now will happen in time. As always, keep the faith and keep trying.

Chapter 10
Autism Truths and Myths

"The voice of parents is the voice of gods, for to their children they are heaven's lieutenants."

—*William Shakespeare*

Some of the most challenging things we face as parents of children with autism are the negative stereotypes prevalent about our kids. Movies and television have improved somewhat in their portrayal of people with autism, but the old stereotype of a person not interested in human relationships—Spock or Rainman—still persists. Sadly, I even hear the word "autistic" hurled about in school sometimes as an insult when a typical kid is being socially inept or slow to understand something. It has become as common as the "R" word when students want to convey that something is weird or stupid. But even beyond the school yard, as common as autism is, I meet parents all the time who believe that autism makes people somehow less feeling, less loving, less human. This is simply not true. I want to address the three most common myths here, and give you the information that you already know in an organized way. Our daughters are loving, attached, and very aware of the world around them. Sometimes they just have trouble expressing themselves.

Truth one: Children with autism are aware of people and things around them

One of the most annoying things that people do is talk as if children with autism cannot understand a word they say. I have had people ask questions about Caroline, often negative ones, when she is standing right beside me. Or they offer their condolences about how hard my life must be! I now say, "Caroline can hear," and then just stare. There is a huge difference between receptive and expressive language (what you hear and what you can say). Studies have shown that our children often have better receptive language than expressive language. So even if your daughter isn't able to express to you how she feels, it doesn't mean she hasn't understood what you have said. Caroline spoke late, and only recently has she been able to offer more than very basic answers to questions. Yet, sometimes she will recollect something that happened, such as a Christmas or summer vacation, from years earlier when she had very limited verbal skills. She now has enough language, at 12, to express thoughts about events that happened when she was four or five. What I have realized is that she was very aware of everything, and was creating lasting memories, when I had no idea what she was processing. It startles me a bit sometimes because I think I was operating at those times almost as if she was deaf. I have always been hopeful about my kids, however, so I pray that I always spoke about her that way in front of her. But it is sobering to realize that my sweet Caroline was fully there all along, even if she wasn't looking me in the eye or responding to me.

Perhaps the best evidence for the silent awareness of children with autism is found in Temple Grandin's book *Emergence*. Ms. Grandin is one of the most famous and accomplished adults with autism in the world. *Emergence* tells the story of her early years, and her mother's devotion in helping her learn to communicate. I found the book amazing because Temple remembers with remarkable clarity and detail all of her life, even the early years when she was preverbal. She didn't begin talking until she was four (Grandin and Scariano 1996). She describes why she did all she did, how the stimming calmed her, and why certain textures, fabrics, and sounds were painful to her. The lesson was clear to me: even without words, our children are still fully people who are feeling and processing and creating memories of their lives. Their experiences and relationships are shaping them in ways we cannot always know or see.

The other beautiful revelation in the book is the way she was silently responding to her mother's love and dedication. Temple knew that her mother was fighting for her and not against her, at times when her mother must have wondered if any of it was getting through at all. Temple is a beautiful translator for all of us who wonder if our children are aware of their surroundings. They are. Even if they don't have Temple's cognitive gifts, they are still hearing our words. Even if they don't understand our words, they are sensing our tone. Children with autism are very aware of the world around them, just not so good at expressing their impressions of it. And they will blossom best when treated with the love and respect that cognizant, feeling people deserve. As Temple's mother once shared with a psychologist at Temple's school:

> When Temple feels love and appreciation, her compulsive behavior dwindles, her voice loses its curious stress and she is in control of herself... She wants someone near her in whom she has confidence...
> in any therapy with Temple the most important point seems to be love. (Grandin and Scariano 1996, p.133)

How simple and profound are the words of Temple's mother and the enormous lesson they provide.

Another amazing testimony to this veiled awareness comes from stories of non-verbal children who learn to communicate through word-processing. One phenomenal story is of Carly Fleishmann, a 16-year-old American girl, who was non-verbal until she was ten. As her mother recalls:

> One day, when Carly was 10, she and a therapist were working with the alphabet screen of a device to type words she knew how to spell. Carly was "fussy" that day and wanted to stop and she typed the word, "no." Then, she typed more words to explain she felt sick. It was the first time her spelling was purposeful and spontaneous. About six months later, Carly's sentences started tumbling out. (Hauch 2011)

Up until that point, Carly was thought not only to have autism, but potentially to be so low-functioning that she was in need of institutional care. Now, she writes extensively in her online blog about everything from politics to boys. I realize her story is extreme, and not all children with autism will make her amazing progress, but it does point out that our children are aware of their loved ones and surroundings, sometimes in ways that are significantly more sophisticated than we imagine.

I remember reading in Dr. T. Berry Brazelton's baby book *Touchpoints* when Lizzie was a newborn about "social referencing." Social referencing describes the way babies as young as nine months take non-verbal cues from their parents about the world around them. More significantly, infants can also sense their parents' positive or negative reactions to them. Dr. Brazelton tells parents that babies "use cues from parents to reference their approval or disapproval" (Brazelton and Sparrow 2006, p.125). Therefore, Dr. Brazelton cautions parents to be aware of the way they talk to and about their children, even before their children have expressive and receptive language skills. I think, as parents, we should always assume even from the beginning of our children's infancies that they are listening to and understanding what we are saying about them because there is no way to know for sure when and to what degree cognition and language develop. This is especially true for our kids because what they understand is an even greater unknown. Even if the learning trajectory for our children to acquire language is much longer— even if it is a lifetime—they are listening. And our words can be the prophecy that shapes both their self-worth and their futures.

Last year I was speaking with a parent of one of my high school students, a girl with autism. The girl is bright and sweet, but she has tremendous struggles with peer relationships. As the girl was standing with her mother, the mom said, "She can't make friends. Just doesn't get it. I have been trying for years to deal with this. I am out of ideas." I wanted to shake her. The poor girl looked at her feet in total shame and defeat. For how many years had the girl heard this message, repeated in front of her probably hundreds of times? How much had that judgment contributed to the girl's struggles with friendships? Contrary to her mother's assessment, this girl understood a lot, including that her mother thought she was incapable of making friends. Now, maybe I am being too hard on the mom, as I am sure she was trying her best. But the bottom line is that she regarded her daughter as not fully present at that moment in the way any other child would be. Would any other mother of a teenage girl describe her daughter that way and live to tell about it?

I had a similar, but more humorous, experience recently with one of Caroline's teachers. He is a sweet guy, well intentioned, but he hasn't quite figured her out. I ran into him as I was picking Caroline up from school one day. He was talking quite candidly to me about her strengths and weaknesses as she was standing there. Then, when he wanted to speak to her, he would stare at her and shout. Kind of what Americans do instinctively and ineffectively when speaking to someone who doesn't speak English fluently. Finally, I had to interrupt him and tell him that she hears just fine, and that she heard and understood everything he had said about her. She looked up at him skeptically out of the corner of her eye, and, at that moment, he got it. Sometimes, just small reminders work the best.

Usually Caroline's teachers have been phenomenal, but I always know when someone is not accepting of her because she shuts down and withdraws more into herself. She had a horrible first grade long-term substitute who told her she was bad and chastised her all day. Caroline had very little functional language at that time, but came home every day and repeated to herself, "No, Caroline. Bad, Caroline." She felt that rejection on every level and learned nothing with that woman. In fact, I bet you have had the same experience with your daughter: that teachers who accept and love her make much more progress than those who aren't so invested, patient, or affirming. If that isn't awareness, what is? And I am sure that you have family members who don't get your daughter, and, consequently, she acts out or shuts down. Again, maybe no words, but she can feel what is going on.

I like to go for walks in the evening, just at dusk, and something occurred to me the other night. In my neighborhood, dusk is when rabbits come out of hiding and nibble on the neatly trimmed, unnaturally green lawns. Rabbits are funny creatures in that they make no sound at all. They are defenseless, except for the ability to run. What they do best is move quietly and quickly, remaining hyperaware of their surroundings. They twitch nervously as they eat, constantly vigilant, listening for sounds of danger. And they never make eye contact, but you know they are watching you in their peripheral vision. They remind me of Caroline. She is not always quiet, but she has the same ability to sense danger or safety, and the same peering out of the corner of her eye, and the same hyperawareness of the people around here, even when she seems tuned out. The truth is our kids are like rabbits: they are silent, but ever aware of who is safe, who is dangerous, who accepts, who loves, and when they can just relax and be themselves.

My heartfelt conviction is that our children are very aware of everything around them, even if it they cannot express it. So speak of them with hope and faith, and make sure those around them do as well. This is why it is so troubling to me when parents speak of children with autism as damaged or ill. We need to surround them with words of confidence and love, and believe they are absorbing that powerful optimism. As my girls have learned to express themselves in words, I have learned that though they seem to hear little of what I tell them to do, they hear and remember everything I say about them. When in doubt, assume they are listening, and tell others to as well. Our daughters are participating in life differently, but, make no doubt, they are present.

Truth two: Children with autism are very attached to people

Most intelligent people know that children with autism are deeply attached to their families and loved ones; yet I hear people reference the lack of attachment in children with autism frequently. Children with autism may not be good at expressing attachment in words, but, as parents, we know our kids love us. And if your personal relationship isn't testimony enough, you can tell people about the many studies that have been done about attachment between kids with autism and parents. A 2004 review of 16 studies on autism and attachment concluded that "Despite the impairments of children with autism in reciprocal social interaction, the majority of the studies found evidence for attachment in these children" (Rutgers *et al.* 2004, p.1123). Another interesting American study published in 2010 concluded that while children with autism have more difficulty establishing attachments, they can do it quite well if certain conditions exist (Seskin *et al.* 2010). The most important condition is the level of belief the parent has in the potential for attachment and the parent's own capacity for attachment. Parents who were most attached and felt closest to their children created a more secure pathway for attachment to occur. The parental ability to attach is crucial for all children, but for children with autism, the parent's attachment to and faith in their child was a much more powerful predictor of attachment (Seskin *et al.* 2010).

Now, I know you don't need any more pressure or guilt. And even if you have the patience and fortitude of Mother Theresa, you may still have a child so developmentally challenged that it is hard at times to gauge attachment. I know there have been times, especially when my girls were younger, when I thought they were oblivious to me. But the good news in this study is that we, as parents, can significantly affect our relationships with our children in positive ways. If we believe in the potential for connection and attachment, we can help it to occur. As with so many things in autism, it is our outlook and faith that help create the outcome. If you regard your daughter with autism as deficient in feeling, and you lose faith in her ability to bond with you, you will negatively affect her ability to do so. But if you keep reinforcing the positive and stay open to the ways your daughter can show attachment, you will create that safe pathway for attachment to occur. Again, thought can create reality.

I think this perception that our children lack emotional attachment may stem from the difficulty some kids have with hugs and affection. The truth is that physical affection is not an emotional issue but a sensory one. Again, Temple Grandin does not like physical affection with her loved ones, and her mother couldn't hug her, which must have been heartbreaking. However, she loves her mother deeply and was incredibly attached to her mother. In every speech she gives, she acknowledges that it was her mother's love and faith that allowed her to thrive. In fact, in one interview, when asked to free-associate words, Temple's response to the word "love" was "mother" (Weiss 2010). Do not mistake the inability to hug due to sensory issues for a lack of feeling. It is not. You may be able to find other ways to express affection. Some kids like deep pressure given through bean bags or cushions, or brushing the skin with sensory brushes. You may be able to sing songs or have games that convey love and affection. I am sure right now there are things that only you can do for your daughter; that she will simply not accept someone else tucking her in to bed at night, or she must have you make her cheese sandwich. This may seem like work but it is also attachment. Your daughter trusts you to meet the needs no one else can. You are the voice, the protector, the comforter, the lifeline in a world spinning in confusion and mystery. Even if you don't get much back for that devotion for a long time, maybe forever, don't think for a moment that you are not the most beloved person in your daughter's life. You are.

For a year, after my divorce, I worked at a preschool for children with special needs, the same school Caroline had attended. I worked with four-year-olds, some of whom were very severely affected by autism, non-verbal, and seemingly not interested in interaction. During certain songs and games, I could see glimmers of the personalities within, and those smiles, however fleeting, were so amazing and worthwhile. On the last day, the kids performed some songs for their parents and graduated from preschool. Their parents attended for the graduation and a picnic. I swear to you, every child watched for his or her parents to arrive, and when they did, you could see the joy in them at seeing their moms and dads. Some smiled shyly, some clapped, and some ran over to their families excitedly.

Afterwards, I was talking with one lovely mother of a beautiful boy who, at age four, had never uttered a word. I listened as she shared her fears and the exhaustion of an infancy that had no end in sight. Although he was walking and growing, he wasn't speaking and was still in diapers. And he was hard on her: at one moment content and the next throwing a tantrum. The truth is, in most cases, infancy lasts just about as long as human beings can stand for it to last. That kind of completely sacrificial relationship is meant to be short-term. Yet, for parents of kids with special needs, it goes on indefinitely. Sometimes we need someone just to recognize that. I told this mom that she was an amazing parent, doing a difficult job with devotion and grace. And I described to her how I had seen her little boy smile when he caught sight of her walking across the lawn. I told her I could see that all her devotion was not lost on him, no matter how difficult he could be or unaware he could seem. She smiled and said, "I know. I love him and he loves me." That was seven years ago. I pray by now she has heard those words from him, but even if she hasn't, they both still know they are true. Love doesn't always speak in words.

Truth three: Children with autism can feel empathy

Empathy is one of the hallmark traits of being human: the ability to recognize another person's pain or suffering, and feel for them in response. It is one of the things we talk about most in my English classes with regard to literature and how it helps us become better human beings. Studies show that empathy must be modeled by a parent or significant role model to be learned and internalized in a meaningful way. As a teacher who sees at least a hundred typical kids on a daily basis, I can tell you that the ability to feel empathy varies widely in people. What I have found is that empathy is not related to intelligence or education, but is more a matter of understanding and the heart. It occurs when parents make it a priority, when they encourage their children to look outward as much as inward, and when helping others is at least as important as getting ahead. You have to make kids aware of other people's feelings and teach them that others matter. That is true for all kids, not just kids on the spectrum. I have very bright typical kids who have little empathy because it has never been asked of them or modeled for them, and I have children who struggle with reading and writing whose hearts flow like the Mississippi when a friend is in need.

In psychological terms, empathy is a two-part process. There is the recognition of another person's feelings and then the empathic emotional response to those feelings. The truth is our children can struggle with the first part. They don't read facial expressions well and often cannot process language quickly enough to identify feelings. There is a time lag in connections and in responses. However, I believe when you make them aware, our children have the capacity to be very empathic because they are full of feeling. A fascinating article on empathy published in 2009 theorizes that people with autism do have the capacity to feel empathy. Although they may lack the cognitive ability to recognize other people's feelings or states of mind spontaneously, when they do feel empathy, they may actually feel it more potently than typical people (Smith 2009). In a sense, as with everything else for people with autism, empathy is an intensely felt experience.

The key component in teaching empathy seems to be directing children with autism to recognize other people's feelings and experiences on a daily basis. Once the awareness of others' feelings is there, the empathy will follow. The process is not different from that for typical children. Human beings do not start off with empathy. Babies are, by necessity, self-absorbed; that is how they survive. Toddlers start to get a sense of others, but it takes a while for empathy to emerge, and it only develops fully if modeled and encouraged. Because our kids tread more slowly along that path of maturation, we may have to endure the self-absorbed period longer than most parents, and redirecting our children to the feelings of others may always take effort. However, teaching empathy is possible, but it must be a concerted effort if you want your daughter to be capable of it.

In her autobiography *Emergence*, Temple Grandin describes teaching kindness and empathy to children on the spectrum this way: "Teach your child love and kindness in a concrete manner, with very specific examples. For instance, an example of kindness would be bringing flowers to an elderly lady in a nursing home" (Grandin and Scariano 1996, p.163). Temple's insightful suggestion points out two essential truths: children on the spectrum can be taught to be empathic and thoughtful, but it must be taught to them in a very concrete way they can understand if you want them to truly internalize it as a value and incorporate it into their daily behavior. It is well worth the effort to help them connect with their loved ones and the world around them.

One of the most interesting articles I have read on teaching empathy to children with autism incorporates a technique many of us may already be doing: imaginative play with dolls and puppets. Through the dolls and puppets, researchers led the children through a series of social vignettes, eliciting empathy in appropriate situations. The article, which describes a 2009 study into teaching empathy to children with autism, concludes that "children with autism as young as 4 years old can learn to demonstrate socially relevant empathy skills in pretend-play settings…these skills can also generate to interactions with real people in nontraining settings" (Schrandt, Townsend, and Poulson 2009, p.30). I found this study so reassuring because that is exactly how I sought to teach my girls empathy. I have mentioned many times in this book my girls' and my own love for dolls. Through playing with dolls, I have acted out with my girls how it feels to be scared or excited, what it means to have your feelings hurt or to be sad. I always found that this worked better than just chastising them to feel for someone, and because it entertained them, they would pay attention to it. Caroline and I still make her dolls talk about what their days in school are like, and sometimes when her dolls are misbehaving, Caroline will reprimand them to "be nice." This study proves that not only can empathy be taught to our children, but it is something a mom and dad can do while playing with their child.

Teaching Caroline empathy

I am not claiming to be some kind of miracle worker. Teaching Caroline empathy was a slow process, and I often wondered if I was making progress. For Caroline, recognizing other people's feelings has been swimming against the tide at times. For many years, Caroline seemed to be on a solo mission in life. She wanted what she wanted when she wanted it. She was determined, no matter what anyone else wanted. She would even giggle when someone else cried or got hurt. That still happens sometimes, and I am not sure if it is a nervous reaction or not. Sometimes her irrational willfulness would bring me to tears. Sound familiar? Still, I would make her look at Lizzie if she was crying. I would tell her, "Lizzie is sad." If I saw something on television, we would practice identifying emotions. And the "dolls" would always speak up to remind her to be nice and think about others. I asked her speech teacher to work especially hard on helping her to recognize other people's feelings. And with both of my kids, I have hammered away at manners. Even if I wasn't sure they knew what it meant, I always insisted on please, thank you, and excuse me. I wouldn't accept autism as an excuse to be rude or selfish or mean. For a long time, I wasn't sure it was working with Caroline.

Within the last two years, from ten to twelve, Caroline has made enormous progress with her emotional connections and awareness. Notice that this has happened long after that mythical developmental window of opportunity at three years of age closed. Our children never stop learning, so you never stop trying. It started with little things. If her sister cries, Caroline brings a tissue. If I say I have a headache, she rubs my head—sometimes too hard and it hurts more, but it's the thought that counts. When the cat cries, Caroline says, "Juliet is sad," although generally the cat just always wants more food. I can see that she is getting it—empathy! I am not sure when it happened, if it has to do with puberty, or if she was just finally ready to make those connections. But after working so long on the first step—awareness of other people having feelings—she has now mastered the second step in empathy—she feels for others! I am so proud of her and her big heart.

This past February my dad passed away after a decade-long battle with Alzheimer's disease. I was blessed to have had a wonderful dad. He was warm, and sweet, and full of affection and feeling. However, my girls never really got to know the dad I had because the disease had changed him and made him irritable and frightened. I was nervous about how Caroline would react at the wake and funeral because she, like many kids on the spectrum, has this tendency to laugh at inappropriate times. When I took her up to say a prayer for my dad, she looked at him and started to giggle. Then she said to me, "Grandpa is asleep. He was tired." I could see that she got it on some level. A couple of days after the funeral, she came up to me and said, "Mommy, Grandpa died. Are you sad?" When I said yes, she hugged me and started to rub my head. Not a sign of a giggle. I cannot tell you how comforting that hug was. Does she still smile and giggle at the wrong times? Absolutely. But does she also love and feel for her family and friends? Without a doubt!

Sometimes it is just that our children do not know how to express what they feel, and art and music can be a beautiful door to understanding and expressing feelings and empathy. I teach a sweet girl with autism who gave me an amazing picture recently. This girl loves to draw cartoons. She has an entire world of cartoon people and is often absorbed in that world of drawing during class when she should be reading or writing. At times she seems unaware of the people around her. I share a lot of stories about my family with my class, just as I encourage them to share their stories when making real-life connections to the literature. So my students knew about my dad and knew he had passed away during the February break. When I returned to school, many of them hugged me and told me how sorry they were. They were the sweet expressions of typical kids, heartfelt and clear. My sweet girl with autism didn't say anything, but at the end of the period she came up and handed me a drawing. It is picture of her hugging me, and tears running down my face. It is one of the most beautiful drawings I have ever seen. All of her feelings that she couldn't put in words or hugs were exquisitely expressed on that paper. I cannot think of a more perfect example of empathy.

One of my dear friends and colleagues is a speech teacher. She runs a social skills group for some of our students with autism and other developmental challenges. Sometimes I join them. It is a quirky group to say the least. Some of them are highly verbal, and some pretty limited in their ability to express themselves, but they all listen. As with all teenagers, they tend to dwell on themselves and their feelings. One session, there was a bit of a mean girl issue going on in the group. Yes, even in this group there is a pecking order. One girl was feeling left out of her group of four friends, and the three others were saying it was her own fault for being a baby. I am giving the abbreviated version; it was a very long, meandering road to make that clear. The speech teacher and I were getting frustrated because no one seemed able to understand the others' feelings, and they were just repeating themselves. Suddenly a boy in the group, also on the spectrum, who is almost always silent and tends to perseverate on his clothes, erupted, rather furiously, "She wants you to like her! She wants you to like her!" He put in words the simple truth of the whole matter. He listened, understood, and he felt for this girl. That is empathy.

Empathy seems like a simple concept, and people say it is natural. So is speech, but you still need to hear it in order to learn how to do it. Just because it is harder for our girls to learn to speak does not mean we give up trying to teach them. We should do the same with empathy. All children, including children with autism, need to have empathy modeled and taught in order to really understand that other people have feelings that are like their own. Our children are just as sensitive as any other human beings—sometimes, I think, more so. As with so many things, it is about working on redirecting them outward and helping them to make those connections. They may never easily read faces or emotion, but they can understand when made aware and care about other people's feelings. And, from that awareness, empathy will follow. It might take a long time, and it may not be obvious, but it will be there.

Choose to believe

> *"You don't have a soul. You are a soul. You have a body."*
>
> —*C. S. Lewis*

I know I have been very blessed with my girls in the last few years. They have grown emotionally in ways many people said they could not. That is why I challenge so many of these myths that make our children sound less than fully human. Awareness, empathy, and attachment are very real in children with autism. It may take longer to get there, and they may not always express their feelings in eloquent or obvious ways, but they have the love, the understanding, and the desire to participate fully in their lives. I think my perspective may come down to a spiritual conviction. I believe in the soul, in something that cannot be quantified or measured by any test or study. The soul of a person with any development challenge is just as rich in spirit and grace as that of every other human being. One of the most hurtful things ever uttered by a parent was written by pediatrician Dr. Jerry Kartzinel in his introduction to Jenny McCarthy's (2007) memoir *Louder than Words*. Kartzinel described autism as something that "steals the soul of a child" (p.xvi). In that same book, McCarthy herself describes her son's autism as "the loss of the soul in his eyes" (p.6). What a horrific and dismissive way to define a child with challenges. Our brains do not give us our souls, nor do our bodies, nor do our parents. Our souls are given to us by God, and nothing can take that grace away.

It is that faith in the souls of my children that fuels my belief in their potential, even in those abilities they haven't quite yet mastered. That is why when I speak of them, I believe they are aware. Why I know they can feel empathy. Why I am certain of their capacity to love deeply the people in their lives. Some of the most amazing love stories I have seen are between parents and their severely challenged kids. They go beyond words to the soul. So keep working with your daughter and believing in the progress she can make. If you can't tell if she is listening or understanding, or if you don't see evidence of empathy or attachment at times, choose to have faith in her. Studies prove your beliefs make a huge difference. We must not characterize our children by their challenges or shortcomings any more than any other parent would. Our children are sacred, soulful, and full of promise. So challenge those myths, and watch your daughter embrace the world.

The heart of the matter about autism truths and myths

1. People with autism are complete and worthy human beings, capable of deep emotions and attachments.

2. Always speak hopefully about and around your daughter; you do not know how much she listens or understands.

3. As parents, we can have a positive effect on the ability of our daughters to feel deep attachment and connection.

4. People with autism are capable of empathy; but, as with all people, empathy must be role-modeled and taught for it to be learned.

5. Always remember that the way we view our children shapes the way they see themselves, and the way the world sees them as well.

Chapter 11

Dark Moments

"Sometimes I lie awake at night and I ask, 'Why me?' Then a voice answers, 'Nothing personal, your name just happened to come up.'" Charlie Brown

---

—Charles Schulz

Shortly after my girls were diagnosed, I became acutely aware of people with special needs all around me. It seemed I kept seeing the big blue buses for the DDS—Developmental Disabilities Services—carrying adults with severe developmental challenges all over my town. I almost felt as if they were following me. I wondered if I was going crazy. Every time I saw the faces of those sad adults with big childlike eyes, staring out those bus windows, I would burst into tears. I am ashamed of this now, but back then I was sad, scared, and angry all at the same time. I wondered if that was the fate that awaited my Caroline. Suddenly, everywhere I went, I would see people who had been invisible to me before, and I didn't want to join their world. The irony is that I had worked with special needs kids for years during college summers, and I had accepted them without question. I see now that I was able to accept them because I never thought it had anything to do with me personally. I was detached and felt, in my own way, "safe" from those problems. I can honestly say now that I don't have that reaction anymore. Thanks to my daughters, my heart has grown, and I now see people where I formerly saw only special needs. That is one of the many blessings my children have given to me.

Still, having children with autism does bring moments of sadness and frustration, and I would not be honest if I didn't admit to feeling down at times. As much as I try to be the eternal optimist, there are days when the world gets the better of me. And there is a fear of the future that I have been chasing away ever since I found out my girls had autism. I try to fight that fear by forging ahead with hope, but I want to share my low moments, so you know that we all have them. I find it best if you let yourself feel the sadness or fear when it comes, and then let it go like a wave when the feeling has passed. Autism is best lived day to day, wave to wave. My biggest emotional challenges are anger, loneliness, sadness, and fear. Here's how I try to deal with them.

Emotional challenge number one: Anger
The anger of "Why me?"

I am, by nature, someone who avoids conflict, and I am more prone to depression than anger, which my therapist tells me is anger turned inward. Still, I have had my moments when I have felt anger about how hard my girls and I have to struggle at times. There is the initial anger of "Why did this happen to me and my kids?" I wondered that quite often after my girls were first diagnosed, and I saw the neighborhood kids whizzing around effortlessly on their bikes, interacting with a natural rhythm and ease. And still sometimes, when I know something is particularly hard for one of my girls, I can feel that righteous indignation rise in me again. But when I look around the world and see so much suffering, I can't linger long in self-pitying anger. And I don't have to look far. As a teacher, I see more than I can handle sometimes of children dealing with illness, loneliness, poverty, and abuse.

When I step back and take a broad look at life, I see that everyone has challenges, and, for whatever divine reason that I cannot fathom, we all have our periods of pain and struggle. From that vantage point, "Why me?" no longer seems a question worth asking. Do I question God at times? Sure, but He always welcomes me back and I find comfort there. My girls are healthy and joyful, so when I feel anger, I try as best as I can to refocus on my blessings. The sooner you can make peace with your life as it is, not as you expected it to be, the more room you will make for happiness. Do I still sometimes feel anger at so much unfairness of things? Sure, I have my moments. But all it takes is a laugh from Caroline, and my anger at fate dissipates like smoke on a windy beach.

Mean people make me mad

Another time I feel anger is when we encounter mean people. And, I am sorry to say, they are out there. Whether it is a snide remark made by a salesperson who doesn't understand why Caroline is talking about the Rugrats to herself, or a classmate who refuses to talk to Lizzie at the bus stop, mean people have raised my blood pressure at times. There have been parents who have openly discouraged their children from being friends with mine, and classmates who refused to invite my daughters to their birthday parties because they were "different." Caroline has had to endure far more of these rejections than Lizzie. I try so hard to be Anne Frank and believe people are good at heart, so these moments still sting me every time. It is excruciating to explain to Caroline that another girl does not want to be her friend. Yet I must, or Caroline will keep trying to befriend the girl because she can't read the subtle language of rejection. How do I do that without breaking Caroline's spirit and her heart? And how do I explain the actions of the mother of that girl who whisks her kids away when we appear? How do I account for the teacher who does not have the patience or heart to teach children like yours and mine? All of these people make me angry. How do I handle the anger? Well, sometimes my husband or a friend will listen while I rant about how lousy people can be, or I will take a fast and furious walk until I calm down. I try not to spend too much time focused on the nasty people of the world because the truth is those people are not worthy of our time and certainly not of our tears. My best coping strategy is to consider them ignorant and to ignore their existence as best I can. When it is not possible to ignore someone's unkindness, however, my anger has been best served by taking constructive action. Sometimes anger can be the catalyst for you to take a stand against mean people and perhaps educate them to prevent future unkindness. The key (and the tricky part) is making sure you don't become a mean person yourself in the process.

Channeling Anger to Create Change

Caroline had a substitute teacher in first grade when her regular teacher left for maternity leave. This woman was downright mean. She did not believe Caroline belonged in the general class, and she resented her presence. This woman would constantly reprimand Caroline, which only made Caroline upset and aggravated her behavior. That year Caroline would come home from school and repeat all the things that had been said to her: "No, Caroline!"; "Bad girl, Caroline!"; "Stop it, Caroline!" Caroline would write these words over and over again on construction paper. She was so sad that year. I called the school countless times, and I was promised the situation would be remedied. The teacher herself refused to meet with me.

One afternoon, the teacher called me because the following day the class was going on a field trip to see a play. She wasn't sure if she should bring Caroline, so she left this message on my answering machine: "I was wondering if Caroline can behave herself at a play because I don't want her to ruin it for all the other children." I think I ruptured several blood vessels when I heard that message. Caroline has never been a behavior problem in school. She sometimes struggles with the academic material, but she has always been a lovely, gentle child. At that point I realized the teacher was incapable of appreciating my daughter, so speaking with her was pointless. When I see that someone's mind is clamped shut, I know to move on. So instead, I called the special education supervisor for the district and let him know about the nasty phone message from the teacher. Since I work in the same district in which my kids attend school, I was able to be especially "candid." He assured me he would speak to the teacher directly. I do not know what he said, but I do know that this teacher ceased to interact with Caroline. Considering the teacher's limitations, that was the best possible outcome until she left the position. Of course, I would like to have seen her fired. At least I was able to vent my anger in the most productive way possible, which helped me calm down, and kept Caroline safe from further hurt. Sometimes with mean people, the best thing you can do is use your righteous anger to put barricades between them and your daughter.

Shortly after that episode, Caroline's regular teacher returned from her maternity leave. That particular experience had been horrible for Caroline. My anger simmered for quite some time. How dare such an ignorant woman hurt my daughter! I spent the next few months reminding Caroline of all the teachers who love her, and in time my anger passed and her fear eased, but that woman definitely took a toll on my sweet Caroline's spirit, and mine.

Ingrates infuriate me

There have also been the aggravating times when I have had to listen to other moms, co-workers and neighbors complaining about their exceptionally gifted child not receiving enough attention or stimulation in school. I have had to listen to many conversations of parents complaining that special education gets too much money; what about the gifted? I want to tell them the gifted have the world at their feet, so stop worrying. I have also had to endure those parents who are not happy with their athletically talented child unless he or she is team captain. There are the parents who cry when their daughter is not homecoming queen, but only runner-up on the court. Sometimes I want to shake them! Don't they get how lucky they are? Is there a drop of gratitude anywhere in them? And there are smug parents who take full credit for having a totally typical child and look at me with a slightly skeptical look of blame when they recognize that Caroline has autism. I guess it comforts them to think they couldn't possibly have a child with problems, but even when I psychoanalyze them, it still bugs me.

Smarmy, ungrateful people can put me in a nasty mood, so I make myself take a deep breath and reflect on how glad I am to be free of these competitions. I think of how having my girls always makes me remember the simple values in life: love, family, and a worthy purpose. A lot of what we occupy ourselves with in life is ego-based and superficial. Just watch reality TV for 15 minutes and you will know what I mean. Having a special needs child makes you leave your ego behind. You realize it's not about you, not about what you wanted; it's about what your child needs. And, really, isn't that the lesson all parents need to learn? Lucky for us, our kids teach us that early in our parenting. So when I feel myself resenting or becoming angry at some parent who is lamenting that his or her child was only accepted to state schools and not Ivy League ones, I just smile and move on because they have not yet figured out that the secret to happiness is being grateful for what you have, not obsessing on what you didn't get.

Avoid getting swept up in the tornado of anger

The bottom line with anger is that it hurts you more than anyone else. Unless you can turn it into positive action that brings change, anger will just deplete your energy. Life is a crazy, uneven rollercoaster ride, and spending time lamenting the car you are in just wastes precious time. The same goes for obsessing on mean people. Remember that the misery they bring to you is probably minuscule compared to the misery they endure being in their own presence on a daily basis. After all, you can leave; they are stuck with themselves. Mean people make the world seem small and cold and empty. But that's only because *they* are. The world is actually full of kind people, so remember that. And erase the meanies from your memory card as soon as possible, to make room for the nice ones. As for the braggarts and the parents involved in the Olympiad of children, forget about them too. As a high school teacher, I can testify that all kids turn their parents' worlds upside down at some point. So exit that foolish race and just keep trotting along at your own pace. We all feel anger sometimes; that's human. It's a part of who we are. The key is not to let it be *all* of who you are. Your daughter needs you happy and hopeful, not angry.

Emotional challenge number two: Loneliness
Lonesome me

Sometimes I just get plain lonely because so few people understand the things that worry me. At times I feel overwhelmed by the enormity of the responsibility I have, not just to raise my girls, but to work so hard to help them overcome certain deficits, not the least of which is the ignorance of the greater world at large. Even my family doesn't understand how often I find myself looking at ordinary life from the outside, trying to find a way for my girls to be included. With Caroline, I am always negotiating the unwritten rules that restrict her entry into the world. How often have I been at a loss for words when Caroline has freaked out about something that I simply cannot explain to anyone who isn't me? And sometimes my loneliness is quite literally because we have spent more time isolated. How many times have we opted to stay home because whatever outing was proposed would be too much to handle? My family usually tries to play it down: "At least Caroline is verbal...your girls are very healthy." That's true enough, but I think they say it more to make themselves feel better than to comfort me. People don't like to look too hard at a tough reality when they can avoid it. Not that I blame them; you don't get it if you don't live it. It's just that sometimes being the only one who gets it is pretty lonesome; at times it's just me and the tumbleweeds blowing by.

Alone in a crowd

It's strange how loneliness can also sneak up on you in the most public of places. Sometimes, when my neighbors or co-workers are talking (bragging) about their kids, I often don't share my experiences because I can't stand the look of pity mixed with nervousness on their faces, even if I am sharing a story about something terrific. It's as if they just see me as someone whose life is utterly and completely different. I think my girls are fabulous, but it is hard to explain that to someone who thinks your life is their worst nightmare. It feels strange to know you scare people. There was one woman I met a while back through mutual friends. She had concerns because her son was not talking at two years old. I had no intention of saying anything to her about it; I had just heard about it from someone else and considered it her private business. I refrain from drawing any kind of conclusions about other people's kids, lest they think that misery, as they see me, loves company. We were at quite a few social gatherings together, and I noticed this woman was avoiding me. She would stand as far away from me as possible, as if I was the Grim Reaper disguised as a suburban mom. It seemed foolish, so at a backyard barbeque one sunny afternoon, I approached her and offered a casual hello. She announced to me, "My son is fine...it's just a speech delay; it's not like with your girls," and then whipped around and power-walked across the lawn before I could respond. I was left speechless, which was ironic given the topic of her brief lecture. I guess she thought I was going to make an irreversible diagnosis or pronouncement of autism right there by the chips and salsa, so she had to cut me off before I "cast my spell." I half expected her to have a wreath of garlic around her neck the next time I saw her.

Bad omen walking

I also find that pregnant women avoid me. Sounds weird, but sometimes I think they believe I am a bad omen. I could be quite friendly with someone at work or in my neighborhood, but as soon as she is pregnant, I am nothing but bad news. When women are sharing pregnancy experiences, I discovered if I shared my stories, they are met with lots of awkward pauses. I guess my stories are seen as cautionary tales with which no one wants to identify, even though both of my pregnancies progressed without complications. So I stopped trying to be part of those conversations. I know I was kind of superstitious when I was pregnant, so I try not to be offended. It's not about me, just about their fears. There's my attempt at psychoanalysis again. Still doesn't make me feel much better. I want to tell them that autism is not contagious, and that I wish them nothing but the best. I am not some bitter crone, stirring a cauldron at night, trying to doom others to my fate. I guess ignorance really does breed fear. And, again, I think my girls are magnificent; that seems to be the part no one understands. So, yes, sometimes I just feel lonely in my life.

Rustle up a friend

The only good solution for that lonely feeling is a good friend. So when I have one of those "lonesome me" moments and I am feeling as outcast as Clint Eastwood in *High Plains Drifter*, I call one of my mom friends with special kids like mine. The funny part is when I tell another special mom the story, we usually end up laughing about how ridiculous the world is, and then I don't feel alone at all. It only takes one other voice in the wilderness to chase the loneliness away. So when you are unwelcome in Dodge, light out for the territory, as they say in the Old West, and find one friend to share a laugh; then you won't even notice the tumbleweeds blowing by.

Emotional challenge number three: Sadness
Night-time blues

My darkest times are those moments late at night when I put the girls to bed. After the busyness of the day is done, I am left with my thoughts. Sometimes I feel overwhelmed by sadness at the things Caroline may never get to do because of her autism. Caroline wants to do so many things in life; she talks about going to college, traveling to Paris where Madeline lives. She likes to joke about which mischievous boy in her class she will marry, and how many babies she will have. Both of my girls have always loved baby dolls, and both of them have just assumed they will be mothers some day. I know Lizzie can be a mom, but for Caroline it is doubtful. I remind myself that Caroline may be just as happy without children, that she may find many other things to fulfill her. And she is so lovable; I am sure she will have a special boy some day. When I feel so sad, I try to remind myself that the future is always full of promise, and every day brings change and possibilities. I find that if I really go deep into sadness, it is hard to pull myself back out. So I let myself cry a bit, and then I force myself to do something else.

If you find that your sadness is unmanageable, by all means talk to your physician. I have a therapist whom I have been seeing for years, and I am not ashamed of that. I challenge anyone to live my life and not need some guidance and therapy. I also take an antidepressant to help with my anxiety and stress. Again, I am not ashamed. Depression runs in my family, so it only makes sense to treat it. I need to be my best self for my girls. So don't let false pride or embarrassment stop you from getting the help you need if your sadness has progressed to depression. Sadness is part of being human, but it is a temporary passerby. Depression moves in and stays. So be kind to yourself if you know you can't fight the sadness alone, and reach out for help.

Emotional challenge number four: Fear
The scary place

Even though I can usually manage my sadness, sometimes my mind goes to my fears. I ponder the question all parents of special needs kids try to avoid: What will happen to my child after I die? Who will keep

Caroline safe and watch over her? I frequently see this one elderly mom in the grocery store, leading her middle-aged developmentally challenged son around the store. She looks so worn-out, and he looks so lost. For the rest of the world, time has moved on, but they have stayed in that mommy and child place for an exhausting eternity. Of course, the problem is that none of us has an eternity in this life. Some day that sweet, devoted mom in the supermarket will die, and her son will be alone, without her guidance. I don't worry so much about Lizzie. She is bright, and I believe she will be fine. Her progress is nothing short of amazing. Will she be quirky? For sure, but so is her mom, and I'm doing okay. But my Caroline, I worry about her. She is so innocent and sweet, but so vulnerable. How can I make sure she won't be like that lost man in the supermarket when I am no longer here?

One night recently I was up late, thinking and crying about Caroline and the future. I looked up and saw Lizzie standing in the kitchen, staring at me. She asked me what was wrong. What could I do but tell her the truth? I told her sometimes I get sad because I worry about who will take care of Caroline when I cannot. As much to comfort myself, I began to tell her about all the wonderful services available in our community for special people like Caroline; I told her there are people with big hearts who devote their lives to helping special adults. A look of surprise came over her, and she said, "Mommy, what are you saying? She's my sister. I'll take care of her." Of course, I don't expect that to be her full-time job; I want Lizzie to have her own life and feel the freedom to explore the world and her talents. But it was so sweet and reassuring to hear how much she loves Caroline. Caroline is her sister, and I am sure Lizzie will help to watch out for her. Their bond is strong and deep. At that moment, I realized that I have to put it in God's hands; there is love in the world, and I have to trust it.

From fear and sadness to action

When I have dark moments of sadness and fear, I make a vow to myself to keep working on both my girls' independent living skills. I remind myself I need to investigate and access all the agencies and professionals out there who work with adults with special needs. My husband works in the mental health field, and he assures me there are truly wonderful people who devote their lives towards helping children like ours when they become adults. I want to create a network of support for Caroline through family and friends. I want to work to provide for her financially. If I do my best now to construct a life for her, then I hope she can thrive when I am not here to be her advocate and guardian. I think the key is not to isolate our girls and our families. Let your daughter know the world, and let the world know your daughter. I am trying to make as many meaningful connections for my girls as possible, so that they will have a community of people in their lives beyond me.

My fears are also what fuel me to keep advocating for my girls and all the kids with special needs whom I teach and who live in my community. When I get scared, I start making lists about what I can do now, to make it better in the future. I need to change the world as much as I can, while I still can, to make it the best place for my children. One of my best contributions is working hard to educate my typical students about their peers with challenges. They are the ones who will grow up and make the decisions about how our daughters are cared for in society. I am also becoming politically active for the first time in my life, trying to push for government support and funding for programs to help our kids. Adult programs are not what they should be; we need to change that. We have come far in our culture with regard to recognizing the value of individuals with challenges. However, much more work needs to be done.

As long as I can, I will keep trying to make the world a place which values and provides for people with autism and other development challenges. We all need to be the voices for our daughters in the world. The more we talk about our kids, the more we educate the world, and the more the world will accept and include them, as well as recognize their moral obligation to provide for them in law and in deed. We must reach out to as many people as possible; and then, as with all children, raise them right, believe in their potential, and keep forging ahead.

Moving on

"Stop worrying about the world ending today. It's already tomorrow in Australia." Charlie Brown

—*Charles Schulz*

Dark moments are tough. Too bad there isn't a psychic nightlight to keep the fears away. Sometimes you just can't avoid the sadness, loneliness, or the anger. It's best to just let it come, and then let it go. Crying actually releases endorphins, which can make you feel better. Of course, there is always chocolate too. I count on prayer, my family, my friends, and the amazing potential and sweetness in my girls to get me through. Life for everyone is truly unpredictable and best lived one day at a time. Try not to look back too often, and try not to look too far ahead. Do your best now; that's all you can do. When I was growing up, and even after I got married in my 20s, I would often get worked up about something that was worrying me. I have been a lifelong worrier. As I said at the beginning of the book, there was lots of crazy turbulence for me when I was growing up. I never had an uncomplicated life; does anyone? My dad was the person I would go to for comfort. He would always say the same simple thing, and it always worked for me. "Babe, it's just a day. If it's a bad one, go to bed early, and it will all seem better in the morning." Sometimes all you can do is wake up tomorrow and try again. More often than not, tomorrow will be better. So keep the faith.

The heart of the matter about dark moments

1. As parents of children with special needs, we feel many emotions deeply. The best thing to do when you are sad or angry is allow yourself to experience the feeling and then let it retreat again like a wave.

2. Try to find the most constructive way to deal with anger by addressing situations calmly and doing the best you can to advocate for your daughter. We cannot help our feelings, but we can control how we react to them.

3. There are people who will never understand our girls or our lives because they can't or won't; that is their problem, not ours.

4. Finding someone to talk with about your feelings is so important, whether it be a friend or a therapist. Don't let pride or shame stop you from getting support and help.

5. When you are feeling overwhelmed, give yourself a break and go to bed early. Everything seems better after a good night's sleep.

Chapter 12

Special Gifts

"Everything has beauty, but not everyone sees it."

—Confucius

I knew little about the special gifts of children on the spectrum until I saw them unfolding before my eyes. Most parents I know who have children with any kind of special needs can tell you about the exceptional sweetness and innocence their children possess. Both my girls are kind and genuine in ways that I rarely find in typical kids. And I have met many children with autism who are gifted in certain areas, such as art, music, math, and spelling. Then there are the gifts of the spirit. Make no mistake, our girls have some extraordinary abilities, and perhaps the most remarkable is what they teach us about trust and love.

Open hearts

One of my girls' most remarkable gifts is the way they accept all people. They never judge people based on appearances. It is almost as if the same lack of social awareness that inhibits them in certain areas allows them to see to the heart of people and not be swayed by the superficial. They sense what really matters. I have always found both of them to be excellent judges of character. Sometimes I am struck by how fully unaware both of my girls can be about things that might bother other kids. For instance, over the years my daughter Lizzie has had a few friends who, for lack of a better description, are not terribly well groomed. She is in middle school now, and unfortunately most kids are obsessed with appearances, but not my Lizzie. One of her dearest friends always looks as if he has just walked out of a tornado, but she only describes him as the best reader and one of the smartest kids she knows. Lizzie always sees what is especially good in people, and this reminds me to do the same.

Honesty

Most children on the spectrum are also especially candid. I laugh as I write this because I know at times their complete honesty can be disarming and downright embarrassing. However, I can tell you that Caroline is incapable of lying, and Lizzie, if she ever attempts to lie, is pretty bad at it. I think their candor is one of their most endearing traits, and I always know where to go for an honest assessment of anything from my hair to my parenting. Just recently Lizzie advised me that at certain angles, especially first thing in the morning, I look exactly like my mother, who is 76 years old. Thanks, Liz! Even though I suffer the occasional insult, I remind myself that the good part is how easy it is to read my girls. While other parents are trying to figure out what's happening in their child's life, take heart that your daughter is probably a pretty open book. Just make sure that whatever you say in front of her is okay for your parish priest or Grandma to hear as well. The kindly older man who is a cashier at our local Home Depot is still recuperating from Caroline's spontaneous, deadpan explanation of my hysterectomy: "Mommy had her uterus removed. Did you know that?" He never answered her question.

Talented folks with autism

It may also hearten you to hear that many famous and successful people are now thought to have had a degree of autism, based on historical accounts of their personal lives, demeanors, and singular devotion to a field of study. Many historians believe Albert Einstein, who, according to some reports, didn't speak until he was four, is believed to have had autism, which may account in part for his scientific drive and lack of concern for his appearance—i.e. crazy hair! Painter Vincent Van Gogh, well known for his eccentricity and social struggles, is also theorized to have possessed traits symptomatic of autism (McGee 2011). Another eccentric talent, writer Emily Dickinson, is thought to have had some personality traits in line with autism, spending the majority of her time in solitude, composing her puzzling but artfully crafted poetry. Bill Gates, Microsoft creator and genius, exhibits many personality traits of someone with Asperger's. Also impressive is that fact that British mathematician Richard Borcherds, the 1998 winner of the Field's Medal (kind of the Nobel Prize for mathematics), has been diagnosed with Asperger's (Lane 2004). And, of course, our beloved Temple Grandin is always a symbol of the potential brimming just below the surface in many individuals with autism. Temple was diagnosed with severe autism as a child, didn't speak until she was three and a half, and yet went on to earn a doctorate from the University of Illinois in animal science and revolutionize the cattle industry in innovative, humane ways. She defied her diagnosis in ways that amaze the world still.

Channeling your daughter's passion

Does this mean that all people with autism have some degree of genius? Unfortunately, it does not. However, it does illustrate that autism does not preclude genius, and in certain instances the ability to focus, almost obsessively, can yield very impressive results if channeled in constructive ways. This is one of the reasons why helping your daughter to identify an interest or passion is so important. There is probably something she already loves—a television show, or a specific animal, or a game. The idea is not to fight this passion, but to find a way to use it to connect to another activity. If her amazing focus can be directed towards a creative, athletic, or academic endeavor, you may just discover there is a hidden talent there. Temple Grandin advises, "Many times I have stated that fixations should be directed into constructive channels. Parents, teachers, and therapists should work with fixations and not against them" (Grandin and Scariano 1996, p.177). If you expose your daughter to a variety of things and see which one is in line with her interests, you may be able to construct a way for her focus or area of interest to become more productive and satisfying for everyone. What she loves could well become the key to her talents and her future.

The arts, music, and more

Visual arts

Gifts in the arts and music are common in kids on the spectrum, and participation in the arts can be incredibly therapeutic because it allows for a unique kind of expression. Children can often draw or express through pictures feelings for which they cannot find the words. Also, children can participate in the arts at any level, and a child can develop skills at an individual rate. Both of my girls love all kinds of artistic pursuits. They have both always loved art class because it uses different parts of the brain, and they are both very visual learners. In addition, art allows them to express their interests in a constructive and enjoyable way. Lizzie will often use a favorite musical as the inspiration for an art project, and Caroline likes to devote her art projects to her favorite television characters. And even though they are focusing on their favorite things, they are learning new skills and finding creative ways to express themselves. Different parts of their brains are being exercised and developed through art.

There is an amazing website called Artism: The Art of Autism (http://artismtoday.com) which showcases the beautiful and moving artwork of individuals with autism. You will be in awe at the works they have created. If you read their biographies, you will see that many of the artists are quite significantly affected by autism. I was so moved looking at the paintings and reading about the artists that I was crying. However, remembering that autism is a communication disorder, it should not surprise us that, given a non-verbal medium, people with autism are able to express so much feeling and insight. Art transcends language and speaks to the heart.

One of my favorite students is a young lady with autism. She is verbal, but it is hard for her to express her feelings at times. However, she is a tremendous artist. She loves cartooning and has created an entire world of original characters intertwined with complex relationships. There is an entire hierarchy of order there that I still don't quite understand. She expresses so much through her beautiful drawings about relationships and friends and growing up. Not only is art an enjoyable endeavor for her, but it is clearly therapeutic as well. When she doesn't want to talk about something, if I ask to see a picture, she will usually show me one that opens a conversation about what's on her mind. She is now taking advanced art classes and thinking about a future in graphic design or even creating her own cartoon strip. Whatever she does with her life, I know art will continue to be a form of self-expression that allows her to process the world and her feelings.

Music

Music is another great way for your daughter to express herself and have some fun. I cannot explain it from a scientific position, but I believe there is a correlation between autism and musical talent. An article in the London *Times* cited this fascinating fact: "Scientists have found that the genes thought to cause autism may also confer mathematical, musical and other skills on people" (Leake 2008). Therefore, there may well be a link discovered between autism and musical genius. At any rate, I have known many students on the spectrum who are especially talented musicians. A dear friend of mine has a son with autism who has struggled tremendously with the academics of school but is a fantastic trombone player. He is in the elite jazz ensemble at his school. Music is appealing to kids with autism for a number of reasons, I believe. First of all, music expresses feelings and moods without words. That is huge. Also, music is well ordered, following specific rules and patterns. It is a controlled world of beauty. As with visual art, music goes straight to the soul and bypasses the stumbling blocks of verbal expression. If you do an online search, you will be stunned by how many stories there are of children with very severe autism who are also musical prodigies. The soul is an amazing thing when it finds a form of self-expression.

One summer at a camp program during my college years, I worked with a little girl who had autism, was blind and significantly mentally challenged, and spoke only a few words. She was a beautiful and sweet child, and one of the exceptional things about her was her gift of music. She loved the sun and the water, and when I would take her in the pool, we would sing. This sweet little girl had perfect pitch and the most angelic voice. At those moments, I did not notice her challenges, only her amazingly sweet voice. Music was a window into all the joy inside of her that found no other means of expression. Whenever we did anything with music at that summer camp, this little girl would light up and engage with the world around her. I am not sure what happened in the years following as I graduated from college and had to find a full-time job, so I didn't return to camp. But I thought of that little girl often and prayed that somehow her musical gift had helped her to connect to her world and given her a voice to express herself.

Lizzie, Frank Sinatra, and cartoons

Lizzie has always loved music. When she was four years old, she loved to listen to Frank Sinatra with me. For Christmas that year, all she wanted was a Frank Sinatra Barbie doll. I got her one: a collectible Barbie doll, the young Frank Sinatra, complete with bow tie and microphone. For about a year, she wouldn't go to sleep unless she had "Frank." It would make me laugh to see this preschooler, holding her Frank Sinatra doll against her little face, fast asleep. Lizzie has always loved to sing; she has a beautiful voice, participates in chorus, and has three times been in her school's musical productions, which has been a tremendous confidence builder and boost to her self-worth. Lizzie also loves to draw original cartoons. Once on a field trip, Lizzie drew cartoons for her classmates, and they were really impressed with her talent. She was so pleased to be recognized as a good artist by her peers and receive this kind of affirmation. Talents like these allowed our girls to be recognized for their positive attributes and contributions.

Caroline and the purple trumpet

Caroline also has a sweet voice and participated in chorus for several years. This past year she got her own purple trumpet and joined her school's band. It took a while for the trumpet to make sense to Caroline, but she was devoted to learning. Eventually, to my amazement, she played a five-note scale, which involves not just pressing different valves, but blowing in different ways to create the higher notes. I couldn't believe she figured out how to do it. Caroline's trumpet teacher was patient with her, and that helped tremendously. The music teachers at my children's schools have always been especially welcoming to children with special needs. I have found the arts, right through high school, to be a haven of acceptance and tolerance for all kinds of children. My daughters have benefited tremendously from their participation in art and music, and it has allowed their peers to see their talents, as opposed to their limitations. Watching Caroline sing her heart out in chorus (although at times a wee bit louder than she ought to), I can see and hear her joy at being included with her peers. And seeing her excited face as she walked onstage with her purple trumpet at the band concert was one of the best moments of my life.

Not quite prima ballerinas

Both my girls also took dance class for many years. I was fortunate to find a school where the owner was sympathetic and patient, and she treated my girls just like all the other kids. Caroline even started before she was talking much, and I could see her trying to keep up by watching the other kids, which is a fine compensatory skill she has today. We even weathered the marathon recitals for a few years, and watching them participate, or at least hang out, on stage was nothing short of miraculous. Is the New York City Ballet in their futures? No, but they did gain some social skills, body awareness, and confidence through their years at dance. A few new synapses started to fire, so it was a good experience. You never know until you try, and every kid deserves a chance to try. If you find the right dance school and teacher, your little girl may just find dance the perfect medium to express herself.

Sports really are for everyone

Many of my friends' children have benefited from sports leagues devoted to giving kids with special needs a chance. You should see if there is one in your area, and if not, start one. There will undoubtedly be many parents and children in your area who will be keen to join. This kind of proactive outreach is also healing for you as a parent, as is the camaraderie you will find with other parents in the process. I am sure we all remember the boy with autism, Jason McElwain, who made the amazing three-point shots at the high school basketball game in

2006 and gained national recognition (Dakss 2006). What a gift he had! More than the three-point shots, Jason said it was participating on the team that made a difference to him. Jason was the manager of the varsity basketball team, and was added to the roster for the last game of the year as a reward for his devotion to the team. The chance to play in that one game yielded three-point miracles. Through his love of basketball, he was a part of something larger than himself and gained the respect, admiration, and friendship of his peers. I am not saying your daughter should try out for the basketball team, just encouraging you to look at ways to help your daughter participate. If she likes sports, perhaps she could do a solo sport such as swimming or running, where there is none of the pressure of team play. Or she could help manage a sports team by assisting the coach with planning and preparation.

Sports help teach discipline, commitment, self-control, and a host of other virtues. You may also find that many of your daughter's behaviors, such as sleep issues, improve when she expends some of the energy in the pool or on the field. I read a terrific story recently about a talented young wrestler from Pennsylvania, Jeremiah Oakes. Jeremiah had a great season this year, advancing to the Eastern National tournament, and he just happens to have autism (Teatum 2011). Stories like that one prove to me that if we channel our girls' boundless energy, we can find outlets to give them a sense of pride and accomplishment, while it also helps them connect with the world.

No matter how challenged your daughter may be, there are resources out there to help her participate in a variety of activities. There are many organizations on a local and national, even international, level that provide opportunities for all children to develop their athletic abilities, be part of a group effort, and just have some fun. The most famous and prestigious, of course, is the Special Olympics. This tremendous organization allows people with all kinds of challenges to compete in athletics, and there are branches in every state in the US and 170 countries around the globe. So, if your daughter likes to run and throw balls and do somersaults, find a sport that just might become her great passion. Even if she doesn't excel on the field, she is certain to have fun and make some friends in the process.

Quirky gifts

You may also be surprised by the quirky talents you discover in your daughter. In fact, there is a higher incidence of exceptionally gifted children in the autistic population than the general population. I like to share that fact with people who appear to feel sorry for me or my children. My kids have a few unusual abilities. Caroline is like a human PalmPilot. She knows birthdates, the school calendar, and everyone's age, and she can tell me when we visited Grandma's house two summers ago to the exact date and day of the week. Caroline is also a perfect mimic; she can do all the voices of the characters on *Family Guy*. She is especially good at doing Lois Griffin. Yes, we have a watched a few episodes of *Family Guy*, always with my hand on the remote; please don't judge me!

Lizzie has an amazing memory as well, and she is very creative. She is constantly writing short stories and poetry, and is even trying her hand at writing a plot for a musical. I swear her writing is more technically accurate and fluid in style than most of the high school seniors I teach. Lizzie is also a virtual Broadway historian and can tell you who starred in the original Broadway version of *My Fair Lady*, right down to the bit parts. There are times, of course, when I attempt to steer their abilities into more functional areas, such as homework and chores. However, I always make sure to applaud their strengths and encourage them to become accomplished at what makes them happy. I think if you love something enough, you may just find a way to make a living at it someday.

If you think about it, even now, there may well be things your daughter is exceptionally good at doing, and these can be windows into her intelligence, talents, and potential. Quirky gifts can indicate much greater abilities if they are developed.

What only our kids can see

"With an eye made quiet by the power of harmony, and the deep power of joy, we see into the life of things."

—*William Wordsworth*

Perhaps the most touching gifts our children often have are what I call spiritual gifts. No matter what your faith or lack thereof, I think you will find children with special needs are more attuned to the truest nature of things. I would even say it is a kind of holy state of being at times with certain children, as if they have purer connections to God. And, in my experience, what is fascinating is that the more significant a child's special needs, the more connected to God or spirituality they seem to be. At times I wonder, because they are not as tied to our "reality," can they see what we cannot? When you think of the trivial nonsense with which our world is so often preoccupied, it makes you pause and wonder: Who are really the developmentally challenged ones?

My friend Cindi teaches a life skills class at our high school, which includes teenagers with significant developmental challenges, everything from Down's syndrome to cerebral palsy to severe autism. One day in her class she was having her students write simple poems to learn about the senses. They would write, "I hear the school bus," "I smell the cookies," and so on. One boy with autism who rarely spoke wrote this poem:

> I hear birds sing,
>
> I taste the apple,
>
> I smell the air,
>
> I feel the warm sun,
>
> I see God's face.

Kind of takes your breath away, doesn't it? She had tears in her eyes when she showed it to me. Who is to say he doesn't see the face of God? Maybe he is open to seeing in a way that we are not.

Caroline's grace

When my girls were about five and seven, and my first marriage was falling apart, I tried to seek comfort in church. I had been raised a very strict Catholic, and church for me had always been a comforting ritual of prayer and quiet contemplation. However, it wasn't really possible to bring my girls, especially Caroline, to the quiet Catholic mass. And, truthfully, at the time I was aching for more reassurance than my church seemed to offer. My sister and brother-in-law were attending a non-denominational Christian church at that time. She invited us to come along one Sunday. I had been feeling far away from God for some time. Between my exhaustion at trying to help my kids and my frustration in my marriage, I had trouble finding God. I am not sure why I said yes, but reluctantly I agreed to take my girls to this church.

When we arrived, the worship portion of the service was underway—a half-hour of music and prayer. Some of the children of the congregation were dancing in the front of the church by the band. Caroline immediately ran up and started to dance. The other kids were holding hands and dancing in a gentle, little circle, but my Caroline was really dancing up a storm. I was mortified. For Caroline at that age, there was rarely moderation in anything she did. I saw the pastor look at her, so I walked towards him to apologize and explain. As I started to talk, telling him about her autism, he touched my arm and smiled. He said the following words to me, and my perspective changed. I will always be grateful to him.

> She is perfect. God made her perfect. Never apologize for her. Don't look at her through the world's eyes. Always look at her through God's eyes.

Of course, I cried at his kindness and acceptance. But, beyond that, I swear it was a moment of revelation for me about my girls. I started to see their gifts. As we continued attending church, Caroline started talking about Jesus a lot. I would ask her who she played with on the playground, and she would say, "Brianna, and Joey, and Jesus." She would talk about Him as if he was another child in class, playing on the swings and running around with her. At Christmas that year, she insisted that we have a birthday cake for Jesus' birthday. He is so real to her. Every year now, having a Carvel ice cream cake at Christmas is part of our family tradition. She also wanted us to have a menorah, so we do that too. Religious symbols seem to captivate her. Caroline loves all things God, and she believes with such a pure faith that it inspires me to believe as well.

When friends of ours lost their son, Brandon, to a chronic heart condition a couple of years ago, Caroline talked about seeing Brandon at the beach that summer. She said he was playing in the sand with Jesus, and she laughed and smiled as if she was looking at them. It was so sweet and sincere. As she has grown and developed, Caroline doesn't mention seeing Jesus as much anymore, although she still says prayers to Him and loves Him. Perhaps she has entered "our" world enough now that the spiritual one isn't as close as it once was. But seeing the "other" world through her eyes was so affirming and comforting to me at a time when I needed it most. Caroline gave me back my faith—just one of the many gifts my daughters have given to me. I guess I named her Caroline Grace for a reason.

What we would lose without autism

Recently I was asked how I would feel if there was a "cure" suddenly discovered that would take the autism from my children. It was an intriguing question, and I found it harder to answer than the person who asked me expected it to be. Of course, I want my children to have as many opportunities for independence as possible and I want them to have all the choices other people have. So, in that sense, of course, especially with Caroline, I would wish for a cure. I would be lying if I said otherwise. But autism brings with it certain gifts that are so interwoven into who my girls are as people that it is hard to imagine who they would be without it.

A recent article in the London *Times* explained that if we were to genetically eliminate autism, we would lose many geniuses from the world (Linklater 2008). And as much as I would want my daughters to experience all they desire, there would be something lost if they suddenly became typical kids. Autism makes them different in some ways, but it also brings out so many beautiful parts of them. Anyone who has spent time with children and adults with special needs knows about the grace and innocence they possess. Our children have many special gifts, even if the world doesn't always acknowledge them. They remind us on a daily basis what matters and what endures beyond the busyness that preoccupies a day. If you help your daughter find her gifts, you may be surprised by how bountiful they are, and how your life is enriched in the process. So let me reassure you, as that pastor reassured me: Your daughter is perfect. Look at her through God's eyes, not the world's eyes, and you will see much that is exceptional and sacred hidden there.

The heart of the matter about special gifts

1. Having autism does not preclude being gifted or having talents.

2. Many children with autism have unique talents for the visual arts and music.

3. Finding a way to channel your daughter's fixations or obsessions into something constructive will make everyone happy.

4. Some kids with autism are also fine athletes. But even those who are not talented athletically can benefit from the camaraderie and exercise of sports.

5. Some of our children's sweetest gifts may be those of the spirit. Keep looking for your daughter's gifts and I know you will find them to be amazing.

Chapter 13

Outtakes, Mistakes, and C is for Crazy

---

*"My mother had a great deal of trouble with
me, but I think she enjoyed it."*

—*Mark Twain*

By this point in the book, you may be getting tired of my optimism.
You may be saying, "Doesn't this woman get how hard this is?" Well,
I certainly do. For four years after my divorce, I did the whole thing
alone, as a single mommy, and had to return to work full-time as well.
My dad had been diagnosed with Alzheimer's at the time, and my
mom was his caregiver, so I had no help at all. When I say alone, I
mean *really* alone. So trust me when I say that I get how crazy, tired,
and frustrated you can feel. I have had my share of less than glorious
moments. And although sharing my mistakes and screw-ups is not my
favorite pastime, I wouldn't be honest if I didn't admit to the many
times I have been less than Polly-Perfect as a mom. It seems I vacillate
between trying to do the super-mommy thing and pulling my hair
out. Raising kids with special challenges is not for the faint of heart,
and there are times when I am pretty close to crazy as I try to rise
to the occasion. As much as I love them, they can make life mighty
tricky at times. For instance, they have a tendency to lack subtlety,
as when they say the absolute worst thing at the worst time, such
as, "Happy Birthday, Grandma. Do you like your present? Mommy
says you will return it like everything else we give you." Oh, for the
smallest bit of social wisdom! Plus, I can feel pretty worn-out from
all the advocating I have to do for them at school. If we wrote the
IEP, why can't anyone read and follow it? But I think my toughest

moments have come when I have come up against the iron wills of my children. In this chapter I want to just share some of the most embarrassing moments, just so you know that we all go through this.

R is for routine

I understand why my kids need routine more than most. The sensory overload of autism is a kaleidoscope of sights, sounds, and smells. Our girls' rituals are like road markers that help them focus in the midst of confusion. So I try to be patient, just as I try to increase their flexibility by changing routines at times. But some of these rituals are hard to break and they can drive me crazy. Caroline has to go to bed at exactly the same time every night. Then there is our after-school routine; Caroline likes to ask me the same questions every day, and she often feeds me my lines. You can project the flat affect in the tone, as you have heard it yourself. This is our conversation every day after I pick her up from school:

> "Mommy, aren't you going to ask me how was art today?" Caroline asks every day after school.
>
> "How was art today, Caroline?" I ask as sunnily as possible, a smile on my face.
>
> "I didn't have art today," she will answer.
>
> Then she continues, "Mommy, aren't you going to ask me how was science today?"
>
> "How was science today, Caroline?" I ask, slightly less sunny.
>
> "Science was good. Mommy. Aren't you going to ask me how was PE today?" Caroline continues, unfazed by the change in my tone of voice.
>
> "How was PE today, Caroline?" I respond, cloudy with a chance of rain.
>
> "I didn't have PE today," she will answer.
>
> She persists in earnest. "Mommy, aren't you going to ask me how was social studies today?"

"How was social studies today, Caroline?" I ask, starting to drizzle.

Dear Lord, I think, how many classes are there in a school day?

We continue until we have gone through every subject and exhausted her schedule. Does it drive me crazy? Yes! Is it her way of conversing? Yes, it is. Do I try to steer her towards more spontaneous conversation? I do, but sometimes I am tired and we just have our little Abbot and Costello routine. Caroline also likes to ask repeatedly questions she knows the answers to, such as "When is Christmas?" and my personal favorite, "How old are you, Mommy?" And she is nothing if not persistent and thorough. She could make a great lobbyist someday!

S is for Sugar Plum Fairy

It is not just the sometimes maddening routines that have caused me to lose my mind. It is the stubbornness that both of my girls possess, the sheer battle of wills, which can make me wacky. When Caroline was in third grade, around Christmastime her class was taking a field trip to see the ballet *The Nutcracker* at a local theatre. Normally she didn't like leaving school for field trips because it disrupted her routine. So I was surprised when she seemed to be excitedly looking forward to this trip. She had taken ballet for several years, so I just attributed the change in her attitude to her love of dance and her increased maturity. At this point I was a newly single mom and had just returned back to teaching full-time. Getting the three of us up and out in the morning was a daily miracle, and we were always rushing. I wanted to be the exemplary employee because I needed my job, and I couldn't be late or my students would be crowded in the hall outside the locked homeroom door.

The morning of the field trip, I dressed Caroline in a lovely holiday dress, hair done in a bow, and Lizzie was all set as well. I went to put on my make-up, congratulating myself on how well I was doing at all this. When I came out into the kitchen to put on our coats and leave, Caroline was standing in the middle of the room wearing a pink tutu about three sizes too small, purple tights, and ballet slippers. Smiling, she announced to me, "Pretty." It then dawned on me that Caroline didn't think she was watching *The Nutcracker*, she thought she was starring in *The Nutcracker*! What happened next was not pretty. I knew I couldn't let her go to school in a tutu in the middle of winter, and I didn't know how to convey to her that she would just be sitting in the theatre watching the dancers. I had no time to discuss it with her, so I just tried to be firm and matter-of-fact, but that didn't work very well. "Caroline," I said with authority, "you cannot wear the tutu. You are watching the ballet from a chair in the audience. We have to put your dress back on." Of course, she would have none of it. It turned into a battle of wills, and an ugly scene ensued. As I fought with her to tug the tutu off and put her dress back on, she kept screaming, "Caroline is the Sugar Plum Fairy!" By the time she was redressed, she and I were both crying, and Lizzie was watching in horror. When I dropped them off at school, Caroline wouldn't look at me. She wasn't fighting me anymore; she was just whimpering, defeated. I felt terrible all day about it. She enjoyed the show, but her teacher did tell me she kept repeating somberly to herself, "Caroline is not the Sugar Plum Fairy.'" It still makes me sad to think about it. Maybe I just should have let her wear the tutu.

B is for bug or buggy

Lizzie's stubbornness has put me through some stress also. When she was about five, she saw part of a documentary on television about bugs that terrified her. I am not sure why, but since she had been a baby, bugs had always freaked her out. Because the show had been on in the evening, she became hysterical if we turned on the television after dark. In her little mind, a direct correlation had been made between night-time and scary bugs on television. Unfortunately, this was in January and the days were mighty short! There is not a whole lot to do in upstate New York on January evenings, and I am the first to admit that television is my welcome escape from reality. However, Lizzie was militant. If we even tried to turn the television on, she would begin to scream that high-pitched scream only little girls can emit. And it was genuine, gut-wrenching fear in her howls. I tried everything to reassure her: comforting words, showing her the television guide and letting her pick just one channel to watch, and giving her the remote to hold so she could turn the television off if anything frightened her. I even went so far as to put a blanket over the television screen to hide the picture, and just have the sound on to try to ease her gently into feeling safe. Nothing worked. She would simply go crazy if the television was on in the evening, even if she was down the hall. I swear Lizzie has bionic hearing!

I remember one evening in particular when I just lost it. She was clutching the remote for all she was worth, and I wanted it. Suddenly, I just had to have the stinking remote. I missed my sit-coms. Her bizarre phobia was controlling our lives. I couldn't take the irrationality of it anymore, so I started to rant to her about bugs and their important role in the food chain and the ecosystem. In the middle of my passionate plea on behalf of insects everywhere, I started to try to pry the remote from her iron little hands. In the midst of the tug of war, I looked at her desperate little face and realized that I was quickly becoming the crazy one. Her bug phobia had made me buggy! So I just kind of gave up on the television for a while. I didn't win; I just let it go. Sometimes the best thing we can learn from our kids is how to surrender. While the snow fell that winter, we read a lot of books and played a lot of Candy Land. I missed the entire Winter Olympics that year, but I spent some sweet time with my daughters. Finally, spring came and the days got longer. The television stayed on later and later. By summer she had forgotten all about it, and the next fall we could watch television in the evening without incident. It's the kind of thing no one can understand unless they have a child like ours. People would say, "Just turn the television on and she'll get over it." What they don't understand is that the Herculean will of a child on the spectrum is nothing short of epic! Times do change, however. This past summer I was throwing a bit of a hissy fit because we had bees on our deck and they were driving me crazy every time I went out there. Lizzie shook her head in dismay and chided me, "Mommy, they're just bees. Get a grip." I bit my tongue, but the small sad pop that followed was my head exploding.

M is for marker

Of course, there are countless other times when I have been less than patient, when I have thought I couldn't handle things. A few years ago Caroline was obsessed with earrings. However, she was too afraid to get her ears pierced, so I bought her stick-on earrings. One morning before school, she ran out of them because she had stuck them on all her stuffed animals and dolls. She was in the midst of a complete Charlie Brown fixation at the time. When she realized she had no earrings to wear, she began to shout her favorite line of indignation, lifted from *It's the Great Pumpkin, Charlie Brown*: "Trick or treats come only once a year. And I missed it by sitting in a pumpkin patch with a blockhead. YOU OWE ME RESTITUTION!" I knew when I heard her recite Sally's speech about missing tricks or treats that I was in trouble. This was a line of echolalia she reserved for only the direst of situations! She refused to get in the car without earrings, and I was going to be really late.

In desperation, I told Lizzie to get me the markers. While Lizzie watched in half-puzzlement and half-shock, I drew little pink dot earrings on Caroline's ears with a marker. No lie, I drew on my daughters ear lobes because it was the only way I could get her in the car. In my defense, they were non-toxic Mr. Fiddlestick markers and it worked. She checked it out in the mirror, and then contentedly hopped in the car with her marker earrings. After I dropped my girls off at school that day, I was thinking as I drove to work, "I actually drew on my daughter's ears! What kind of a mother am I?" But I know my Caroline's iron will, and I had to get to work. I am not proud of that moment, and I recommend against drawing on your children as a rule, but sometimes desperate times call for desperate markers...uh, I mean measures.

B is also for butterflies

My favorite Caroline story that describes life on the spectrum has to do with her class trip to the Bronx Zoo in the third grade. My girls' elementary school makes a big deal of the third-grade year. They learn a lot about animals and biology, and the year culminates in a day trip to the Bronx Zoo, a three-hour bus trip from our home in Saratoga to the Bronx. I had chaperoned when Lizzie went, so I was more than happy to go with Caroline. Caroline wanted to attend the trip, but was nervous because she has a fear of elephants. She says they are too loud, which is comical for a girl whose occasional shrieks can shatter crystal, who speaks loudly in all situations, and who chose to play the trumpet in band. However, I reassured her that we would not have to visit the elephants, but could see the quieter animals. So, to the zoo we decided to go, with Caroline dressed in pink shorts and top, pink socks, a magenta visor, and her favorite sneakers which lit up like sparklers as she walked. We departed school as the sun rose at 6 a.m., arriving at the zoo around 9.30. We had until 4.30 to explore the zoo. That's right, seven hours total in one place!

Well, Caroline seemed determined to run through the exhibits, fearing elephants at every turn. And by 11.30, we had seen nearly every exhibit, chomped on pretzels, popped popcorn, dripped ice cream, slurped slurpies, and she wanted to "go home on the bus." We sat on a bench by the sea lions for a while; actually, I was sitting, and she was sprawling on the bench, whining to go home. She decided she didn't really like the zoo, and we had five more hours there. I was really questioning my decision to go on the trip. I always want to give my children the chance to participate in everything, but sometimes I overestimate what they can handle. We were both hot and miserable when I spotted the butterfly house. It was an enchanting-looking solarium with giant metal butterflies decorating it. Caroline always loved butterflies. She had butterfly books when she was little and has a butterfly pillow she sleeps with every night. So it was easy to convince her we could spend some time in the butterfly house.

The exhibit was tight on security because inside the butterflies flutter free. You have to go in one door and shut it tightly behind you, and then only when it is shut to the satisfaction of the guard can you enter the next door into the butterfly room—a very Wonka-esque chocolate room. There was an exceptionally grave woman inside the door, a kind of butterfly head librarian, who scolded us in a raspy whisper that we must do the same when we exited on the other side. I guess butterflies are disturbed by loud voices—uh-oh. We stepped inside and I could see Caroline's mouth gape open in amazement. The butterfly room was amazing. Inside, thousands of exotic butterflies fluttered around in streaks of purples and pinks and golds. Sunlight streamed through walls of windows. It was truly ethereal, and Caroline was mesmerized. She was smiling so big, wandering around in heaven, looking angelic. I sat down on a bench to rest, relieved to have her so happily occupied. It was peaceful in the solarium. Plus it was air-conditioned, so the little bugs didn't perspire. A perfect place to stay for a while.

For a long time, Caroline was content just to look at the butterflies, and I was congratulating myself on always knowing how to handle every situation. Yes, I was actually starting to relax. In fact, I was staring into space when I saw her dart suddenly across the room. I guess she had become so happy with the butterflies that she decided she wanted to take one or two of them home. So she started grabbing at them, gently at first, but then, with each failure to catch a butterfly, she became more determined. Soon it was a furious grab; she looked as if she was on a game show in a glass booth snatching at the air for dollar bills. I tried to stop her discreetly by motioning to her, but that didn't work, so I started to yell, "Caroline, no hands!" It was a phrase from preschool used to stop Caroline when she was grabbing at something that wasn't hers. However, it didn't have the intended effect. She stopped grabbing all right, and started stomping at the butterflies that were flying close to the ground. By God, that child has quick reflexes! Those pink sneakers were lighting up like a slot machine, and butterflies were dropping, well, like flies. As soon as I could reach her, I dragged her towards the door. I was yelling at her, and the butterfly librarian was screaming at us. Caroline got scared and broke away from me. She blasted through the first door, then immediately blasted through the second door, letting sunlight and a gust of wind invade the sanctuary of the butterflies. I could hear the butterfly lady screaming in horror, but we just kept running and panting down the path away from the scene of the crime.

When we finally stopped in front of the great ape house, I was screaming, my hands waving like one the less evolved ape house occupants. I yelled at Caroline for running, for stomping, for embarrassing me, and for getting me in trouble with the Queen of Butterfly Hearts. I was not super-Mommy; I was crazy-screechy Mommy. Eventually we just started walking, both of us whimpering quietly. The day ended five long hours later, after several hot dogs and about a dozen rides on the Bug Carousel where Caroline glanced fleetingly at a butterfly, and then martyredly rode a cricket. As we traveled home on the bus, I winced at the vision of some ancient custodian sweeping up the crushed carcasses of exotic butterflies. But I winced more at the way I yelled at Caroline. She was asleep all the way, looking innocent and exhausted from the day's drama. I regretted my rant, for worrying more about the way we looked to strangers than the way Caroline felt. I hoped there weren't too many insect casualties, but I realized that I couldn't blame Caroline for wanting one of those butterflies. They were spectacular, and it isn't every day that she sees something as rare and exquisite as she is herself.

I think the key to sanity is laughing. How else can you get through the play-date where other kids mold animals and your kid eats the Play-Doh? Or the times you have to leave a restaurant because some unacceptable food has touched your daughter's plate? Or the times you bungle a mild situation, only making it worse? We have all been embarrassed, humbled, and made crazy by our kids at times. If you haven't, you are either a saint or heavily medicated. I can say I have never spanked my girls and I never will. I always love them more than life, even if there are times I think I will lose it. They have made me a more patient, kinder, better person. I have a perspective on life now about what really matters. And even if I occasionally lose my perspective in a moment of craziness, I think I am doing a pretty good job. Parents don't have to be perfect. Our kids need to see us make mistakes, and they need to see we are people too. Even though they have challenges, they need to learn to be kind and considerate as well. So forgive yourself for occasionally messing up. It happens to all of us. We are being called to do something that takes a lot of strength, and at times we are just tired. When I feel as if I can't do it anymore, I just go to bed early. It always seems better in the morning. Oh, and hugging your daughter always helps too!

The heart of the matter about craziness

1. Craziness is part of the job description of being a special parent. It's okay.

2. The best thing is to expect the unexpected. The moment you think you have it under control, you're toast.

3. We have all made bizarre accommodations to appease our kids; we just don't admit it. Don't worry: you are not a pushover, just a human being.

4. We all lose it at times. Just apologize to your daughter if you yell or cry. She loves you and she will forgive you, sometimes too readily. Always remember her feelings matter more than what strangers think, even butterfly librarians.

5. If you are going to survive, you have to learn to laugh loudly and often. Seeing the humor in life is the only way to make it through and have some fun along the way.

Chapter 14

Relationships

> *"Let us be grateful to people who make us happy; they are the charming gardeners who make our souls blossom."*
>
> —*Marcel Proust*

I struggled with how to write this section. I have shared my experiences helping my daughters establish friendships. So I think it is important to talk about my relationships as well, because your special circumstances with your daughter may impact your relationships. As with any challenging event in life, people will have a variety of reactions to your daughter's special needs, and your relationships with them may improve or fall away. For me, over time it was as if someone had given "character truth serum" to everyone I knew, and revealed things at times I did not want to see. I did discover through my experiences, however, that I have some truly wonderful people in my life, some family and some friends. And I have had the great fortune to find more along the way. Support will come to you from the most unexpected of places.

But first I should address the not so supportive folks you may meet. They may be family or they may be friends, but, either way, they are anything but helpful.

Bad news blamers

The most painful people are the blamers—people who want the autism or the autistic behaviors to be your fault. Although we do not know what creates autism, we do know it is not caused by anything that a mother or father does in the care or raising of a child. So people who are blamers need to be moved immediately out of your sphere of existence. I actually had a family member tell me at one point, in anger, "Look, you need to make that child be normal!" It remains one of the most ignorant and hurtful things anyone has said to me. I realized at that moment not to listen to what that person had to say. She was frustrated with my daughter, but, knowing that her frustration was inappropriate, chose to blame me. Sometimes, when people lack the adequate patience or compassion to deal with something, they want to attack, rather than admit their own failings. Blaming you for your child's autism is a way to avoid their own inability to deal with it.

Other people need to find some way to make it your fault, so they can feel they can protect themselves from it. If you caused it, then they can make sure they prevent it. It is similar to the unkind reaction some people have to others' illnesses. Often when someone is diagnosed with a terrible illness, someone else says that the person didn't take care of him or herself, attributing blame. When people can ascribe blame or explain a cause for something, they can comfort themselves that it won't happen to them. It's crazy because most difficult things in life are, as my students would say, "totally random." Whatever the reason, people who blame you are detrimental to your well-being and you should avoid them as best you can. The truth is that what you are facing just plain scares them, and their fear is toxic to you.

Aggravating advisors

Equally discouraging are people who are full of advice but little understanding. It may be your mother or mother-in-law, but someone will see a 30-second spot on the evening news and tell you what you should do. Suddenly they are an expert and you are not doing enough. I know they may be trying to be helpful, but it always feels like more pressure to me. When I have spent the day dealing with my girls' frustrated tears, battling teachers, and researching therapies, in addition to working full-time, the last thing I need is to be told about one more thing I "must" do if I love my child. That is one of the reasons I find the current rash of "healing" stories so upsetting. When a celebrity goes on television telling the world she has "healed" her child, people think anyone can. I cannot tell you how many people have recommended I read certain books, so I can "fix" my kids. As if it is easy or desirable to change who people are. I had one woman at my daughter's dance class chastise me when I told her Caroline had autism, "You know, there's a diet that cures that." I could think of a couple of choice things she could shove in her mouth! I think people with typical kids often want to feel that their good fortune is attributable to their virtue; therefore, our children's challenges are reflective of our flaws. And from that faulty logic on high, bad advice will flow. Their kids are easy, they were born that way, and it is luck. When I spot one of those self-aggrandizing helpers, I run as fast as I can. Information is helpful. Lectures and pressure to fix your daughter are not.

Fleeting and fleeing friends

I have to say there was a pretty marked attrition rate to my friendships in the years following my girls' diagnoses. Maybe it is just reflective of the middle-class community in which I live, or maybe it is just our culture, but a good number of parents I know are fiercely competitive and have mighty aspirations for their kids. Some of the moms I knew from my girls' nursery schools just weren't interested in having their kids be friends with mine anymore, and thus weren't interested in continuing friendships with me. These are people for whom social status is everything, and they are focused on moving their kids up the social ladder. The irony is that when I see them now, they are still not satisfied. If their child is on the soccer team, it is not enough because he is not the star. If their daughter is in the school musical, they are not happy unless she is the lead. They don't get it. They don't appreciate their good fortune, and some of them do not even seem to be enjoying their kids. I consider myself lucky to have shed those people along the way. In their race to the top of the class, or the homecoming podium, or Harvard, or wherever the heck they are going, they are not enjoying their kids' childhoods and the gift of family. And the truth is life is so crazily unpredictable that to build your life on social status and vain pursuits is to set yourself up for one Willy Loman of a fall anyway. But if I told them that, it would just sound like bitterness, and I am sure there is some bitterness in there. So I just say adios and welcome the room in my life for a better batch of friends.

Friends of the heart

> *"Friendship is born at that moment when one person says to another: 'What! You, too? Thought I was the only one.'"*
>
> —C.S. Lewis

My true friends are those who accept me and my children just as we are. And as with so many other things, my children have been a blessing in this way. For one thing, Caroline especially is drawn to people with kind hearts and warmth, and I can see her visibly withdraw around people who are cold and superficial. She has a tremendous instinct about people's internal goodness. Furthermore, if someone is not comfortable around my kids, that tells me volumes about their character. Good people don't judge and don't limit whom they can accept and love. Some of my dearest friends are people who either have kids like my girls or work with kids who have special needs. There is simply no substitute for understanding and true empathy. Joining a parent support group can be a great way to find friends who get it. I have family members who are terrific and those who are not. I limit the time I spend with those who lack understanding and compassion. I will not subject my children to people who make them feel bad about themselves, or make me feel bad about my parenting. I have learned to rethink family. Family to me is the people who love and support you unconditionally, and those are the people with whom I want my girls to spend time. They have several "adopted" aunts and uncles who are their family as they know it.

Love and marriage, or something resembling it
Marriage

Romantic relationships can be another quandary in the life of a special parent. My girls' dad and I divorced when they were six and eight, after 14 years of marriage. We had been together since we were in our early 20s, for 17 years total. I do not want to say too much about my first marriage out of respect for my ex-husband's privacy, except that the end of our marriage was sad and life-changing. Divorce in families where there are children with autism is estimated to be anywhere from 50 percent to 80 percent, depending on the study you read. I don't believe this is the fault of the children, and I am always careful to make sure my daughters know this. As with so many other things, our children's presence just brings to light dynamics that are already there. I think, with my first marriage, the stresses of parenting just revealed the fault lines that had always existed. I believe this is true for all parents, whether their children have special needs or not. That said, there are unique stresses when raising special kids, and there are a few crucial things couples need to do in order to support the marriage.

When a child is diagnosed with a developmental challenge, both parents must commit to being a part of their child's life and participate in parenting. You both need to make peace with the new reality of your lives and seek counseling to help you both adjust. There needs to be agreement between the two of you about how best to approach helping your daughter. If there is disagreement, it is essential that you talk about it and resolve it before taking action. That means both parents need to be educated about treatment options and educational philosophies. Even if one parent is the main caregiver, the other parent needs to take the time to listen and learn. Also, you need to be a team and support each other as you parent. That involves giving each other breaks from parenting and sharing the responsibilities as equally as you can. Try not to take your frustrations out on each other. This happens frequently. There are stresses, and because you certainly cannot become angry with your daughter for struggling, sometimes you may unknowingly turn your anger toward your spouse. Remember, your spouse is your partner in this, not your adversary, and it is no one's fault. Dealing with the challenges of parenting special children does not have to be a strain on a marriage. I know couples whose marriages were strengthened by their joint commitment to helping their children. So I encourage you to keep talking and sharing, and really commit to being in it together. It is the best thing for your children and your marriage.

You also still need to take time to be a couple and enjoy being with each other. Being parents doesn't mean you have to give up being people. However you can manage it, hire a babysitter and go out as a couple. In any marriage, keeping the connection between spouses strong is essential. With all the added busyness of raising a child with special needs, it is easy to lose each other along the way. You share a very special bond as the parents of an extraordinary daughter, and no one loves or understands her as you do. Your spouse will understand how you feel better than anyone if you just take the time to share your feelings and listen to his or hers. Also, sometimes go out and don't talk about the kids at all—just have fun. You have to cultivate the happiness in your marriage because it is the air your child breathes. So devote time to your marriage; it is better for you and your special little girl.

A word for dads

There is so much pressure having a child with special needs, not the least of which is worrying about finances. In many of the families I know, the moms are staying at home to oversee the children's programs and interventions, and the dads are working overtime to support the family. If this is your situation, I know both people can feel overtaxed and under-appreciated. I know moms can feel isolated and lonely, and at times it is hard to see progress for all your effort. So while I know dads are doing their best, just remember that, as hard as you are working, you are having a chance to escape the never-ending needs of the child and be someone else for a while. Try to remember to give your wife some time to be alone. Encourage her to get out of the house for a while when you get home and have some time to herself. This will also give you a chance to connect with your daughter, and your wife will be very appreciative of the support.

When your special child is a daughter, it may seem logical as a dad to let your wife handle the majority of the parenting. Please do not bow out of the parenting. As a mother and teacher, I have seen how critical it is for all girls to feel loved and valued by their fathers. It is even more critical for a little girl to feel totally accepted and loved by both parents when she is facing so many challenges outside the home. Find some parenting jobs that are yours to do with your daughter—maybe the bedtime routine, or teaching her how to ride a bike, or play a sport. If your wife is shouldering most of the work, be good to her and give her support and praise. It is not easy to be the nurturer, teacher, and role model. However you and your wife configure your family, be sure you are there for your daughter and that she knows how much you love her and accept her just as she is.

Dating and other situation comedies

For me, there was life after my first marriage, but it took some time to take form. If anyone reading this is the single parent of a child with autism, take heart. You also deserve to be happy and have a life outside of parenting. There must be balance, and your daughter must come first, but you are not selfish for trying to have something for yourself. Actually, having time away from your children, spent with another adult, is both rejuvenating for you and healthy for your kids. I think many parents feel they must focus 100 percent on their children, but this is detrimental to everyone involved. Children need to know they can be okay apart from their parents for a while, and parents need to remember to be people. Our parenting jobs can be consuming, and if you lose perspective and joy, that is not helpful to your kids. You may begin to see you children as a burden, and they will feel your resentment. Likewise, if you don't carve out a life of your own, your daughter may eventually feel the pressure of being your whole purpose in life. I have met parents who depend so much on their child for purpose and identity that it actually causes them subconsciously to impede their child's independence. The bottom line is that having a life of your own is good for you and your special girl. So whether it is white-water rafting or online dating, do your best to make time to be a person, and don't feel guilty about it!

If you do decide to date, all I can say is dating as a single parent of any child can be a comical, if sometimes impossible, task. When your child has challenges, it can be even more daunting. But if you stay optimistic, it can work out. After I was divorced, I was terrified to start dating again, so I let friends set me up. The first thing you should know is that once you hit 35 your friends have only one criterion for setting you up with someone: it is the only single person they know! That's it—he could be an unemployed, humorless, Ichabod Crane look-a-like, and they will set you up with him because he is single and you are single. I went on quite a few bad dates, and I mean *bad* dates. And after the tremendous effort it took for me to arrange my life to actually leave my house, that was mighty disappointing. However, it was an educational experience for me.

As with friendships, I found the way people responded to the fact I had girls with challenges to be a great filter. Any man who had a negative reaction wasn't worthy of being in my life or theirs.

It would always hurt my feelings when a man acted dismayed or put off by my girls, but it was also informative and saved me a lot of time. The few times my girls did have occasion to meet a man I dated, I found both my girls' reactions and the man's reactions tremendously revealing. Since my girls never held back, I always knew exactly what they thought. So rather than worrying about how or when to tell someone you are dating about your daughter's autism, I say just tell them. Hiding it makes it seem as if it is something bad, and it is not. Be open about who your kids are and you will find someone worthy of your heart and your children's time and love.

After a series of misadventures, I met a very special man, who is now my husband and my girls' stepfather. From the very beginning, my husband never hesitated for a minute when I told him my girls have special needs. He was open and willing to know them and love them. He thinks they are great kids, and he doesn't treat them any differently than he would typical children. Because of this, he has helped me to see more fully their potential and ability. It took time to find the right person and at times I was ready to give up, but I am glad I didn't. I believed God would send someone right for us, and my husband was worth the wait.

A better life

Your life as the parent of a special child will affect your relationships, but it need not be in a negative way. As a mother of special girls, I have gained the courage to confront ignorant people and the wisdom to know when to walk away from a person who has nothing to offer to us. My girls and their special gifts have refined my relationships, allowing me to recognize and invest in the most valuable ones. The friends I have now are people whom I trust deeply with my children's feelings as well as my own. They are people who have generous hearts and emotional depth. Because of my children, I have met extraordinary parents of other extraordinary kids who have enriched my life immeasurably. I have been lucky enough to find a man to share my life who loves my girls and me just as we are. All of my relationships have been redefined, but strengthened and improved, I believe, through the privilege of being Caroline's and Lizzie's mom.

The heart of the matter about relationships

1. You have the right to have helpful, supportive people in your life.

2. Toxic people, blamers, and know-it-alls, be they family or not, should be kept as far away as possible. No one should give unsolicited advice because, unless they are living it, they don't have a clue.

3. True friends and family will love and accept you and your children just as you are. Being able to see who is a true friend is one of the blessings of having special kids.

4. Protect your marriage; it is your daughter's foundation and her model for a happy, healthy adult relationship.

5. You still deserve to be you and have time to yourself. Having adult friendships and relationships will support you and make you a better parent.

Chapter 15

Taking Care of You

> *"A good laugh and a long sleep are the best cures in the doctor's book."*

—Irish Proverb

While you are navigating the myriad of ways to help your daughter, one of the things you must not forget to do is take care of yourself. As parents in general, but especially as parents of special kids, we often put ourselves last on our own list of priorities. However, remember the advice you receive when you are on an airplane. The parent must get the oxygen mask first, so they can be sure to take care of the child. Your daughter's survival and success depends on yours, so protect her best friend, advocate, and teacher. Take care of you!

Eat, sleep, and be merry... Oh, and exercise too!
Get off the computer and go to sleep!

First and foremost, you must get enough sleep. If your daughter is not a good sleeper, focus on remedying that immediately. Prioritizing what needs to be addressed first for your family is essential, and sleep is priority number one. You need to be sufficiently well rested to run the family. I remember all too well the walking-zombie days of no sleep, and, I can tell you, life is so much more manageable now that I can sleep through the night. Have your daughter's pediatrician address this immediately if it is an issue. Also, don't keep yourself up late working on things once your daughter is asleep. The housework can wait; it just gets dirty again anyway. Resist the urge to surf the net looking for treatments and therapies. Have a cup of chamomile tea, and tuck yourself in at a reasonable time. Sleep is an absolute necessity!

Try to eat healthily most of the time

The second priority has to be eating right. As best as you can, try to eat healthy foods, with the occasional treat! One of the good things about examining your daughter's diet for food allergies is that it makes you more conscious of what your whole family is eating. We really do feel better when we put healthy stuff in our bodies. Also, be sure to take a multivitamin every day. Facing the sometimes confounding behaviors of kids with autism is much harder when you are sick. So the better you can eat, the healthier you will stay. I know I tend to seek comfort in food. As a matter of fact, I love food. I will definitely allow myself treats sometimes—ice cream, cheese and crackers, chips. I just try to make sure I don't do it every day. I try to find other indulgences such as baths and good books because food can get *too* comforting! As with all things, try to keep your comfort foods to a minimum. Remember how important you are to your daughter's well-being, and treat your body with respect.

Exercising your demons

I know telling you to exercise may make you grimace. It seems like one more chore to do. However, that endorphin rush can really make you feel a whole lot better. I cannot get to a gym, ever! So I bought a NordicTrack second-hand from a neighbor, and I keep it in my basement. I try to use it for about 40 minutes, three to four times a week. And, yes, I am often interrupted by the kids, and it is hard, and I struggle. But I do feel better after I am done. And lest you think it is easy, let me describe how it goes.

I arrive home from work and help Caroline with her shower. She still needs assistance washing her hair. Afterwards, I have to blow dry and straighten her hair. Then the girls and my husband eat dinner while I sort out laundry and other chores. After that I make sure the girls are set with homework and then off on their leisure activities—Wii, computer, reading, and so on. My husband watches them and I head to the basement. My basement is not finished—it is the musty elephant graveyard for old clothes, furniture I haven't quite given up on, my husband's old Air Force stuff, and artificial Christmas trees. In the middle of the floor are my NordicTrack and my boombox. When I say boombox, I am not kidding—this boombox is vintage; it could have been a prop from the movie *Car Wash* or *Xanadu*. I usually put on my 1980s retro CDs and begin to sweat. Typically it's the Ramones or Poison, but sometimes it's Broadway show tunes. My attire is any old T-shirt and shorts. This and the beet-red face I immediately get upon exerting myself are why I can't be seen at a gym. Many times as I sweat and pant, I will hear the basement door open, and one of my girls will come halfway down the stairs and ask me a question, or ask me to do something. I scream over the music, "Leave Mommy alone. Let me exercise." They reluctantly leave, but they will return. As I get sweatier and more fatigued, when they return, I can only manage to yell, "Privacy!" It is an ugly scene, to say the least. As I am sure you experience, privacy is the one thing I long for the most sometimes. In fact, I think my tombstone should read, "Alas, she never got to pee in private." But I don't give up—I ski forward in my basement, while staying paradoxically in place, through frustration and the smell of mold.

And when I am done, I feel tremendous relief. I feel calm and ready to deal with a whole new list of issues. I hate doing it, but I like how I feel when I am done. When I finally arrive at the top of the stairs to rejoin civilization, I am a sweaty mess, my hair all curly and puffy and sticking up all over, and my face tomato-red. If I have worked out hard enough, Caroline will usually look at my Krusty the Clown hairdo and calmly proclaim, "Mommy, you have Grandma hair." Mission accomplished.

This parenting job can bring a lot of stress, not necessarily from your daughter, but from dealing with the ignorance of other people. Exercising has helped to keep the middle-age spread down and my spirits up. Don't set crazy Olympic goals for yourself; you don't have to run a marathon. Exercise because it will make you feel better when you are done. If you make it part of your routine, you will find it easier to manage. Even though my kids bug me, they have pretty much accepted that I am not going to search for anything in the house or prepare a snack during my 40 minutes of exercise. They complained at first, but now they just begrudgingly accept it as part of life. Do not feel guilty about taking the time to exercise. You deserve to be healthy and sane!

Just be you for a night

You also deserve a night out, so get out of the house without your children once in a while. I know this can seem like a mighty task, but it is so worth it. Remembering you are an actual person, and not just a mom or dad, can feel great. Go have dinner or coffee with a friend. Go to a movie and just zone out for a while. Try to cultivate a list of people who can watch your daughter comfortably; maybe trade off babysitting with other parents of kids on the spectrum. That way there is no worrying or explaining about some of your daughter's more unusual behaviors. You have to really make an effort to do this, but you will be glad you did. We all need a break from our kids, especially when our kids require extra TLC. Sometimes they need a break from us as well! Get dressed up, put on some make-up, and paint the town. Just being a person once in a while can help make you a better parent all the time.

Have a happy list

> *"Happiness is two kinds of ice cream, knowing a secret, climbing a tree." Charlie Brown*
>
> —*Charles Schulz*

Find small things that make you happy. I think this is really the key for anyone to be happy. Life is never perfect, and sometimes it is really a struggle. However, if you have a few things that make you happy, life can seem more manageable. There are the obvious, such as hugging your kids or your spouse. But it also helps to have a list of things you know always make you smile. I try to reserve some of my time for things that make me happy. One thing is music. I always have music on in my house, and my girls love to sing. Whether it is the soundtrack of *Oliver!* or Taylor Swift, my kids are always listening to music. My own list of happy music includes Stevie Wonder, Jimmy Buffet, and Frank Sinatra. I know if I put on *Songs in the Key of Life*, I will be smiling, and life will seem a bit better. Same goes for watching *House Hunters* on HGTV, shrimp cocktail, Gene Kelly movies, baking tollhouse cookies, talking on the phone to my college roommate, bad reality TV shows, shopping at Macy's, and having my husband rub my feet while we're watching British mystery shows on DVD. This may sound hokey, but you need a "Happy List." I mean you literally need to write down a list of things that you know make you happy. Then you need to make a point of letting yourself have these things on a regular basis. Giving your children a happy home and a happy childhood can only happen if you are a happy person. Joy expands exponentially, so put on the Jackson Five and start to dance!

Life is what happens while you are growing your bangs (fringe) out

I like to share this motto I came up with a while back. I think it might help you relax more about your kids and your life. Basically it means that life is what happens while you are waiting for things to be perfect, which is never going to happen. When I was young, I hoped there would be a point in my life when I would have the right job, have an ever-blissful marriage, be skinny enough, finally have good hair, have an immaculately clean and well-decorated home, and be the mother to amazing kids. Then I would be in a permanent state of happiness. Ha, ha, ha. How deluded was I? The truth is this life is not meant to be perfect. Jobs are good but hard, spouses are lovable but frustrating, you're always chubbier than you want to be, houses seem permanently messy (at least when people live in them), and hair frizzes. However, my kids are amazing, just not in the ways I expected. The only way to really be happy is to accept the imperfections in life and even enjoy them. And no one is permanently happy; happiness, like sadness, comes in waves, so you just have to enjoy those moments when you can. But you may find if you can embrace your reality, those happy waves will roll into shore a lot more often.

Be good to yourself

As a parent of a daughter with autism, you have been given a very special and at times challenging path in life. It is okay to take occasional rests along the way. Nothing is so urgent that you can't go to bed early one night if you need to, or just plop on the couch and watch a silly movie from time to time. Most of us with children on the spectrum are so focused on finding help for our kids that we forget that we are their most important teachers, therapists, and role models. You need to find ways to keep yourself happy, so that you in turn can model and share that happiness with your daughter. Remember, you are the resource she needs the very most. So conserve that invaluable resource by taking good care of yourself.

The heart of the matter about taking care of you

1. The only way for your daughter to thrive is for you to thrive, so you must take care of yourself.

2. Sleeping enough, eating well, and exercising are simple ways to take care of yourself.

3. When you are feeling overwhelmed at all you have to do, take a break. Watch dumb television shows or eat cookies. This is a long journey; you are allowed to have breaks along the way.

4. It is okay to spend an evening out just being a grown-up. Your daughter will be fine, and you will be better when you come home.

5. You deserve to be happy, and your happiness will give comfort and joy to your daughter. So remember to be kind to yourself, and do the small things that make you smile.

The Future

"Hope is the thing with feathers that perches in the soul and sings the tune without words and never stops at all."

—Emily Dickinson

So, where do we go from here? The future is, of course, the great unknown, and I would be lying if I said it doesn't scare me at times. However, I cannot emphasize enough how many kind people I have met since my girls were diagnosed—so many people who have truly enjoyed working with them and seeing them blossom. I have faith that there are wonderful people out there committed to helping people of all ages with special needs. I still have very high hopes for my girls and their future potential, and I will never stop believing that they can achieve much more than anyone initially predicted. Perhaps the greatest thing I can say to them, after I say "I love you," is "I believe in you." I know I still have a lot of work left to do. I do my best to be positive, think of how far they have come, and enjoy every moment with them.

Lizzie is amazing!

Lizzie is now a full-fledged adolescent and she is a very typical 14-year-old. She is emotional at times, happy one minute and sad the next minute, and she frequently finds me a tremendous embarrassment. As her self-awareness has grown with age, Lizzie has questioned what it means to have Asperger's, and sometimes she worries about it. I know this is a normal part of adolescence; all kids just want to fit in. I just keep reassuring her that having Asperger's is not a bad thing, just a different thing. And in many ways she is blessed by Asperger's because it is a sign that she is smart and focused and insightful. Plus, Lizzie has already proven to everyone that she is much more than a one-word description. She is special and gifted in so many areas; she is not lacking anything. I tell her this as often as she will let me because I want her to believe in herself. I am doing my best to keep our relationship open and honest as we navigate together the sometimes murky waters of her adolescence. Lizzie's future is wide open, and I have no doubt that she will go on to college, marry, have children of her own, and have a remarkable career as a writer or teacher or Broadway star, or anything else she chooses.

Caroline is fearless!

For Caroline, the future is still a bit of a mystery; she has made so much progress already that I still believe her potential is tremendous. Caroline is also now in middle school, and she is yearning for more independence as well. She is disappointed at times because she wants to do everything the other kids do: dances and parties and sleepovers. It is tricky at times to know when to protect her and when to let her fly. I remind myself I need to listen to her, especially as she continues to grow over the next few years. She is just on the brink of adolescence, so I am sure there are many challenges awaiting me. I know she will surprise me; she always does. Ever since she was that energetic, smiling baby, Caroline has always had a mind of her own. She is fearless, and she is my inspiration. She still has that absolute belief that she can do anything she wants to. That is why she is learning the scientific method, doing long division, playing trumpet in the school band, and whooping everyone's butt at Mario Kart. I swear sometimes her will is supernatural! I know Caroline will make valuable contributions to the world in whatever she does.

I am blessed

Writing this book, I have realized how quickly my girls' childhoods have passed. Looking back, I would have worried far less about what other people think. I would have enjoyed those fleeting moments more and fretted less about what the future would bring. I am grateful for the sweet times I have had with my girls, and sometimes I miss those younger days, as hard as they were at times. Try not to be so busy trying to help your daughter that you forget to enjoy her. Your daughter needs to know she makes you happy. This is her only childhood, whether she has special needs or not. It flies by way too fast, and you will long for it when she grows older.

My wish for you

My experience over the past ten years with my girls has not been the typical parent's journey, but it has been a much richer experience than I ever could have chosen. Life on this side of the looking glass is joyous, sweet, and deeply fulfilling. I know it will be for you as well. I truly believe the greatest gift you can give your daughter is acceptance of who she is. All children flourish when they are loved and accepted unconditionally. It is then, paradoxically, that they are free to make the most progress. When you stop wishing for something other than what is, you can make the most of what you have. Your faith in your daughter can shape her future, and your love is the most powerful therapy of all. You will be amazed how much your daughter will grow and how much you will learn from her in the process. So many of the accomplishments my daughters have made are things some of the experts said they would never do. They didn't do them when other kids did, but in time I saw many miracles. So I end this book with the same thoughts that began it: all your daughter really needs from you is patience, hope, and love. That is what I learned from my precious daughters. Lizzie and Caroline are truly my heroes; they have taught me that the most miraculous things happen when we love our children just as they are, encourage them to develop their gifts, and believe in all they can become.

References

Autism Science Foundation (2011) "Beware of Non-Evidence-Based Treatments." Available at www.autismsciencefoundation.org/what-is-autism/autism-diagnosis/beware-non-evidence-based-treatments, accessed on October 3, 2011.

Autism Speaks (2011a) "Symptoms: Physical and Medical Issues that may Accompany Autism." Available at www.autismspeaks.org/what-autism/symptoms, accessed on September 28, 2011.

Autism Speaks (2011b) "Floortime (DIR)." Available at www.autismspeaks.org/what-autism/treatment/floortime-dir, accessed on September 29, 2011.

Autism Speaks (2011c) "Treatment for Biological and Medical Conditions Associated with Autism: Sensory Integration Therapy (SI)." Available at www.autismspeaks.org/what-autism/treatment/treatment-biological-medical-conditions-associated-autism, accessed on October 3, 2011.

Autism Speaks (2011d) "Treatment for Biological and Medical Conditions Associated with Autism: Is there a cure? Is recovery possible?" Available at www.autismspeaks.org/what-autism/treatment/treatment-biological-medical-conditions-associated-autism, accessed on October 3, 2011.

Autism Treatment Center of America (2011a) "What Makes the Son-Rise Program Different?" Available at www.autismtreatmentcenter.org/contents/about_son-rise/what_is_the_son-rise_program.php, accessed on October 3, 2011.

Autism Treatment Center of America (2011b) "History of the Son-Rise Program." Available at www.autismtreatmentcenter.org/contents/about_son-rise/history_of_the_son-rise_program.php, accessed on October 3, 2011.

Bacon, A.L., Fein, D., Morris, R., Waterhouse, L., and Allen, D. (1998) "The responses of autistic children to the distress of others." *Journal of Autism and Developmental Disorders 28*, 2, 129–42.

Baker, J.P. and Clements, D. (2010) "Do Vaccines Explain the Surge in Autism?" Online, DukeHealth.org, May 17, 2010. Available at www.dukehealth.org/health_library/advice_from_doctors/your_childs_health/do_vaccines_explain_the_surge_in_autism, accessed on October 3, 2011.

Bazelon, E. (2007) "What Autistic Girls are made of." *The New York Times* Magazine, August 5, 2007. Available at www.nytimes.com/2007/08/05/magazine/05autism-t.html, accessed on September 28, 2011.

BBC News (2008) "Autism 'may be Missed in Girls.'" Online September 16, 2008. Available at http://news.bbc.co.uk/1/hi/health/7616555.stm, accessed September 28, 2011.

BBC News (2009) "Genes 'have Key Role in Autism.'" Online April 28, 2009. Available at http://news.bbc.co.uk/2/hi/health/8020837.stm, accessed on November 17, 2010.

Brazelton, T.B. and Sparrow, J.D. (2006) *Touchpoints Birth to Three: Your Child's Emotional and Behavioral Development* (2nd edition). Cambridge, MA: Da Capo Press.

Brown, A. (2011) "Clear Answers and Smart Advice about your Baby's Shots." Online, Immunization Action Coalition. Available at www.immunize.org/catg.d/p2068. pdf, accessed on June 6, 2011.

Burns, J.F. (2010) "British Medical Council Bars Doctor who Linked Vaccine with Autism." Online, *The New York Times*, May 24, 2010. Available at www.nytimes. com/2010/05/25/health/policy/25autism.html, accessed on August 11, 2011.

Caldwell, N. (2008) "Intelligence Testing and Autism." Available at www. psychologytoday.com/blog/positively-autism/200805/intelligence-testing-and-autism, accessed on May 29, 2008.

CDC (2011a) "Facts about ASDs: Causes and Risk Factors." Available at www.cdc.gov/ ncbddd/autism/facts.html, accessed on September 28, 2011.

CDC (2011b) "Autism Spectrum Disorders: Data and Statistics." Available at www.cdc. gov/ncbddd/autism/data.html, accessed on September 28, 2011.

CDC (2011c) "Timeline: Thimerosal in Vaccines (1999–2008)." Available at www.cdc. gov/vaccinesafety/concerns/thimerosal/thimerosal_timeline.html, accessed on October 3, 2011.

CDC (2011d) "Autism Spectrum Disorders: Related Topics." Available at www.cdc.gov/ ncbddd/autism/topics.html, accessed on October 3, 2011.

Childs, D., Salahi, L., and Mazzeo, P. (2010) "A Gluten-Free, Casein-Free Diet No Remedy for Autism." Online, ABC News, May 19, 2010. Available at http:// abcnews.go.com/Health/Autism/gluten-free-casein-free-diet-remedy-autism-study/story?id=10690766, accessed on August 10, 2011.

Coplan, J. (2010) *Making Sense of Autistic Spectrum Disorders: Create the Brightest Future for Your Child with the Best Possible Options.* New York, NY: Bantam Books.

Cutler, E. (2010) cited in "Temple Grandin's Mother Offers Words of Hope" by Jean Winegardner. *Washington Times*, 22 February 2010. Available at http:// communities.washingtontimes.com/neighborhood/autism-unexpected/2010/ feb/22/temple-grandins-mother-offers-words-hope, accessed on 8 February 2012.

Dakss, B. (2006) "Autistic Teen's Hoop Dreams Come True." Online, CBS News, February 23, 2006. Available at www.cbsnews.com/stories/2006/02/23/ earlyshow/main1339324.shtml, accessed on August 19, 2011.

Denoon, D.J. (2010) "Study Linking Autism to Vaccine Retracted." Online, WebMD, February 2, 2010. Available at http://children.webmd.com/vaccines/ news/20100202/study-linking-autism-to-vaccine-retracted, accessed October 3, 2011.

Doheny, K. (2010) "'Autism Diet' May Not Improve Symptoms: Study Casts Doubt on Effectiveness of Casein-Free and Gluten-Free Diets." Online, WebMD, May 19, 2010. Available at www.webmd.com/brain/autism/news/20100519/autism-diet-may-not-improve-symptoms, accessed January 9, 2012.

Dominus, S. (2011) "The Crash and Burn of an Autism Guru." Online, *The New York Times Magazine*, April 20, 2011. Available at www.nytimes.com/2011/04/24/ magazine/mag-24Autism-t.html?pagewanted=all, accessed on October 3, 2011.

Emond, A., Emmett, P., Steer, C., and Golding, J. (2010) "Feeding symptoms, dietary patterns and growth in young children with autism spectrum disorders." *Pediatrics 126*, 2, e337–42. Online, August 1, 2010. Available at http://pediatrics. aappublications.org/content/126/2/e337.abstract, accessed on June 17, 2011.

FDA (2011) "Thimerosal in Vaccines." Available at www.fda.gov/ BiologicsBloodVaccines/SafetyAvailability/VaccineSafety/ucm096228.htm, accessed on October 3, 2011.

Frankl, V. (2006) *Man's Search for Meaning.* New York: Beacon Press.

Ghosh, P. (2010) "Study Identifies 'Many More' Autism Genes." Online, BBC News, June 10, 2010. Available at www.bbc.co.uk/news/10275332, accessed on June 3, 2011.

Giarelli, E., Wiggins, L.D., Rice, C.E., Levy, S.E. *et al.* (2010) "Sex differences in the evaluation and diagnosis of autism spectrum disorders among children." *Disability and Health Journal 3*, 2, 107–16.

Gilman, S.R., Iossifov, I., Levy, D., Ronemus, M., Wigler, M. and Vitkup, D. (2011) "Rare de novo variants associated with autism implicate a large functional network of genes involved in formation and function of synapses." *Neuron 70*, 5, 898–907.

Grandin, T. and Scariano, M. (1996) *Emergence: Labeled Autistic* (second revised edition). New York, NY: Warner Books.

Grandin, T. (2010) cited in "Life Among the 'Yakkity Yaks'," The Weekend Interview by Bari Weiss. *The Wall Street Journal*, 23 February 2010. Available at http:// online.wsj.com/article/SB10001424052748703525704575061123564007514.html, accessed on 8 February 2012.

Gray, C. (2011) "What are Social Stories™?" Online, The Gray Center for Social Learning and Understanding. Available at www.thegraycenter.org/social-stories/ what-are-social-stories, accessed on September 29, 2011.

Greenspan, S.I. and Wieder, S. (2006) *Engaging Autism: Using the Floortime Approach to Help Children Relate, Communicate, and Think.* Cambridge, MA: Da Capo Lifelong Books.

Harmon, K. (2010) "Large-Scale Autism Study Reveals Disorder's Genetic Complexity." Online, *Scientific American*, June 10, 2010. Available at www.scientificamerican. com/article.cfm?id=autism-genetic-complexity, accessed on August 25, 2011.

Hauch, V. (2011) "Unlocking Carly: Using one finger, autistic teen uses iPad, laptop to communicate – Parentcentral.ca." *Parents, Parenting, Child, Teenagers, Babies, Pregnancy, Education, Family, Health, Activities – Parentcentral.ca*, February 21, 2011. Available at www.parentcentral.ca/parent/familyhealth/children'shealth/article/944466-- unlocking-carly-using-one-finger-autistic-teen-uses-ipad-laptop-to-communicate, accessed on October 14, 2011.

Hoecker, J.L. (2010) "Is Chelation Therapy an Effective Autism Treatment?" Online, Mayo Clinic, December 9, 2010. Available at www.mayoclinic.com/health/ autism-treatment/AN01488, accessed on August 19, 2011.

International Society for Neurofeedback and Research (2011) "Definition of Neurofeedback." Available at www.isnr.org/information/index.cfm#Def, accessed on October 3, 2011.

IOM (2011) "About the IOM." Available at www.iom.edu/About-IOM.aspx, accessed on October 3, 2011.

Johnson, C.K. (2011) "Fraternal Twins with Autism: Is risk in the womb?" Online, Yahoo! News, July 5, 2011. Available at http://news.yahoo.com/fraternal-twins-autism-risk-womb-200138403.html, accessed on August 24, 2011.

Kane, K. (2006) "Death of 5-year-old Boy Linked to Controversial Chelation Therapy." Online, *Pittsburgh Post-Gazette*, January 6, 2006. Available at www.post-gazette. com/pg/06006/633541-85.stm, accessed on August 7, 2011.

Keller, H. (2004) *The Story of My Life: The Restored Edition*. New York: Modern Library Publications.

Kim, J.A., Szatmari, P., Bryson, S.E., Streiner, D.L., and Wilson, F.J. (2000) "The prevalence of anxiety and mood problems among children with autism and Asperger syndrome." *Autism 4*, 2, 117–32.

Knowles, D. (2011) "Dr. Andrew Wakefield Falsified Study Linking Vaccines to Autism, Journal Says." Online, AOL News, January 5, 2011. Available at www.aolnews. com/2011/01/05/dr-andrew-wakefield-falsified-study-linking-vaccines-to-autism, accessed on August 11, 2011.

Kotz, D. (2011) "Few Risks Associated with Vaccines, Specialists Conclude." Online, Boston.com Daily Dose, August 25, 2011. Available at www.boston.com/ Boston/dailydose/2011/08/few-risks-associated-with-vaccines-experts-conclude/3iaNwF4WLUi9W7Hf8eNIjI/index.html, accessed on August 25, 2011.

Lane, M. (2004) "What Asperger's Syndrome has Done for us." Online, BBC News, June 4, 2004. Available at http://news.bbc.co.uk/2/hi/3766697.stm, accessed on August 6, 2011.

Leake, J. (2008) "Autism Genes can Add up to Genius." Online, *Times Online*, October 5, 2008. Available at www.timesonline.co.uk/tol/news/uk/article4882699.ece [subscription only].

Lewis, C.S. (1960) *The Four Loves*. Los Angeles, CA: Fount.

Lewis, C.S. (2001) *Mere Christianity*. San Francisco, CA: Harper San Francisco.

Linklater, M. (2008) "If we Screen out Autism, we Run the Risk of Losing Genius, too." Online, *Times Online*, January 12, 2008. Available at www.timesonline.co.uk/tol/ comment/columnists/magnus_linklater/article5496799.ece [subscription only].

McCarthy, J. (2007) *Louder than Words: A Mother's Journey in Healing Autism*. New York, NY: Dutton.

McGee, S. (2011) "Famous People with Autism." Online, Love to Know: Autism. Available at http://autism.lovetoknow.com/Famous_People_with_Autism, accessed on August 5, 2011.

Maugh, T.H., II (2010) "Andrew Wakefield Responds to Article about Journal Retraction of Autism Study Report." Online, *Los Angeles Times*, February 3, 2010. Available at http://latimesblogs.latimes.com/booster_shots/2010/02/andrew-wakefield-responds-to-article-about-journal-retraction.html, accessed on August 11, 2011.

Mayo Clinic (2011) "Autism: Definition." Available at www.mayoclinic.com/health/ autism/DS00348, accessed on September 28, 2011.

Myers, S.M. and Johnson, C.P. (2007) "Management of children with autism spectrum disorders." *Pediatrics 120*, 5, 1162–82.

National Institute of Mental Health (2011) "Treatment Options: Medications Used in Treatment." Available at www.nimh.nih.gov/health/publications/autism/treatment-options.shtml, accessed on October 3, 2011.

Nichols, S., Moravcik, G.M., and Tetenbaum, S.P. (2009) *Girls Growing Up on the Autism Spectrum: What Parents and Professionals Should Know About the Pre-Teen and Teenage Years*. London: Jessica Kingsley Publishers.

Offit, P.A., Quarles, J., Gerber, M.A., Hackett, C.J., *et al.* (2002) "Addressing parents' concerns: Do multiple vaccines overwhelm or weaken the infant's immune system." *Pediatrics 109*, 1, 124–9.

Partnership for 21st Century Skills (2011) Home page. Available at www.p21.org, accessed on September 29, 2011.

RDIconnect (2011) "Restoring the Guided Participation Relationship." Available at www.rdiconnect.com/pages/Restoring-the-Guided-Participation-Relationship.aspx, accessed on September 29, 2011.

Roan, S. (2011) "Autism Linked to Hundreds of Genetic Mutations." Online, *Los Angeles Times*, June 9, 2011. Available at http://articles.latimes.com/2011/jun/09/health/la-he-autism-20110609, accessed on June 29, 2011.

Rochman, B. (2011) "For Siblings of Autistic Kids, Risk is Far Higher than Thought." Online, *Time* Healthland, August 15, 2011. Available at http://healthland.time.com/2011/08/15/autism-affects-far-more-siblings-than-suspected, accessed on August 23, 2011.

Rope, K. (2010) "The End of the Autism/Vaccine Debate?" Online, CNN, September 10, 2010. Available at www.cnn.com/2010/HEALTH/09/07/p.autism.vaccine.debate/index.html, accessed on June 21, 2011.

Rutgers, A.H., Bakermans-Kranenburg, M.J., van Ijzendoom, M.H., and van Berckelaer-Onnes, I.A. (2004) "Autism and attachment: A meta-analytic review." *Journal of Child Psychology and Psychiatry 45*, 6, 1123–34.

Salahi, L. (2011) "Report Linking Vaccine to Autism 'Fraudulent' Says British Medical Journal." Online, ABC News, January 5, 2011. Available at http://abcnews.go.com/Health/Autism/link-vaccine-autism-link-fraud-british-medical-journal/story?id=12547823, accessed February 15, 2011.

Schechter, R. and Grether, J.K. (2008) "Continuing increases in autism reported to California's developmental services system: Mercury in retrograde." *Archives of General Psychiatry 65*, 1, 19–24.

Schrandt, J.A., Townsend, D.B., and Poulson, C.L. (2009) "Teaching empathy skills to children with autism." *Journal of Applied Behavior Analysis 42*, 1, 17–32.

Seskin, L., Feliciano, E., Tippy, G., Yedloutschnig, R., Sossin, K.M., and Yasik, A. (2010) "Attachment and autism: Parental attachment representations and relational behaviors in the parent–child dyad." *Journal of Abnormal Child Psychiatry 38*, 7, 949–60.

Smith, A. (2009) "The empathy imbalance hypothesis of autism." *The Psychological Record*, 59, 273–94.

Stein, R. (2011) "Vaccines Generally Safe, National Academy of Sciences Says." Online, *The Washington Post*, August 25, 2011. Available at www.washingtonpost.com/national/health-science/vaccines-are-generally-safe-national-academy-of-sciences-says/2011/08/25/gIQA7XAjdJ_story.html, accessed on August 25, 2011.

Stratton, K., Gable, A., and McCormick, M. (2004) "Immunization Safety Review: Vaccines and Autism." Online, The National Academies Press. Available at www.nap.edu/openbook.php?record_id=10997&page=21, accessed on August 19, 2011.

Szabo, L. (2011) "Siblings of Autistic Children at a 20 Times Higher Risk." Online, USA Today, August 15, 2011. Available at http://yourlife.usatoday.com/health/medical/autism/story/2011/08/Siblings-of-autistic-children-at-a-20-times-higher-risk/49963574/1, accessed on August 23, 2011.

Szatmari, P. (2011) "Is Autism, at Least in Part, a Disorder of Fetal Programming?" Online, *Archives of General Psychiatry*, July 5, 2011. Available at http://archpsyc.ama-assn.org/cgi/content/full/archgenpsychiatry.2011.99, accessed on July 29, 2011.

Teatum, A. (2011) "Wrestler with Autism Advances to Junior National Tournament." Online, *The Times-Tribune*, April 25, 2011. Available at http://thetimes-tribune.com/sports/wrestler-with-autism-advances-to-junior-national-tournament-1.1137107#axzz1UHYMUYJS, accessed on August 6, 2011.

Thomas, J. (2009) "Standard IQ Test may Undervalue People with Autism." Online, HealthDay News, June 19, 2009. Available at http://health.usnews.com/health-news/family-health/brain-and-behavior/articles/2009/06/19/standard-iq-test-may-undervalue-people-with-autism, accessed on June 29, 2011.

Tsouderos, T. and Callahan, P. (2009) "Autism Treatment: Science hijacked to support alternative therapies." Online, *The Baltimore Sun*, November 23, 2009. Available at www.baltimoresun.com/health/chi-autism-science-nov23,0,3526417.story, accessed on August 19, 2011.

Wakefield, A.J., Murch, S.H., Anthony, A., Linnell, J., *et al.* (1998) "Ileal-lymphoid-nodular hyperplasia, non-specific colitis, and pervasive developmental disorder in children." *Lancet 351*, 9103, 637–41.

Weiss, B. (2010) "Life Among the 'Yakkity Yaks.'" Online, *The Wall Street Journal*, February 23, 2010. Available at http://online.wsj.com/article/SB10001424052748703525704575061123564007514.html, accessed on June 16, 2011.

Zarembo, A. (2011) "Autism Study Downplays Role of Genetics." Online, *Los Angeles Times*, July 5, 2011. Available at http://articles.latimes.com/2011/jul/05/health/la-he-autism-20110705, accessed on July 29, 2011.

Index